God's Minute

A Book of 365 Daily Prayers Sixty Seconds Long for Home Worship – A Collection of Biblical Wisdom and Spiritual Guidance for Christians

By 365 Eminent Clergymen and Laymen

In All Thy Ways Acknowledge Him and He Shall Direct Thy Paths.

- *Prov. 3: 6.*

**PANTIANOS
CLASSICS**

Published by Pantianos Classics

ISBN-13: 978-1-78987-377-1

First published in 1916

Contents

A Call to Prayer

Let us put by some hour of every day
For holy things! — whether it be when dawn
Peers through the window-pane, or when the noon
Flames, like a burnished topaz, In the vault,
Or when the thrush pours in the ear of eve
Its plaintive monody; some little hour
Wherein to hold rapt converse with the soul,
From sordidness and self a sanctuary,
Swept by the winnowing of unseen wings,
And touched by the White Light Ineffable!

Clinton Scollard.

A Word from the Publishers

THIS little volume is sent forward with the prayer that it may assist many Christian people whose early religious training, education and experience have not been such as to enable them to give reverent expression to their spiritual needs, and this book is aimed to aid all such to formulate their thoughts, and train them along devotional lines. The arrangement of the prayers in calendar form should prove a constant reminder to them of their privilege to talk to their Heavenly Father at the beginning of every day.

No printed prayer can always present the individual soul wants, but some of the most effective prayers are the printed ones. Those by the Psalmist have been appropriated by many who found in them the spiritual expression of their soul's inmost needs.

Some may claim that they have no time for such worship. It requires only 25 seconds to repeat the model prayer that our Lord taught His disciples. The name given to this volume, "God's Minute," conveys the idea that these prayers of about two hundred words in length will require about a minute to give each reverent expression.

Every contributor, representative of both the religious and the intellectual forces in the English-speaking world in the pulpit and in the pew, did his work willingly and gratuitously, so that the volume could be sold at a price within the reach even of people with humble means.

May God bless every reverent user of this little volume, and the many good people who have so generously aided us in making its publication possible.

January

Open to me the gates of righteousness: I will go in to them, and I will praise the Lord. — Psalm 118: 19.

OUR Heavenly Father, we pause at the opening of this day to place ourselves in harmony with Thy great plans. We know that it is unwise and sinful to oppose or attempt to hinder Thy purposes. Hear our humble appeal for Divine wisdom, for spiritual sensitiveness to Thy messages, for broader views of our duty, and for the peace of God which fills the soul when working in full harmony with Thee. Let each of these blessings be given to all whom we love. Incline them to stop and pray — to watch and act, under the impulses which come from Heaven. Make known Thy love and law to all people in all lands, and hasten the era when all mankind shall accept the teachings of Thy Son, and of the Holy Prophets, and thus in sincere agreement live in peace with all, and in full obedience and devotion to Thy Holy Will. We ask these great blessings in the Name of our Lord Jesus, Thy Son, and our Redeemer. *Amen.*

Russell H. Conwell, D.D.,
Philadelphia, Pa.

JANUARY SECOND

His love is perfected in us. — I John 4: 12.

HEAVENLY Father, write Thy new, best name of Love upon our hearts this morning. Help us to remember Jesus Christ. During the busy hours bring Him often to our thought. When the mind is free from some set task may it revert to Him, as the needle turns to the pole. Keep us from wounding Him in thought or word. Make our communion with Him sweet. Give us of His strength, of His wisdom, of His winsomeness. Forgive the professions which have been but empty words. Forgive the sins which have brought a reproach upon Thy church. Forgive us if we have made it difficult to distinguish between the church and the world.

Save us from the sin of despair. Light the lamp of hope in every heart. Fill us with the spirit of expectancy. Teach us that ruined lives may be rebuilt, and that in Christ is sufficiency for all our needs. We are thankful that Christ is the way to our Father's house, that there is forgiveness for all, the bread of life for all, and a welcome. Cleanse us from the defilement of the way; blot out the memories of the far country; clothe us with the garment of righteousness, and give us the joy of knowing that Thou dost own us as Thy sons and daughters. *Amen.*

Frederick T. Keeney, D. D.
Syracuse, N. Y.

JANUARY THIRD

Make His praise glorious. — Ps. 66: 2.

O GOD, our gracious Father, we look to Thee now for Thy benediction. We are Thy suppliant children, who subsist under the cover of Thy patience. We praise Thee for all Thine extraordinary mercies. Thou hast made us like Thyself in the desire and in the capacity for fellowship. May fellowship with Thee be the basis and supreme blessing of our fellowship with each other. May flowers of devotion breathe their fragrance every day upon the family altar. Teach us how to be abased and how to abound. Keep our feet from unbidden paths, and our eyes from tears; or if the tears must come, let the Comforter come as well, that He may wipe them all away. Temper to us the long night watches of pain and sorrow. If weeping endure for a night, bring joy in the morning; and when the long afternoon shadows deepen toward the eventide of this earth's life, bring us very gently to the turn of the road from whence we may catch the vision of the home eternal. May this our present habitation be a promise and a foretaste of the house which has foundation whose builder and maker is God. Help us in our social joys and pleasures to remember Thee. Grant us all to face all life's tasks bravely, and perform them earnestly. And bring us in the end with joyful hearts and glad faces to abide with Thee, through Jesus Christ our Lord. *Amen.*

Charles F. Wishart, D. D.,
Chicago, Illinois.

JANUARY FOURTH

Keep yourselves in the love of God. — Jude 21.

O THOU Eternal Love, Whom Jesus has taught us to call our Father, and in Whom we are learning to trust as our Brother, our Comrade, our Closest Friend, we are not seeking Thee, for we know that Thou art nearer to us every moment than we are to ourselves; we are only wishing and hoping that often, through this day, the thought of Thy nearness to us, of Thy presence with us, may spring into our consciousness, that we may see what Thou art showing us, and know what Thou art telling us, and be ready to take what Thou art giving us, and to do what Thou art bidding us. Help us to feel more than once today that the good thoughts and the good wishes which we find in our hearts are signs of Thy presence there; and may we learn to look for Thee thus, within our own lives, and to rejoice when we find Thee there, and so to become aware, more and more, of what we mean when we speak of the fellowship and communion of the Holy Spirit! We know that Thou art working in us to will and to do of Thy good pleasure; and we know that Thou findest Thy good pleasure in lives made fruitful and beautiful in Thy service. So help us to work with Thee, this day and every day, through Jesus Christ, our Lord. *Amen.*

Washington Gladden, D. D., LL.D.
Columbus, Ohio.

JANUARY FIFTH

O Lord, my God, I will give thanks unto Thee forever. — Ps. 30: 12.

OUR eternal Father, we thank Thee that Thou hast brought us into the close and loving relationship of children, by the death of Jesus Christ, Thy Son, our Saviour, through Whom we are adopted into Thy divine family and become Thy children.

We thank Thee that Thou Who wast the Creator of all men hast brought into Thine own family those who accept the love and sacrifice of Thy dear Son. We thank Thee that Thou dost share with us not only our sorrows, but our joys; that Thou art delighted when life delights us, and when virtue and faithfulness lead us to higher levels of thought and purpose.

We thank Thee for Thy Holy Word, and pray that our faithfulness in studying it may result in spiritual growth and development. May we "hunger and thirst after righteousness" and after the food of Thy Word. May we never dare to enter upon the duties of a single day without the nourishment and support of the Word of God!

Bless, we pray Thee, all who are dear to us, and give to us all an interpretation of friendship which centers in our divine Friend and Saviour, Jesus Christ. We ask it in His holy Name. *Amen.*

John Timothy Stone, D. D.,
Chicago, Illinois.

JANUARY SIXTH

I thank Thee and praise Thee, O God. — Dan. 2: 23.

OUR Father in Heaven, we approach Thee in the name of Jesus Christ, Thy Son, our Saviour, that we may render praise and thanksgiving to Thee; and that we may seek the forgiveness of our sins, the continued manifestation of Thy favor, and the guidance of the Holy Spirit in the choices of our lives, and in the rendering of service to Thee. We realize, our Father, the shortness of our vision, the imperfection of our judgment, and the weakness of our effort, but Thou hast said, "Commit Thy way unto Jehovah, trust also in Him, and He will bring it to pass." It is sweet to rest upon this promise, and to feel that thus we can walk hand in hand with Thee, and that our ways shall be Thy way.

In order that we may be true to our high calling, give us the sympathetic heart, the kindly look, the golden speech, the helping hand. Make us a channel of blessing to those about us, that we may be the true children of Abraham, who was blessed that he might bless. And now, dear Lord, give us the strength for that which is immediately before us according to the promise, "As thy day is, so shalt thy strength be," and Thy name shall have the glory, through Christ, our Lord. *Amen.*

J. A. Duff, D. D.,
Aspinwall, Penna.

JANUARY SEVENTH

Behold what manner of love the Father hath bestowed upon us. — I John 3: 1.

IN Thee, God, we live, and move and have our being. If Thou wert to withdraw Thy hand for a moment we should sink into nothingness, as when a drop of dew exhales into the air.

We thank Thee for all that makes life worth living; for home and kinship and loving friends, for happiness, the hope and the opportunity of doing good. We thank Thee for life and immortality brought to light in the Gospel, and for a strong staff to lean on as we journey toward the immortal life.

Pardon our sins, for Jesus' sake, that we may not be dragging a hopeless chain after us. Sanctify us by Thy Spirit, that we may run in the way of Thy commandments; and enlarge our hearts that we may constantly be doing good as we have opportunity unto all men. Look graciously on the sick and suffering; and incline the hearts of those who know Thee not to come running unto Thee.

Hear and answer, Father of all mercies; not for any worth or worthiness in us, but because we ask in the all-prevailing name of Christ, our Saviour and Thy beloved Son. *Amen.*

David J. A. L. Burrell, D. D.,
New York City.

JANUARY EIGHTH

I will love Thee, O Lord, my strength. — Ps. 18: 1

LORD God Almighty, creator and preserver of all things, we humbly

9

bow down before Thee in worship and supplication. We come without a single plea of merit, except that we have been redeemed through the suffering, death, and resurrection, of Thine only begotten Son, Jesus Christ. We thank Thee for the blessings that Thou hast bestowed on us so generously in the past, and we ask wisdom and guidance from Thee in order that each one of us may become a blessing to all with whom we come in contact. We pray for the forgiveness of our sins. We ask Thee to walk with us today; be Thou our friend, our counsellor, our guide, our brother, the sure staff on which we may lean. May love for Thee and for our fellowmen always fill our hearts, and shine out of our lives so that all men may see that we have been walking with God.

Thou hast never promised to supply all our wants — many of them are not for our good, but Thou hast promised to fill all needs, and we ask Thee for the gift of contentedness, of being satisfied with what Thou doth send. These, and all other things which will satisfy our souls and increase our capacity for service in the Kingdom, we ask for Jesus' sake. *Amen.*

William Anthony Granville, LL.D.,
Gettysburg, Penna.

JANUARY NINTH

Give thanks unto the Lord, call upon His name. — Ps. 105: 1.

DEAR Heavenly Father, as we gather at Thy feet today as a family, we ask Thy blessing on our home and Thy guidance to each one during the hours of this day. Help us to realize Thy nearness to us at this hour. May we realize Thy reality, and be conscious of the fact that Thou art not a God afar off — the Great King of Heaven, the Mighty Judge of all the earth enthroned in infinite space above us, but that we can claim Thee as our Saviour and our Friend.

Help us throughout this day to realize that Thou canst be nearer to each one of us than the nearest and dearest of friends.

Let us hear Thy voice today. Let us feel the inspiration of Thy presence, and with willing feet enable us to walk in the path on which Thy light and blessing can fall.

Give us this day some work to do for others, some kindly word to speak, some helpful unselfish deed to fulfil in Thy Name. Be with us each and every hour of this day, and may we so live that Thy will may be done and Thy Kingdom come within our hearts. *Amen.*

Mrs. Maud Ballington Booth,
New York City, N. Y.

JANUARY TENTH

"I will bless the Lord at all times." — Ps. 34: 1.

O LORD and Father of us all, we come with glad hearts to this hour of prayer. When we recall the infinity and eternity of Thy power and wisdom and goodness, we bow in reverence to Thee. *Love* invites imitation, and we choose Thee as our example. May Thy Spirit change us into likeness to Thyself. *Love* craves the privilege of service, and loving Thee we ask, "Lord, what wilt Thou have us to do?" Help us as parents to wisely order our household. May we train our children for useful lives here, and to be fitted for their true home beyond this life. As a family we are very near each other. Help us so to live that proximity may not evoke confusion and strife. May we be "kindly affectioned one to another." Grant us, Lord, that winning gentleness which is the sweet offspring of truthfulness and love.

We pray, our Father, for all who are in trouble; for the sick, the poor, the afflicted, for any good cause. Bless the lonely — those who suffer, weep, and struggle alone. Grant that they may find companionship and comfort in Thee. Since every good gift and every perfect gift is from above, we thank Thee sincerely and heartily for the good things we enjoy. May this prayer, O Lord! find acceptance with Thee, through Jesus Christ, our Lord and Saviour. *Amen.*

Charles Randall Barnes, D. D.,
Hoboken, New Jersey.

JANUARY ELEVENTH

Hear, and in Thy faithfulness answer me. — Ps. 143: 1

OUR Father, our hearts overflow with gratitude when we recount Thy mercies. We feel our unworthiness when we remember all of Thy loving kindnesses toward us. Oh, gracious Father, patiently bear with us we pray Thee.

Deliver us from the bondage of our lower and selfish desires, and make us free to give to Thee all of the love and service that should be Thine own. May we not work against Thee, or apart from Thee, but may we be one with Thee, and share in Thy purposes, Thy work, and Thy joy.

How great is our unbelief! How Thou must be grieved at our doubts and our fears! Lord, increase our faith! When mountains of difficulties loom in our pathway, grant that we may have the faith to remove them. Help us to live forgetful of self, and may our service be such that we, like Paul, shall bear in our body the marks of the Lord Jesus.

Deliver us from the formal religious life, and may the Holy Spirit lead us into the fulness of God's life for us, and within us. In the Name of the Father,

11

and of the Son, and of the Holy Spirit. *Amen.*

Rev. Justin N. Green
Cincinnati, Ohio.

JANUARY TWELFTH

The faithful God, which keepeth covenant. — Deut 7: 9.

OUR Heavenly Father, we come to thank Thee for Thy many mercies, and to invoke Thy protection and guidance for all the way of life. We rejoice that we may know Thee and love Thee and serve Thee and be like thee. Grant us grace to please Thee in all that we think and plan and do. Help us to live in such fellowship with Thee that Thou canst not only dwell in us, but work through us. Help us to share our blessings with others, and to find in our privileges an obligation to minister to those who need what we have. Bestow upon us strength for our daily tasks; courage in the face of fears; comfort in sorrow; quiet in the midst of tumult; hope in the presence of uncertainty; high motives for humble as well as high deeds; self-control in the hour of provocation; gentleness and forgiveness when tempted to revenge; and the peace which passeth all understanding. Hold in Thy holy care all our loved ones, and keep guard over our interests in life. Give us to see the speedy coming of Thy Kingdom among all men, and let us have an increasing share in its establishment. Fill our hearts with songs of expectation, and flood our faces with morning light, and when the day is done, let the weariness of work make welcome the rest of home, we beg in our Redeemer's name. *Amen.*

James I. Vance, D. D.
Nashville, Tenn.

JANUARY THIRTEENTH

If any man lack wisdom, let him ask of God, and He will give it him. - James 1: 5.

INFINITE Father, we have tried the world and found it a great emptiness; we come back to Thee Who art eager to fill our souls with everlasting truth and mercy. We come with a song in our hearts, for the list of Thy benefits is beyond our counting.

We thank Thee for the stirring days of the present, with their opportunities for improvement and service, their concern for the poor and ignorant. We thank Thee for the mysterious, inviting days which are to come, laden with secret stores for our replenishing, hidden delights, and dark experiences for our training. We thank Thee for the silent heroisms of the home; for the hallowed drudgeries of the sick chamber. We thank Thee that despite the cleverness of wicked men and the foolishness of good men, the Kingdom makes steady advance.

Thy bounty unto us is without boundaries. And yet we baffle Thy plans, thwart Thy love, and wander wretchedly from the way of Jesus. We return unto Thee this morning to have our stains removed, our petty shams stripped away, and our hearts fortified. Have compassion upon us, and bring us all by and by to our Father's home, through Jesus Christ, our Lord. *Amen.*

Rev. Hugh Elmer Brown,
Seattle, Washington.

JANUARY FOURTEENTH

Remember the Sabbath Day — Exodus 20: 8.

A Prayer for Sunday Morning.

WE give Thee thanks, O Lord our God, for the rest we have enjoyed during the night, and for the light of another day. We give Thee thanks for Thy guidance during the week past, for labor and its rewards; for friendship and its enjoyments; and home, with its comfort and love. We are glad for the coming of another day of rest. May this Sabbath remind us of Him Who on the first day of the week rose from the dead. May we not forget that this is His day — and ours to use for Him. We ask for pardon of all past offences, and for deliverance from all habits of thought, speech, and conduct which dishonor Thee. Deliver us from impatience and anger. May we be tenderhearted, pitiful and courteous. We thank Thee for the Church, and pray Thee to make it a blessing to us, and make us a blessing to it. Bless all ministers and teachers of Thy Word. When the record of this Sabbath ends, may we have nothing to regret — no wasted opportunities, no misspent hours. And may we carry with us into the work of the week which is to come, an abundance of courage and self-control. Preserve our lives from harm and our hearts from evil. May the Master be our daily comrade and our constant guide. For His Name's sake. *Amen.*

Charles Carroll Albertson, D.D.,
Brooklyn, N. Y.

JANUARY FIFTEENTH

For Thy Name's sake, lead me, and guide me. — Ps. 31: 3.

LORD, hear our prayer in the morning. We need Thee all the day, through all the days. We have our call to prayer at any hour, but particularly when the night is spent, and Thou hast kindled the dawn as if Thou hadst made the day for us and only for us. Then we have strange need that Thou shouldst take our hand in Thine and our heart in Thine and our brain in Thine, and that our feet walk the road where Thy footprints should show the way though Thou shouldst need to leave us for a moment. We pray our morning prayer; we lift our singing hearts to Thee and praise Thee that all the ways we take we shall surely have the good companionship which on a day long since made hearts to burn, and turned a funereal day into one of laughter and great dreams. Blessed be the Lord, Who has guided our going all these years, and Who will continue to be our help and our rejoicing. We will make melody all day; we will walk modestly all day; we will work helpfully all day; we will do things which shall not need to be undone all day; and since these matters are too large for our accomplishment, we ask Thy mighty aid. Fail us not, our God. Smile on our many activities and bid them Godspeed to the end, that at set of sun all may be well with our hearts, and we may be bidden by Thyself a kindly good night. *Amen.*

Bishop William A. Quayle,
St. Paul, Minnesota.

JANUARY SIXTEENTH

The Lord shall guide thee continually. — Isa, 58:11.

O GOD, we pray for the grace which we need for the labors and duties of the day. Our hearts are open; our spirits wait upon Thee. The sensitive conscience which leads to right decisions is Thy gift. The loyalty and fidelity which we desire in living as worthy children of our Heavenly Father, Thou alone canst make possible. The patience we so much need to endure the buffetings of life is born of the Divine patience, and must come from Thee. The forbearance which we must have in dealing with others, we derive from Thee. The tenderness and love which lead us to seek out the needy and minister to them, Thou canst supply out of Thine unwasting fulness. We confess our sins, and ask that Thou wilt forgive us as we forgive those who trespass against us. Enlarge our hearts that we may have a great vision of personal holiness, of civic righteousness, of business integrity, of social service, and of missionary conquest. Give us as the ruling passion of our lives, the desire to bring in Thy Kingdom. To this end make us liberal with our gifts, responsive to the call to service. Above all, give us constant fellowship with Thyself, through Thy Holy Spirit. May the truth as it is in Jesus make us free and joyous as Thy children. May our daily lives be filled with thanksgiving to Thee for Thy manifold mercies, and chiefly for the gift of eternal life through Jesus Christ our Lord. *Amen.*

Pres. Edgar Y. Mullins, D. D. LL. D.
Louisville, Kentucky

14

JANUARY SEVENTEENTH

Offer unto God thanksgiving. — Ps. 50: 14.

WE implore Thy blessing, our Father. Deliver us this morning from all our doubts and all that repels, and draw us near to Thee by all those encouragements which comfort the soul and which strengthen our faith, our hope, and our fidelity to Thee. We confess our sinfulness and we beseech of Thee, day by day, to forgive our sins, and everything in us which offends. Give us not only clearer light, but grace to walk in that light. We pray that Thou wilt make our strength great when our burdens are heavy; that each of us may have a consciousness that God thinks of him, and overrules all things for his good. May the sweetness of Thy presence and the light and the joy which spring from Thy heart, be the portion of each of us. May we be more and more devoted in prayer; more and more earnest for the salvation of men; more and more vigilant in looking after those who are around us; more and more desirous of helping one another, bearing one another's burdens, and succoring those who need help. Wilt Thou comfort such as in bereavement mourn the loss of those who were dear to them. We again pray for the forgiveness of all our sins, and the consciousness of Thy continued favor and presence.

And to the Father, Son, and the Spirit shall be praises evermore. *Amen.*

Rev. J. W. Somerville
Wichita, Kansas.

JANUARY EIGHTEENTH

Let all those that put their trust in Thee rejoice. — Ps. 5: 11.

OUR Heavenly Father, we bow in Thy presence in child-like confidence, knowing that Thou art able and willing to hear our supplication, and graciously answer our prayer for Thy guidance during this day, which will be a day of opportunity, of blessing, of responsibility, and of testing. Grant us as a family Thy benediction and the special direction of the Holy Spirit, so that in all our ways we may acknowledge Thee, and in all our undertakings and in the performance of our tasks we may please Thee, and worthily represent Thee. Bless us individually and collectively, and make us a blessing to all over whom we shall have the opportunity of wielding an influence to-day. May the meditation of our hearts and the utterances of our lips be acceptable in Thy sight, and may the gracious promise be fulfilled on our behalf: "As thy day, so shall thy strength be." Since each day hath its own peculiar temptations and trials, may we be able this day to cope with all our adversaries and successfully conquer them, leaving our impress for good on all with whom we may come in contact. May we realize this day, as never before, the truthfulness of the promise: "The path of the just is as a shining light that shineth more and more unto the perfect day." In Jesus' name we ask it. *Amen.*

Rev. W. H. Bucks,
Cleveland, Ohio.

JANUARY NINETEENTH

And which of you with taking thought can add to His stature one cubit? If ye then be not able to do that thing which is least, why take ye thought for the rest? Consider the lilies how they grow; they toil not, they spin not; and yet I say unto you, that Solomon in all his glory was not arrayed like one of these. If then God so clothe the grass, which is to-day in the field, and to-morrow is cast into the oven; how much more will He clothe you, O ye of little faith? — Luke 12: 25-28.

O GOD, Who knowest our necessities before we ask, and the manifold temptations we meet with day by day, help us to put our whole trust in Thee when despair and misgivings assail us. Suffer us not, we beseech Thee, to become the prey of useless forebodings, nor to lose the things which belong to our peace, through the habit of morbid and sinful worry. So guide us, in all our way, that we may keep our faces always toward the light, that our shadows may lie behind us. Of Thy great mercy enable us to perceive our blessings, that we may always serve Thee with a glad heart and quiet mind, through Jesus Christ our Lord. *Amen.*

Bishop Charles E. Woodcock, D.D., LL.D.,
Louisville, Kentucky.

JANUARY TWENTIETH

Walk in love, as Christ also hath loved us. — Eph. 5: 2.

WE thank Thee, O God our Heavenly Father, for all of life's blessings. All we have comes from Thee, and all we do is by the strength Thou dost give us. Help us to love Thee with all our heart, and serve Thee with all our strength.

We bring our family to Thee, with all its members, in whatever place or condition they may be, for Thy gracious care. If some are sick, or troubled, or tempted, be to them a great physician, a comforting friend, and a mighty Saviour.

Bless our daily occupations, and, if it please Thee, make our way prosperous. If adversity be better for us, make us patient and faithful in trial. Help us in all our perplexities to know Thy will, and make us ever ready to do what Thou desirest. Make us a blessing in our church, and make our church a blessing to others. May Thy Word be a light unto our path, and a lamp to guide all who are in any darkness. Bless the work of this day, fit us for its duties and responsibilities, overrule all our mistakes, and pardon all our sins. We come to Thee as children to a dear Father, asking these and other things we need, for Jesus' sake. *Amen.*

S. S. Waltz, D.D.,
Louisville, Ky.

JANUARY TWENTY-FIRST

In His love and His pity, He redeemed them. — Isaiah, 63: 9.

OUR God, Father of our Lord and Saviour Jesus Christ, *our* Father through Him, we thank Thee most heartily for Thy very gracious disposition towards us. In Thy love Thou hast redeemed us, in the fulness of Thy grace Thou hast given unto us Thy Holy Spirit, the blessed Word, and all things needful for our spiritual welfare.

We are grateful, our God, for Thy good providence, whereby we enjoy the comforts and blessings of the life that now is. We humbly and earnestly pray for faith, hope, and love; for purity in our lives, for a discernment of divine leadership, and that trust in Thee whereby anxiety is banished.

We pray for family happiness, for Thy presence in our home and in each of our hearts; and we ask Thee, most merciful God, to grant us pardon for all our sins which we freely confess. We ask for a rich blessing upon the household of God upon earth, upon the nation in which we live, and upon all people.

We present our recognition of Thee, our thanksgiving, our petitions, and confession in the Name of Jesus, Who taught us to pray, and for His sake. *Amen.*

Rev. Robert W. Thompson,
Pittsburg, Kansas.

JANUARY TWENTY-SECOND

Wherefore come out from among them, and be ye separate, saith the Lord, and touch not the unclean thing; and I will receive you. And will be a Father unto you, and ye shall be my sons and daughters, saith the Lord Almighty. - 2 Cor. 6: 17, 18.

OUR Father, help us to be true to-day; help us to be faithful; help us to be kind. May Thy presence go with us and watch over us so that no evil may surprise us. Keep us from falling, keep us from stumbling. If temptation assails us, may we be given strength to resist it; if trouble awaits us, may we go forth courageously to meet it and may Thy grace be sufficient for us in the hour of our need.

Especially we pray Thee that sin may have no dominion over us; save us from becoming hardened by its deceitfulness, or softened by its false soothing flattery.

Make us generous in our judgments, tender-hearted in our feelings, sweet spirited and loving in all our dealings. Preserve us from being impatient and irritable.

Implant within our hearts a genuine hatred for every form of defilement, and a sincere love for what is pure and Christ-like. Whatsoever things are honorable, whatsoever things are just, whatsoever things are lovely, may we think on these things to-day. For Christ's sake. *Amen.*

Malcolm James MacLeod, D.D.,
New York City.

JANUARY TWENTY-THIRD

Blessed is the man that maketh the Lord his trust. — Ps. 40: 4.

ALMIGHTY GOD, our Father, we come to Thee in the early morning hour to give thanks for that loving care which has kept us during the night, to renew our strength, and to seek preparation for the work and responsibilities of the new day. In our blindness we cannot see what is before us, but Thou knowest; so we place our hands in Thine, that we may be led in a way that will glorify Thee, and make better and more fruitful our own lives. Share Thy richest morning blessings with our dear ones wherever they may be, and put about them Thy everlasting arms. Graciously manifest Thyself to the needy and distressed, to the sick and dying, and to all who look for salvation from sin. May the Holy Spirit of promise and power manifest Himself to all hearts and homes, and thus energize and make effective the agencies ordained for the saving of the whole world. Pardon our sins. May great peace fill our souls, enabling us to constantly walk in the quiet of Thy presence. At the close of the day may we possess consciences void of offense toward Thee, and toward all men, and realize that we have made another day's journey toward the heavenly home. Worthy is the Lamb that was slain to receive riches, and wisdom, and glory, and dominion, for ever and ever. *Amen.*

Bishop William M. Weekley, D.D.,
Parkersburg, W. Va.

JANUARY TWENTY-FOURTH

He ever liveth to make intercession: for them. — Heb. 7: 25.

GRACIOUS GOD, our Father in Heaven, we bless Thee that hour by hour our lives have been enriched with the knowledge of Him who graciously interpreted the Infinite to our finite minds, and Who in reconciling love and saving mercy, brought us near to our Father in Heaven.

Remembering our wilfulness of heart and proneness to sin, we would humble ourselves before Thee. Though, indeed, we have sought to do Thy holy will, yet have we fallen short in many things. We now confess our sins: "forgive us our trespasses."

Once again, we ask that by the Holy Spirit given unto us, we may find our delight in the ways of God, and so be enabled in our daily walk to commend the Gospel of Christ to those among whom we move.

Further, we beseech Thee to hear us on behalf of loved ones far and near, that they may share the blessings which we now ask for ourselves. And may Thy Kingdom come, and Thy will be done on earth as it is done in Heaven.

These and other favors we beg in the Name of our Lord and Saviour, Jesus Christ. *Amen.*

James W. Thirtle, D.D., LL.D.,
London, England.

JANUARY TWENTY-FIFTH

The righteousness which is of faith. — Rom. 9: 30.

HOLY FATHER, we thank Thee for the sweetness and goodness of Thy love. Thou hast sheltered our home, daily bearing our burdens, carrying our sorrows, and supplying all our needs.

We thank Thee for Jesus our Saviour, for the Holy Bible, and for the Church. We praise Thy Name for the Gospel, and for all who are making known the goodness of salvation.

We pray that Christian brethren may dwell together in unity, and put on love which is the bond of perfectness. May Thy righteous and peaceful Kingdom come, till all men everywhere may hear and know of Jesus, and learn to live as He lived, and love as He loved.

Teach us to be kind one to another, tender-hearted, forgiving. Give to us patience, meekness, gentleness, goodness, faith. May we have the blessedness of the pure in heart, and of the merciful. Fill us with the light of Thy presence, and lead us forth to do good unto all men. Keep Thou our going out and our coming in, from this time forth, and for evermore. Through Jesus Christ our Lord. *Amen.*

Rev. Robert E. Elmore,
Cincinnati, Ohio.

JANUARY TWENTY-SIXTH

Bless thou the Lord, O my soul. — Ps. 104: 35.

OUR Heavenly Father, we are Thy children, and we come to Thee, bringing our sacrifice of praise and thanksgiving. Thou hast made us, and Thy love of us is unceasing. Thy love is the light of our life and Thy grace the strength of our hearts. Save us from forgetting Thee and Thy claims upon us. May we welcome our common duties and discharge them as in Thy sight; rejoice in the ties of kinship which bind us to one another, and never forget them; courageously face our difficulties and carefully redeem the time, seeing that the days are evil. Help us to resist every temptation and especially those that assail our thoughts and stain our imagination. Give us power to hush the tumults of the flesh, and fortitude to bear the burdens of life cheerfully. Deliver us from anxiety about the future, and strengthen in us the conviction that all things work together for good for those that love Thee. Enable us to profit by Thy patient and loving discipline. Fill us with the mind of Jesus, and make us ready for any sacrifice for Thy Kingdom of righteousness and peace and joy in the Holy Ghost. Quicken us, Lord, that we may seek first Thy Kingdom and Thy righteousness, and calmly wait Thy will, in the assurance that whatever else is best will be given us. In the Name of Jesus Christ, our Lord. *Amen.*

John Clifford, D.D.
London, England.

JANUARY TWENTY-SEVENTH

I love the Lord because He hath heard my voice. — Ps. 116: 1.

O THOU Who art the light of all who must walk alone in the path of shadows, teach us to so trust Thee that fear may no longer beset us. We confess that we have often faltered when we have put our own thoughts and imaginings in the place of Thine omniscience. We lament our constant reckoning with human weakness when Thou hast promised the joy of the Lord which shall be our strength.

Teach us more of the power of purity, and forgive our sin of distrust of Thy love. If we cannot see beyond the turn of the road, may we yet be conscious of a companionship that leads us in confidence toward each new experience. Grant us the peace of Christ to quiet our feverish hearts, and lend courage for life's daily test of faith and discipleship. We covet the refreshing of Thy grace to lend strength for each new duty, and to enlarge our hearts to receive the fulness of Thy blessing. Lead us, we pray, into the green pastures and beside the still waters, that our spirits may be renewed at the fountains of Infinite Love — so shall we be heartened, and enabled to serve Thee more worthily in the name of Jesus Christ our Saviour. *Amen.*

Charles Gorman Richards, D.D.
Auburn. N. Y.

JANUARY TWENTY-EIGHTH

I was glad when they said unto me, Let us go into the house of the Lord. Our feet shall stand within Thy gates, O Jerusalem. Pray for the peace of Jerusalem: they shall prosper that love Thee. Because of the house of the Lord our God I will seek Thy good. — Ps. 122: 1-2; 6; 9.

For Sunday Morning.

O LORD, Jesus Christ, Who on this day didst arise from the grave, send forth Thy quickening Spirit, we beseech Thee, upon Thy people, that they may rise to newness of life. Drive away worldly cares, lift up our minds to high and noble thoughts, and to spiritual desires.

Hear the prayers of all that are offered in public and in private, for themselves and for their brethren. Grant that all who can may attend the public worship of Thy church, and approach Thee with reverence and confidence. Bless the ministrations of Thy Word and Sacraments. Inspire those who speak and act in Thy name, with the spirit of truth, and love, and power.

Meet the varied needs and fulfil the desires of Thy people. Bind us in fellowship one with another, as with Thyself. Enable us to go forth from the worship and instruction of Thy holy day with renewed strength and courage to perform the duties and bear the trials which are appointed for us.

Grant this, and all our petitions, for Thy Holy Name's sake. *Amen.*

Bishop Arthur C. A. Hall,
Burlington, Vermont.

JANUARY TWENTY-NINTH

If My people pray, I will forgive their sin. — II Chr. 7: 14.

HELP us now, Lord, to draw near to Thee as a family. Incline our hearts to seek Thy face, and graciously withdraw the veil that we may be conscious of Thy presence.

We ask Thee graciously to forgive all that Thou hast seen amiss, and to cleanse our hearts by the inspiration of Thy Holy Spirit, that we may perfectly love Thee and worthily magnify Thy Holy Name. Help us, who have had much forgiven, to forgive others, even to seventy times seven. Keep us from envy and jealousy, from pride and passion, and from every thing that would grieve Thy Holy Spirit. May we indeed be dead unto sin, and alive unto righteousness, through Jesus Christ.

Bless those whom we love. Comfort and help them in whatever circumstances they may be placed; and may they and we be finally gathered to the house of many mansions. Have mercy on all men, and bring them to the knowledge of the truth. These and all other petitions we offer in the name of

Jesus Christ, our Lord and Saviour, and pray Thee to do for us exceeding abundantly beyond all we ask or think, for Thy mercies' sake. *Amen.*

Rev. F. B. Meyer, B. A.,
London, England.

JANUARY THIRTIETH

Ask counsel, we pray thee, of God. — Judges, 18: 15.

OUR Heavenly Father: Thou hast made us for Thyself. We are the tender objects of Thy solicitude and care; Thou art more thoughtful of us and ours than we ourselves are.

We are conscious of our weakness. Temptations assail us. Our lives are often in the shadows, and we are inclined from the right. Awaken in us, O Lord, a sincere desire for Thee, for Thy house, and for Thy welcome. Help us to feel that we can never satisfy our souls until we satisfy them in Thee.

We feel deep within us the call of God to do our best. Do not permit us to rest in false security, in pleasant sins, or in popular falsehoods of whatever kinds. When we are satisfied with what we have done, show us the danger of losing our ideals of perfection. And when the way seems hard, and the by-paths pleasant and enticing, give us Thy gracious help.

Hear us, our Father, in the forgiveness of our sins. May Thy Kingdom come in power, that all men everywhere may know Thee as Lord and Master. May Thy will be done in our lives, and in the world, near and far, as it is in Heaven. Through Jesus Christ our Lord. *Amen.*

Bishop Lawrence H. Seager, D.D.,
Waterville, Illinois.

JANUARY THIRTY-FIRST

With thanksgiving let your requests be made known unto God. — Phil. 4: 6.

OUR Father in Heaven, we praise Thee for the mercy-seat to which we can come, and before which Thou art so pleased to have us bow. Help us to approach it with pure hearts and with sincere motives. Teach us our need of Thee. Show us how dangerous it is to live without the consciousness of Thy presence. Walk with us as Jesus walked with His two companions to Emmaus. Help us to commune with Thee as friend with friend. Prevent us from wilful sin. Subdue our heart's rebellion, and keep us at peace with Thee.

Help us to be patient and sympathetic with all who may need our help. If we have wronged anyone, give us the grace of repentance and confession. If any have injured us, enable us to forgive and forget.

Bless our home, and all who are dear to us by the ties of kinship and friendship. Inspire and strengthen us so that we will be able to glorify Thee in home, in school, in the factory, or shop. Forgive us wherein we may in any way have grieved Thee, and aid us in our efforts to avoid the mistakes of yesterday. Our prayer is in the name of Him Who loved us, and gave His life to save us. *Amen.*

H. W. Crews, D.D.,
Woodstock, Ont., Canada.

February

FEBRUARY FIRST

Blessed is he whose transgression is forgiven. — Ps. 32: 1.

ALMIGHTY GOD, we praise Thy name and worship Thee. Thou art infinitely holy. Through Jesus Christ, our Elder Brother and Mediator, Thou art *our* Father. We pray Thee to come very near to us, as we come to Thy throne of grace.

Help us to trust Thee more each day. Thou dost send the days as Thou wilt; sometimes in darkness and storm; sometimes in brightness and peace. Make us submissive to Thy will in all things, only come Thou with all the days, that each may be full of Thee, and a step nearer to Thy sweet Home.

Bless us all in this home — regard each one of us tenderly as we are bowed in this family circle: father, mother, children, all the loved ones. Make our home a resting place of security. In our outgoing and in our incoming be Thou our Light, our Guide, and our Defence. Give us each grace lovingly and trustfully to give ourselves into Thine hand, to be defended, instructed, and directed as Thou wilt, that in us Thy will may be done on earth as it is done in Heaven. Make all our lives musical with Thy praise; pardon our sins; grant unto us "the joy of Thy salvation," through riches of grace in Christ Jesus our Lord. *Amen.*

W. H. Dunbar, D. D.,
Baltimore, Md.

FEBRUARY SECOND

Pray and make supplication. — II Chr. 6: 24.

O LORD Our God, we thank Thee for Thy Fatherhood, and that Thou hast revealed Thyself unto us through Jesus Christ, Thy Son, Who is our Saviour. We thank Thee for Thy loving care of us through another day — for life and health and all the comforts we enjoy. Bless us as parents and children. Keep us from sinning against Thee. Help us to be faithful in our work, thoughtful of each other, kind and considerate and helpful to all. Watch over us through the night. If it please Thee, give us sleep, and bring us in safety and comfort to another day. May every day bring us a more perfect trust in Thee, so that with our days we may learn how better to walk in Thy ways, and to do Thy Holy Will, and to become more like Him Who has taught us to pray, saying:

"Our Father Who art in Heaven, hallowed be Thy Name. Thy Kingdom come. Thy will be done in earth as it is in Heaven. Give us this day our daily bread, and forgive us our debts as we forgive -our debtors; and lead us not into temptation, but deliver us from evil, for Thine is the Kingdom, and the Power, and the Glory forever." *Amen.*

Charles H. Robinson, D.D.
Wheeling, W. Va.

FEBRUARY THIRD

Finally, my brethren, be strong in the Lord, and in the power of His might. Put on the whole armor of God, that ye may be able to stand against the wiles of the devil. For we wrestle not against flesh and blood, but against principalities, against powers, against the rulers of the darkness of this world, against spiritual wickedness in high places. — Ephes. 6: 10-12.

OUR Heavenly Father, we thank Thee for the rest of the night, and the light of this new day. We also thank Thee for food and raiment and for every other blessing which in Thy goodness and wisdom Thou hast provided for our need and comfort.

We beseech Thee, grant us grace for the temptations of the day, and strength for every duty that may lie in our pathway. Help us truly to represent Thee to-day, and to this end may we hide "Thy Word" in our hearts, that we may not sin against Thee or our fellow men. Grant us the guidance and help of Thy good Spirit. Do Thou protect and defend us from all harm and danger, and when the day's work is done, bring us all again in safety to this, our home.

These things we ask in the Name and for the sake of our Lord and Saviour, Jesus Christ. *Amen.*

James M. S. Isenberg, D.D.,
Philadelphia, Pa.

FEBRUARY FOURTH

For this cause we also, since the day we heard it, do not cease to pray for you, and to desire that ye might be filled with the knowledge of His will in all wisdom and spiritual understanding; That ye might walk worthy of the Lord unto all pleasing, being fruitful in every good work, and increasing in the knowledge of God: Strengthened with all might, according to His glorious power, unto all patience and long suffering with joyfulness; Giving thanks unto the Father, which hath made us meet to be partakers of the inheritance of the saints in light. — Coloss, I.

OUR Father! worthy of all honor and praise, and Whom we desire to worship in spirit, and in truth, help us humbly come to Thee in prayer in this quiet hour.

May Thy hand, that hovered over us during the past night with protecting care, and measured to us the rich blessings of peaceful slumber and refreshing rest, now guide our feet to the duties of the day, and there shield us from harm. There give us Thy spirit of love and tenderness, Thy grace to sustain us in temptation and trial, Thy presence by Thy Spirit, to help us in all we may do.

Dwell in this home ever. Lead us on to glorify Thee in all things, until at last, life's duties finished, receive us to Thyself above. *Amen.*

Rev. P. H. Balsbaugh,
Columbia, Pa.

FEBRUARY FIFTH

Whatsoever ye ask in prayer, believing, ye shall receive. — Matt. 21: 22.

OUR Heavenly Father, gratefully we acknowledge Thy continued, loving kindness in protecting us sleeping and waking, and in providing for our daily needs. Forbid that the regularity with which Thy mercies come should ever make us forgetful that they come from Thee. If Thou shouldst withhold a single one, we should plead for its renewal.

Help us to meditate upon Thyself — Thy majesty and power, Thy tender compassion, Thy grief at our sinfulness, Thy grace to help in our time of need. May every gift of Thine come as a messenger from the Throne, summoning us to deeper devotion in heart and life.

Above all, we thank Thee for the Son of Thy love, Thy most gracious Gift to men.

Help us to tread aright the unknown path of another day. Lead Thou us on. And at its close may we be able to look back thankfully that by Thy grace we have heard Thy voice and followed Thee. Guide us in our perplexities; restrain us in our joys; comfort us in our sorrows; guard us in our temptations; and forgive us all our sins; for the sake of our Lord and Saviour, Jesus Christ. *Amen.*

Rev. G. E. Morgan, M.A.,
London, England.

FEBRUARY SIXTH

To all which believe, He is precious. — I Peter 2: 7.

HEAVENLY FATHER, Thou Who art the author, sustainer and developer of life, from Whom we came, in Whom we live and move and have our being, and to Whom we shall go, we pray that our souls may be conscious of the larger life of which we are a part, that we may find its deepest realities, understand its eternal principles, experience its mighty forces, and move with its persistent current toward its divine goal. We thank Thee for Jesus, for His consciousness of the largeness of Thy life. We thank Thee that faith in Him and the reception of His spirit and the adoption of His life principles make real to us the same divine life that was so vital to Him. Forgive us for ever tainting or circumscribing Thy life within us, for living only within the narrow confines of our own little lives, for failing to realize the largeness of the great spiritual world around us, for keeping aloof from any part of human life, and for devoting our energies and time to the sinful or lesser life objectives. We pray Thee to widen and deepen our life experiences, to keep us in sympathetic touch with all mankind, to help us make our lives genuine contributions to the progressive and divine life movements of the world, and to have a real part in bringing all members of the Father's family to know the length, breadth, depth and height of the fullness of His life. *Amen.*

Charles Herbert Rust, D.D.,
Rochester, N. Y.

FEBRUARY SEVENTH

Behold, God is my salvation; I -will trust, and not be afraid. — Isa. 12: 2.

OH, Lord God, help us to pray that this day we may come nearer the Christ ideal than ever before. Grant that by every thought and act we may bespeak His character to ourselves and to those with whom we shall come in contact. Forbid that we should neglect any opportunity that may come, to be living witnesses for Him.

Through the dangers and temptations, seen and unseen, which compass us about, bring us in safety to the close of day and to the close of this earthly pilgrimage. Bless those who are near to us by ties of home or friendship; and especially to those who know Thee not, manifest Thyself in power to-day.

May the Gospel note of love ring out more clearly this day than ever before, and may the sunshine of truth enter all hearts where ignorance, superstition and sin hold sway. May it bring cheer to the desolate ones, and hope to the despairing ones who may be near us, and yet who seem beyond our power to help. We pledge ourselves anew to the work of lifting the burdens of men and the upbuilding of Thy Kingdom. *Amen.*

Rev. W. M. Gross,
Cincinnati, Ohio.

FEBRUARY EIGHTH

Ye have not because ye ask not. — James 4: 2.

OUR Heavenly Father, it is with rejoicing hearts that we approach Thee in prayer. Thou hast, through Thy dear Son, brought "life and immortality to light." Thou hast revealed to us "the Lamb of God that taketh away the sin of the world." We come with confession upon our lips and penitence in our hearts, asking to be forgiven. Wilt Thou not bless us this day with the manifestations of Thy presence, of Thy peace, and of Thy power? Wilt Thou not use us in Thy service, and make our bodies to be the temples of Thy Spirit? We are Thy "living sacrifices." Our eyes shall see for Thee; our ears shall hear for Thee; our lips shall speak for Thee; our hands shall work for Thee; our hearts shall beat for Thee. We are Thine. Bless Thou the members of this family circle. Thou hast given them the shelter of the roof, the warmth of the hearth, the nourishment of daily bread. Give them also the food that comes from Heaven, the robe of Christ's righteousness, and the assurance of an "inheritance which is incorruptible, and undefiled, and that fadeth not away." Protect them in the hour of danger, and deliver them in temptation. Keep them from evil, and make them to be a positive force for righteousness. Hasten the full coming of Thy Kingdom, the complete proclamation of Thy Gospel, and the universal acknowledgment of Jesus Christ as King of kings and Lord of lords. We ask it in His Name. *Amen.*

Rev. DeWitt M. Benham, Ph.D.,
Baltimore, Maryland.

FEBRUARY NINTH

And it shall come to pass, that before they call, I will answer. — Isa. 65: 24.

OUR Heavenly Father, we thank Thee for our home and our work and our friends. The morning calls us to the joy and toil and trial of a new day, and we want to begin it right, in the sense of Thy nearness and care.

Give us strength to meet the common duties of the day, and to live with our kindred and friends happily and helpfully. In our school life, in our homemaking, and in our business, may we be guided by the purposes of Jesus. If it be Thy good will, keep us from great temptation to do wrong; and furnish us with strength for the trials which Thou wiliest us to endure.

May Thy healing and comfort abide with those we love, who are in sorrow and sickness; make them brave and hopeful.

We pray Thee to prosper us in our work, in order that we may use all our gains for the good of others.

May our home and family be the abiding place of Him Who promised to be in the midst of those who love Him. In His Name. *Amen.*

Ozora S. Davis, D.D., Ph.D.,
Chicago, Ills.

FEBRUARY TENTH

Hast thou faith? Have it to thyself before God. — Rom. 14: 22.

ALMIGHTY and living God, Father of our Lord Jesus Christ, of Whom the whole family in heaven and earth is named, we beseech Thee to look with love and mercy on us, Thy children, throughout this day. Keep us in Thy faith and fear. Give us grace to resist the devil, and to renounce all his works and temptations. Guard us from the lusts and sins of the flesh. Shield us from the corruptions of the world. Make us diligent and faithful in our appointed work. Keep us patient under trial. In anxiety and worry, help us to find trust and peace in Thee. To Thee we offer our thoughts, words, and actions of this day, and beg that Thou wilt bless them. In ills of the body and vexations of spirit, be Thou our healing and our strength. Bless our friends and neighbors. Increase their joys and soothe their sorrows and their sufferings. Protect Thy Holy Church spread throughout the world, that it may abide with steadfast faith in the confession of Thy Name. Take the dying to Thy rest, and comfort the departed with larger and larger measures of holiness and happiness. Dwell in our hearts, and guide us with Thy counsel, that after this life Thou mayest receive us with glory. All of which we ask through Jesus Christ our Lord and Saviour. *Amen.*

George McClellan Fiske, D.D.,
Providence, R. I.

FEBRUARY ELEVENTH

He is faithful that promised. — Heb. 10: 23.

OUR Heavenly Father, we thank Thee that Thy watchful care has brought us safely into another day with its obligations, labors, delights, and trials. Give us strength to resist evil, and to cleave to that which is good. Help us to let our light so shine that others may see our good works, and glorify Thee. Be with those of us who go to work, and those of us who go to school, and those of us who take care of the home. Bless with us all other families who remember Thee, and grant that in many homes who know Thee not, family altars may be erected, so that Thy Name may be glorified in the family life. Bless the officers, members, workers, and enterprises of our Church, and of all churches that seek to enhance Thy Kingdom. Thrust more laborers into the Kingdom, and through increased missionary efforts let the world speedily be filled with the knowledge of the glory of the Lord. Bless our country and those who are directing its affairs. Give them grace, wisdom, and courage to promote righteousness at home and in our relations with other countries. Bless all the other nations of the earth, with their statesmen and rulers. May the spirit of fairness take possession of all of them, so that they will project into all international relationships, peace and harmony. We ask these favors in the name of our blessed Lord and Saviour, Jesus Christ! *Amen.*

Rev. Chr. Staebler,
Cleveland, Ohio.

FEBRUARY TWELFTH

He forgave their iniquity. — Ps. 78: 38.

O LORD, who hast proven that we may trust Thee, we seek Thy blessing in the beginning of the day, that we may carry its influence with us into the toil and trial of our busy life. We claim Thy sufficient grace, that we may be equal to every severe test.

Give us wisdom, that we may undertake our tasks and do them as those who have learned of the Divine Workman. Take possession of our minds that to-day they may think Thy thoughts after Thee, and be intent upon working out Thy great plans through the best lives we can live.

So rule us with Thy Spirit that our senses may be harnessed for Thy uses. Save us from falling into shameful sin. Prevent us from being mean, small, disagreeable, irritable, unsympathetic, as we touch other lives. Be our unseen Companion as we earn our daily bread — and help us to earn it honestly.

Make us wholesome; keep us sweet. May others know to-day by our unobtrusive goodness that Jesus lives at our house. May we somehow be instrumental in opening the doors of other homes for the incoming of this Heavenly Guest.

We ask these favors in His Name. *Amen.*

J. Bradley Markward, D.D.,
Harrisburg, Penna.

FEBRUARY THIRTEENTH

I have loved thee with an everlasting love. — Jer. 31: 3.

WE thank Thee, our loving Father, for Thy watchful care over us through another night. Thou dost neither slumber nor sleep, and Thy ever wakeful eye has been upon us in our unconscious moments, and Thy protecting and upholding hand has been underneath and about us. Thou art setting before us a new day, with all of its opportunities and possibilities for good or evil. This is one of the days concerning which Thou hast promised, "As thy day so shall thy strength be." Is not this one of the days for which Thou hast made such bountiful provision? Let us not venture forth upon the day's duties or difficulties without Thy guiding, upholding, protecting hand. Thou art able to do for us exceedingly abundantly above all that we can ask or think. Give us strength to conquer every temptation. Surround us with Thy gracious presence as a shield from every danger. Bless with us all whom we should specially remember at the Throne of Thy Grace. Wherever we can send a thought, Thou canst send a blessing. Let Thy blessing be suited to the capacities and needs of every one of them. May every heart be turned to Thee as the morning-glory turns to the light, and may their souls and ours be enlivened, purified, and strengthened by the light of Thy health-giving countenance. *Amen.*

R. J. Miller, D.D.,
Pittsburgh, Penna.

FEBRUARY FOURTEENTH

Unto the upright there ariseth light in the darkness: he is gracious, and full of compassion and righteous. A good man sheweth favor, and lendeth: he will guide his affairs with discretion. Surely he shall not be moved forever: the righteous shall be in everlasting remembrance. — Ps. 112: 4-6.

ALMIGHTY GOD, our Heavenly Father, we thank Thee that Thou hast taught us to call Thee "Father." In the strength of Thy Name we go forth to meet the temptations and the duties of this day. May we be worthy of being called Thy children. May we have Thy patience and tenderness in our dealing with others, especially with the members of our own household. May we have pity for all weak and tempted persons, and lend them our strength, as Thou dost lend Thy strength to us. Clothe us this day with the armor of light. May we have Thy purity, the horror of all evil thoughts and all unholy desires, and may they be overcome and cast out of our hearts by a passion for holiness. Whatever we have to do, may we do it so that it shall be well pleasing to Thee. Help us to adorn the doctrine of God our Saviour in all things. Preserve us in all danger; keep us in the way of life; and bring us at last to our Father's house in peace. Through Jesus Christ our Lord. *Amen.*

Henry Evertson Cobb, D.D.,
New York City, N. Y.

FEBRUARY FIFTEENTH

Wait on the Lord, and He shall save thee. — Prov. 20: 22.

IN the Name of the Lord Jesus we bow in Thy holy presence, O God, to thank Thee for all Thy goodness and mercy to us as a family and a household, and to ask Thy forgiveness for all wherein we have sinned and grieved Thy Holy Spirit.

We pray for grace and guidance that we may so walk as to please Thee. Grant us Thy protecting care to shield us from accident and danger. And above all, we pray that, thus walking in Thy fear and love, we may know the joy of Thy salvation.

And what we ask for ourselves, we pray for all who are dear to us. And very specially we commend to Thy Fatherly goodness any who are in sickness or sorrow or trouble, that Thou wilt graciously bless and sustain and comfort them.

Thou hast given Thine only begotten Son that whosoever believeth in Him may have eternal life. Such is Thy love to the world. But Thou hast a still tenderer love for those who believe in Christ and are one with us in Him. For them we make our prayer to Thee.

Hear us and bless us, we pray Thee, for the Lord Jesus Christ's sake. *Amen.*

Sir Robert Anderson, K.C.B., LL.D.
London, England.

FEBRUARY SIXTEENTH

Ask thy Father and He will show thee. — Deut. 32: 7.

ALMIGHTY and Eternal Lord, we come by Thine own appointed way to Thee. The Name above every name is our only plea, and for His sake Who bears it Thou wilt hear and answer. What infinite grace Thou hast for all needy ones; what love and what compassion! Our souls adore and worship Thee for all Thou art, and for all that Thou hast done. W r e praise Thee for Thy Son, and for all that He has become to Thy trusting ones. Especially do our souls go up to Thee in adoring wonder as we think of His cross and passion. It is in the cross we find our hope. And now, Lord, wilt Thou create within us a simple faith in Thy Word, and cause us to see that naught of all Thou hast promised can ever fail of fulfilment. Evermore increase our faith. Keep us walking with Thee: safeguard us from all attacks of the evil one, and if it be Thy good pleasure, take us into the circle of Thy anointed ones, that we may effectively serve Thee. Help us in our daily duties, whether these lie in our home or business; therein may we honor and glorify Thee, and prove a blessing to our fellow men. Speed the coming of Thy Kingdom, and hasten the day when our Lord shall take His own Throne and reign gloriously. In the Name of Him Who loved us and gave Himself for us. *Amen.*

Rev. Joseph W. Kemp,
New York City, N. Y.

FEBRUARY SEVENTEENTH

Sing unto the Lord with thanksgiving. — Ps. 147: 7.

HEAVENLY FATHER, we thank Thee for opening to us the doorway of a new day; and now that our feet stand upon the threshold of this great opportunity, we pray for guidance, wisdom, love and power. Thou hast seen fit to draw a curtain before our eyes, so that we know not what a day may bring forth. As we journey into the wilderness of the future, a pillar of cloud has hovered about us so that we cannot tell what enemies shall meet us to-day, what duties shall present themselves for performance, what temptations may grapple with us by the wayside, what sloughs of despair may await our unwary feet, yet we know that with Thy divine help we shall be more than victors through Him Who loved us. Keep us, God; our boat is so small, and Thy ocean is so vast. Enable us to lay aside every weight and sin which does so easily beset us. May Thy Fatherly protection be over those who are dear to us. Bless our enemies, if we have any, and give us right spirits to all mankind. Hasten the coming of Thy Kingdom, when injustice, impurity, un-happiness, and sin, shall be put down, and when love, truth, honor, and jus-tice shall prevail in the Name of the Lord. Hear us now in this, our prayer. In Jesus' Name. *Amen.*

Rev. Charles C. Selecman,
Los Angeles, California.

FEBRUARY EIGHTEENTH

He hath inclined His ear unto me, therefore will I call upon Him. — Ps. 116: 2.

OUR FATHER, Who art in Heaven, may it be of Thy good pleasure, now in the light of a new morning, to look favorably upon Thy dependent children here kneeling as a united family of worshipers within the home which Thou hast appointed us, and to receive our humble thanksgivings for the perfect protection of Thy care, and for the refreshment of a healthful sleep granted by Thyself through the darkness of the night that is gone.

And do Thou now, we beseech Thee, ordain to us for yet another day Thy watchful providence for our guard against all sickness and bodily peril; Thy wise counsel for our guidance into every right thought and unto every fitting word; Thy sufficient grace for our defense from all temptation to wrong, as likewise for our enablement unto all fidelity in duty, and Thy atoning love to cover all our sins.

Following Thee, may our hearts be cleansed from every motive unworthy of those who bear Thy Name, and may we be led to walk in charity and helpfulness among all those who surround us, making manifest to every companion and acquaintance some forecast of Thy coming Kingdom, and dedicating our several lives to the service of Thy blessed will — through Jesus Christ, our Lord. *Amen.*

Nolan R. Best,
New York City.

FEBRUARY NINETEENTH

I will lift up mine eyes unto the hills, from whence cometh my help. My help cometh from the Lord, which made heaven and earth. He will not suffer thy foot to be moved: He that keepeth thee will not slumber. — Ps. 121: 1-3.

O GOD, Giver of light and power! We thank Thee for our Mountains of Transfiguration, for hours of insight and joy. But vision has not insured effectiveness in service. Like Thy disciples at the foot of the Mount of Transfiguration, "We are not able," and we come to Thee with the great question, "Lord, why could we not cast it out?" We know that all things are possible to him that believeth and that faith-filled prayer, whether it be fellowship with Thee or intercession for another, is efficient prayer. Help Thou our unbelief. Help us to come so closely and truly into Thy fellowship that we shall be filled with power not our own. May we be truly identified with Thee. May we perfectly imitate Thy mind, and so be filled unto all the fulness of God. So teach us in the school of true prayer, that this day may be one of continued joy because Thy power has free course in us. This we ask in the name of Jesus Christ, our Lord. *Amen.*

William Horace Day, B.D., D.D.,
Los Angeles, California.

FEBRUARY TWENTIETH

He forgetteth not the cry of the humble. — Ps. 9: 12.

DEAR LORD, our Friend and our Saviour: Thy children come to Thy feet and look up into Thy face, for we know that Thou dost love us and that Thou art waiting for us. Be Thou ever the centre of our family life, and make us find our peace and our happiness in Thy presence. Our home can be blessed only when we know that Thou art with us, Help us to love one another as Thou dost love us; to be gentle and unselfish and forgiving; to be good children of our Heavenly Father. When we are troubled, do Thou quiet our fears. When we are tempted, do Thou grant us the victory. When we are sick, may Thine everlasting arms enfold us; and when we go astray, O dear Shepherd, seek us and bring us home again. May our hearts be glad in the knowledge of Thy love. May our thoughts be pure because Thou rulest them. Let the sunshine of Thy favor drive away all shadows, and may we sing in the gladness of our spirits, since Thou art our Guardian and Friend, and therefore no harm can befall us. Help us to grow daily more like Thee, and at last take us to Thy Home, where we shall be happy forever.

Hear our prayer, dear Christ, and help us and bless us, for Thine own dear sake. *Amen.*

Floyd W. Tomkins, B.D., LL.D.
Philadelphia, Penna.

FEBRUARY TWENTY-FIRST

God hath attended to the voice of my prayer. — Ps. 66: 19.

O THOU GOD of all grace, Father of mercies, the Hope of believers, Saviour of the penitent soul, hear our prayer.

Thou hast revealed Thyself in such lovely characteristics and endearing relations, that we may remove all fear, and be encouraged in all trouble, and be led to say, "Let us draw nigh to God."

Teach us, Lord, because we know not truth of ourselves. May we see divine things in a heavenly light, so that our minds may be informed and at the same time our hearts be sanctified.

Consecrate our whole life to Thy service and glory. Search us, O God, and know our hearts; try us, and know our thoughts; see if there be any wicked way in us, and lead us in the way everlasting.

Accept our thanksgiving and praise for Thy generous blessing in material refreshment and spiritual strength. Keep us under Thy guardian care so that whether we eat or drink or whatever we do, we may do all in the Name of the Lord Jesus and to the glory of God, through Christ our blessed Redeemer and Friend. *Amen.*

George M. Diffenderfer, D.D.,
Carlisle, Penna.

FEBRUARY TWENTY-SECOND

This, the love of God, that we keep His commandments. — I John, 5: 3.

O LORD, Thou art the high and lofty One Who doth inhabit eternity, Whose Name is Holy: Thou dwellest in the high and holy place, with him also that is of a contrite and humble spirit.

We bow before Thee, humbly asking Thy pardon of our sins, through our Saviour. We thank Thee that Thou didst so love us as to give Thy beloved Son that we might live; and we rejoice that no one shall be able to pluck us out of Thy hands.

We pray Thee that Thy Kingdom may come, and Thy will be done on earth as it is in Heaven. Do Thou support and empower everyone who labors for Thee at home or on the mission fields. Do Thou comfort and uphold all who are sick or bereaved, or troubled. May these trials bring them closer to Thee.

We do desire that Thou wouldst give us grace and power to live rightly to-day, to do our work and to glorify Thee. Oh, keep us from falling or doing anything to grieve Thee or to bring sorrow to ourselves, or to anyone.

We ask all in the Name of our Saviour. *Amen.*

D. T. Reed,
Pittsburgh, Penna.

FEBRUARY TWENTY-THIRD

He that hath My commandments and keepeth them, loveth Me. — John 14: 21.

MOST gracious God Almighty, all wise, all loving, our Heavenly Father, we rejoice that Thou hast called us to be Thy children.

We confess before Thee, that we are indeed like little children, with all their weakness and imperfections, but without their humility, purity, teacha-bleness and trustfulness. Cleanse us from our sins. Grant us joy and peace in believing in Thee. May we have the love that believeth all things, hopeth all things, endureth all things.

In our home, in our daily work and recreations, and in all our relations to others, make us strong and steadfast to do the right and shun the wrong. Bless us, that we may become a blessing to others.

Remember, we beseech Thee, all classes and conditions of men — the sick, the sorrowful, the poor and needy, the widows and orphans, the little children with their sweet faith and childlike joys, the young and vigorous, bearing the responsibilities of life.

Bless the missionaries at home and abroad. Be pleased to make Thyself known in the labors of the faithful pastors and teachers, and let Thy truth and righteousness govern the nations of the earth, through Jesus Christ, our Lord. *Amen.*

Rums W. Miller, D.D.,
Philadelphia, Penna.

FEBRUARY TWENTY-FOURTH

Continue in prayer, and watch. — Col. 4: 2.

O FATHER, God, we thank Thee to-day for life — the privilege of living. Help us to-day to remember that "we live in deeds, not years; in thoughts, not breaths; in feelings, not in figures on a dial. We should count time by heart-throbs." May we ever be reminded that "he lives best, who thinks best, feels the noblest, acts the best." Help us to-day to so act that we may show our appreciation for life by our work.

We thank Thee, too, God, for the chance to serve. May we to-day overlook no opportunity to reach out a helping hand, to speak a kind word, to show sympathy; and above all, help us to appreciate every service rendered by those who work with and for us. May we, O Lord, in all that we do this day, do our level best; may we think the highest and best thoughts; may we strive to use our best efforts. Help us to strive to-day "not as though we had already attained, but that we might reach after" the spiritual life we long for. Then help us to "give to the world the best we have, that the best may come back to us." Hear us, Father, in the Name of Thy dear Son, our Lord Jesus Christ! *Amen.*

D. Walter Morton, A.M., C.P.A.,
Eugene, Oregon.

FEBRUARY TWENTY-FIFTH

Likewise the Spirit also helpeth our infirmities: for we know not what we should pray for as we ought: but the Spirit itself maketh intercession for us with groanings which cannot be uttered. And he that searcheth the hearts knoweth what is the mind of the Spirit, because he maketh intercession for the saints according to the will of God. And we know that all things work together for good to them that love God, to them who are the called according to his purpose.

- Romans 8: 26-28.

THE way is long, our Father, and sometimes very weary. We crowd and bruise one another in passing, and often we forget the goal in the heat and hurry of the pilgrimage. Start us forth, we pray, each day with fresh courage, and whisper in our hearts a little song to gladden our steps as we take up our burdens anew. Grant that the lightest of these may ever be our conscience, and that we may never be too laden with personal troubles to carry the balm of sympathy for friend and foe. Above all, grant us the gift of clear vision, that we may pierce the doubts and fears of the passing moment, and dwell with unfaltering confidence upon the ultimate fact of Thy love. *Amen.*

Alice Hegan Rice,
Louisville, Ky.

FEBRUARY TWENTY-SIXTH

O, satisfy us early with Thy mercy; that we may rejoice and be glad all our days. Make us glad according to the days wherein Thou hast afflicted us, and the years wherein we have seen evil. And let the beauty of the Lord our God be upon us; and establish Thou the work of our hands upon us: yea, the work of our hands establish Thou it. — Ps. 90: 14-17.

DEAR LORD, let us do our work each day, and if the darkened hours of despair overcome us, may we not forget the strength that comforted us in the desolation of other times. In these times of backsliding, when so many allurements are held out by the world, let that great force which turned our life from darkness into Thy most marvelous light be ever present, and the "refining fire go through our hearts, illuminating our souls." May Thy blessed Word be a lamp unto our feet, and a light unto our path. Lift our eyes from the earth; forbid that we should judge others, lest we ourselves be condemned. Help us to understand Thy precious Word, and at this stage of the world's history may we be constantly looking for Thy glorious reappearing. Let us be like the wise virgins, constantly having on the wedding garments. *Amen.*

Rev. A. Sheldrick,
East Northfield, Mass.

FEBRUARY TWENTY-SEVENTH

The Lord looseth the prisoners: The Lord openeth the eyes of the blind: the Lord raiseth them that are bowed down; the Lord loveth the righteous: The Lord preserveth the strangers; He relieveth the fatherless and widow; but the way of the wicked He turneth upside down. The Lord shall reign for ever, even thy God, O Zion, unto all generations. Praise ye the Lord. — Ps. 146: 7-10.

OH GOD, our Father! How precious to us is the privilege of having Thy Name linger on our lips, giving us new assurance of the fact that we are in the circle of Thy love and care. May this confidence drive away all fear and anxiety, and help to keep out of this day all other enemies of our souls. In the moment of our temptation, may we realize Thy promise and Thy presence. When burdens become heavy, may we find the strength necessary in Thee. In face of all difficulty and every problem, may we be brave because of our faith. For whatever these hours bring, may Thy grace be sufficient. Whatever we do, may we do it all to Thy glory. May this day bear the divine mark in the calendar on earth, and in Heaven.

We leave our prayer where all prayer belongs — in the shadow of the Cross. *Amen.*

Cortland Myers, A.B., D.D.,
Boston, Mass.

FEBRUARY TWENTY-EIGHTH

As many as I love, I rebuke and chasten: be zealous therefore, and repent. Behold, I stand at the door, and knock: if any man hear my voice, and open the door, I will come in to him, and will sup with him, and he with Me. To him that overcometh, will I grant to sit with Me in My throne, even as I also overcame, and am set down with My Father in His throne. — Rev. 3: 19, 20, 21.

O LORD, Thou art ever knocking at the door of our souls, seeking entrance into our lives. Help us to recognize Thy knockings, and to open to Thine entrance.

We would have our hearts open to Thee at all times — in sunshine or in shadow, in joy or in sorrow. Whether Thou comest in the time of the singing of birds, or in winter's chilling blasts, may we receive Thee joyfully.

Show us that we need Thee more than anything that Thou mayest give us, and that Thou, Thyself, art more than all Thy gifts. So, when Thou knockest, Lord, may we open to Thee, and receive Thee as an abiding guest. *Amen.*

H. H. Beattys, D.D.,
New Rochelle, New York.

FEBRUARY TWENTY-NINTH

The Lord hath dealt bountifully with thee. — Ps. 116: 7.

(The Extra Day)

O GOD, in Whose hand is our breath, Thou hast given and received our yesterdays, and dost know what our to-morrows hold for us. We thank Thee for to-day. We seek to keep pace with the goings of Thy sun and, therefore, add this day to our year. But we cannot ever keep up with the glory of Thy gifts, since Thou dost do for us exceedingly abundantly above all we are able to ask or to think.

We praise Thee that, when we give ourselves to Thee, Thou dost give us "good measure, pressed down, and shaken together, and running over." Thy extra gifts come to us in pleasant surprises, in our enlarging selves, in beautiful experiences here that "eye hath not seen, nor ear heard, neither have entered into the heart of man," in the exhaustless Christ, and in Thy forgiveness.

Fill our hearts with greater tides of love that in the depths of our souls we may increasingly abound in gratitude to Thee for all Thy gifts that are more than can be numbered. Help us to forsake our murmurings, to forget our bitterness in penitence for our sins, and daily to look for the joys that belong to that perennial newness of life into which Thy holy grace has called us. Through Jesus Christ, our Lord. *Amen.*

W. C. Bitting, D.D.,
St. Louis, Missouri.

March

MARCH FIRST

Let them that love Thy Name be joyful in Thee. — Ps. 5: 11.

MOST Gracious Father, we lift up our hearts unto Thee, from Whom alone comes our strength. Help us to trust Thee so wholly that we trust Thee in the dark. Thy mercies are fresh every morning and renewed to us every night. Help us to praise Thee for Thy goodness and to rest in Thy love. Thou knowest what we have need of before we ask Thee. Grant us all that Thou seest we need. Save us from suffering and want, from sickness and misery, from doubt and perplexity, from temptation and sin. Teach us that Thou carest for us, and nothing can harm us or separate us from Thy love. Relieve us from anxiety and fear, that our minds may be at leisure from themselves to soothe and sympathize. Make us useful in the world in which Thou hast placed us, and zealous in service to Thee. Forgive us our sins, in Jesus Christ; give us Thy Spirit to dwell within us, and grant us the joy of conscious communion with Thee. Conform us ever more closely to Thine image as Thou hast revealed it to us in Jesus Christ; lead us in the paths of holiness; and take us at last unto Thyself to dwell forever in Thy presence, the recipients of Thy favor and love. And. all we ask, we ask in the Name and for the sake of Thy Son, Jesus Christ our Lord. *Amen.*

Benjamin B. Warfield, D.D., LL.D.
Princeton, N. J.

MARCH SECOND

Make the voice of His praise to be heard. — Ps. 66: 8.

OUR FATHER, we thank Thee for the day which is before us. Its light awoke us with gladness; and its evening shadows will beckon us to rest. It is an emblem of Thy gift of life to us. For life is made up of joy and sorrow, like the clouds with the sun shining through, and of toils and responsibilities, and hopes like the morning, and memories glorifying all like the rays of the sunset. Help us to be grateful and worthy of Thy gift. Lord, we are thankful above all for this household of ours. Through its ministry we better understand Thee. What we are to our little ones Thou art to us; and what our children are to us, we are to Thee. When we think of it, love sweeps over us like the summer, and we know the joy of Thy favor, and feel the security of Thy care. In parenthood Thou dost come close to us, and in childhood we draw close to Thee. Bless Thou our children and all our loved ones, and make each one of us worthy of love and confidence human and divine. We are sorry for the harsh word and the unkind act. Even as we are sorry for our own faults, we forgive one another. Do Thou forgive us each one, O Father, for every indifference and sin against Thee. Guard us and keep us to-day. *Amen.*

N. McGee Waters, D.D.
Brooklyn, New York.

MARCH THIRD

He will be our guide even unto death. — Ps. 48: 14.

ALMIGHTY and most merciful Father, we begin the day conscious of our helplessness, and Thy supreme and sovereign power. As Thou didst give us life, so we implore Thee to sustain it and to make us ready and fit for our larger service. For Thy care and protection through the night we praise Thee; the day and the night to Thee are both alike. As Thou hast watched about our beds, so we believe Thou knowest and plannest all our ways. Do Thou prepare us for all that Thou art preparing for us. If perchance we should fail in our fulfilment of Thy plan concerning us, do Thou gently correct us and restore us to Thy love and favor. If disappointments or sorrows should attend us, make us strong to bear our burdens, and enrich us with Thy sustaining grace. Make us ever faithful in each particular duty; loyal to every high claim, responsive to every obligation to Thee and to those about us. Give us to know the way that leadeth unto life eternal, and fill us with the peace that passeth understanding. May the shadows and the sunshine alike develop and ennoble our characters. Bind us as a household with the ties of a sacred love, and make us worthy of Thy continuing care and favor. May we live this day as heirs of eternal life, and rise ever more and more unto the measure of the stature of the fulness of Him Who for our sakes became poor, that we through His poverty might be made rich — Thy Son, our Saviour, Jesus Christ. *Amen.*

James E. Freeman, D.D.,
Minneapolis, Minn.

MARCH FOURTH

For we know that if our earthly house of this tabernacle were dissolved, we have a building of God, an house not made with hands, eternal in the heavens. — II Corinthians 5: 1.

OUR Father Who art in Heaven, we thank Thee for the mercies of the past day and night; for food and clothing, for sleep and shelter; for the companionship of our fellow men, and for daily opportunities for usefulness. By our receiving these mercies may we also recognize the duties which they imply. May our love to Thee and our love to our fellow men ever grow stronger by their daily exercise.

Give us grace to face the future with equanimity. We profoundly believe in the future life, and that Thou hast not created the wonderful minds of the past and the present — minds so fruitful in searching out the secrets of nature and of the human mind and body, and in devising the many means and methods by which man's comfort, intelligence, and general welfare are so wonderfully promoted — only to vanish into oblivion at the death of the body, which is mortal. We believe that Thou hast given to each of us an immortal soul, capable of dwelling with Thee in everlasting bliss. May we so order our lives in this, our temporary home, as to be fitted by Thy grace to inhabit our eternal home. Help us by precept and example to influence our fellow men to accept Jesus Christ as their personal Saviour, and to enjoy this same faith in the future life. All of this we ask in the Name and for the sake of our Lord Jesus Christ. *Amen.*

William W. Keen, M.D., LL.D.,
Philadelphia, Penna.

MARCH FIFTH

God forbid that I should sin in ceasing to pray. — I Samuel 12: 23.

FATHER in Heaven, we turn unto Thee in the morning of this new day, in loving gratitude for Thy care over us through the past night. We thank Thee to-day for home and food and clothing, for service to which Thou hast called us, and for a measure of health and strength to serve Thee, for friends to love and serve, and above all, for the revelation of Thyself through Jesus Christ, our Lord.

We pray Thee to bless cur home to-day; guard every one of us in the hour of temptation; keep our feet from the paths of sin; keep us from using selfishly any of the blessings that Thou hast bestowed upon us. Fill our lives with the joy and peace and satisfaction that comes from living in obedience to Thee.

Cleanse and purify Thy Church, and strengthen it for the service for which Thou hast redeemed it, empowering all those who preach and teach Thy blessed Word in our land and in distant lands. Fill Thy Church with a passion to finish the task Thou hast given it to do.

Grant to every one we love Thy richest and fullest blessing for this day. We pray in the Name of Jesus Christ. *Amen.*

W. B. Anderson, D.D.,
Philadelphia, Penna.

MARCH SIXTH

We give thanks to God always for you all, making mention of you in our prayers; Remembering without ceasing your work of faith, and labor of love, and patience of hope in our Lord Jesus Christ, in the sight of God and our Father; Knowing, brethren beloved, your election of God. For our gospel came not unto you in word only, but also in power, and in the Holy Ghost, and in much assurance.

— I Thessalonians 1: 2-5.

ETERNAL GOD, our Father! Ere we go out into the world to meet its trials and temptations, we come to Thee for strength to fortify our spirits. Give us Thine own armor — Truth in our thoughts and motives, our words and actions; a sense of obligation in our work and in all our relationships; courage to face difficulty, because we know we are true and therefore have the Father with us. May our daily tasks, whether commonplace or exalted, be glorified in the consciousness that we are doing our Father's bidding. Give us patience with the shortcomings of others, and wisdom in the disciplining of our characters. May no evil blight this day, and mar the finished structure of our lives, but may we keep ourselves unspotted from the world. And as we go our several ways, wilt Thou watch between us while we are absent one from the other. Grant us this prayer in Christ's name. *Amen.*

Charles A. Eaton, D.D., M.A.
New York City, N. Y.

MARCH SEVENTH

Seek ye first the Kingdom of God and His righteousness, and all these things shall be added unto you. — Matt. 6: 33.

OUR Father in Heaven, we bless Thee that Thou art near at hand, and not afar off. We thank Thee for Thy protecting care and Thy sustaining grace. We rejoice in our material comforts and our social joys. We recognize Thy Hand in all the good of life.

Forgive us our sins that are past through the mercy and forbearance of God. Make us pure and strong and true this day. Bless us and ours, and all

42

mankind. May Thy Kingdom come! May righteousness and peace and good will prevail in all the relationships of mankind.

May we go forth to our tasks to-day in the fear of God, and with a rejoicing sense of Thy presence with us, and when the evening shadows gather may we go to rest with the assurance that He Who keepeth us doth not slumber nor sleep. May we do our work well through life, and when the day of life is over, when our work is done and the night comes on, at eventide may it still be light unto us. In Jesus' Name. *Amen.*

Rev. A. S. Tuttle, M. A.,
Medicine Hat, Alta, Canada.

MARCH EIGHTH

Ask of God, and He will give it Thee. — John 11: 22.

OUR Father, we thank Thee for the home with its protection and loving fellowship. Whatever else it may or may not be rich in, make it rich in the presence of Thy Holy Spirit in fulness and power.

Forgive and forget, we beseech Thee, for the sake of our Saviour and Thy dear Son, the sins of our lives, and cleanse us in His precious Blood.

Send each one of us forth filled with the spirit of our Master, which is the spirit of unselfish service. Strengthen us to do every proper task, teach us to be kind and helpful to others in Christ's name, make of us blessed channels of Thy mercies, and lead us into that pathway of life in which we can best glorify Thee and serve our fellowmen.

Make our home life continually more Christ-like, and may that life as well as our individual lives react for good on all with whom we come in contact. Hasten, through the service of our lives, the coming of Thy world-wide Kingdom, and the crowning of King Jesus, in Whose Name we pray. *Amen.*

Prof. William J. Martin,
Davidson, N. C.

MARCH NINTH

The Lord is good to the soul that seeketh Him. — Lam. 3: 25.

INFINITE FATHER, Thou art our life and light, our hope and redemption. We have tried the world and found it a great emptiness; we come back to Thee Who art eager to fill our souls with everlasting truth and mercy.

We come with a song in our hearts, for the list of Thy benefits is beyond our counting. We thank Thee for the stirring, stimulating days of the present, with their opportunities for improvement and service, their concern for the poor and ignorant. We thank Thee for the mysterious, inviting days which

43

are to come, laden with secret stores for our replenishing, hidden delights, and dark experiences for our training.

We thank Thee for the silent heroisms of the home; for the hallowed drudgeries of hospital and sick chamber. We thank Thee that, despite the cleverness of wicked men and the foolishness of good men, the Kingdom makes steady advance. Thy bounty unto us is without boundaries. And yet we baffle Thy plans, thwart Thy love, and wander wretchedly from the way of Jesus. We return unto Thee this morning to have our stains removed, our petty shams stripped away, and our hearts fortified. Have compassion upon us, and bring us all by and by to our Father's home, through the riches of grace in Christ Jesus. *Amen.*

Rev. Hugh Elmer Brown,
Seattle, Washington.

MARCH TENTH

We are more than conquerors through Him that loveth us. — Rom. 8: 37.

HEAVENLY FATHER, the strength of all who put their trust in Thee, be with us each day, we pray Thee, to uphold our hands and guide our hearts that we may give of our best to Thy service.

Thou knowest our weakness, how much we care for the opinion of others. Give us of Thy strength, that we may never be afraid to do Thy will. Each day there come temptations, sorrows, successes; may we be ready to meet each with a clear faith in Thee and an earnest trust in Thy goodness.

Help us as we go about our daily task, in the mill or the office, the school or the home, to have pure thoughts and clean lips.

May we try to give ourselves in helpfulness to those with whom we come in contact, each day making some one happier by word or deed, so that, as the evening comes and the shadows lengthen, we may go to our rest happy in having been of service to the world.

Grant that we may, by our surrender to Thee, and our sacrifice for others, gain the strength to bear the cross, following His footsteps, in Whose Name we offer this, our imperfect prayer. *Amen.*

Rev. Edward H. Bonsall, Jr.
Morton, Penna.

MARCH ELEVENTH

He knoweth our frame; He remembereth. that we are dust. — Ps. 103: 14.

O LORD, we come to Thee in the name of Jesus, Who is the way, the truth, and the life. Thou art a great God, and we would approach Thee with feelings of reverence and holy fear. But Thou art also our Father, having created and redeemed us, and we come with the love and confidence of children. We thank Thee that we have a friend and advocate in Heaven, ever our Saviour, Who was tempted in all points like as we are, yet without sin, and W T ho can be touched with the feeling of our infirmities. We adore Thee, the Triune God, Father, Son, and Holy Spirit.

Every good gift is from Thee. All our hopes are in Thee. Cast us not away from Thy presence. Look with compassion upon us, and blot out all our sins.

Teach us Thy will, and lead us in a plain path. Make us willing to be used in Thy Kingdom. Forbid that we should lay a stumbling block in the way of another. As we grow in years, may we grow in grace. Prosper Thy Church in this and all lands. Speedily bring all nations to accept Jesus as Lord and Saviour. We ask it in His Name. *Amen.*

Charles P. Wiles, D.D.,
Philadelphia, Penna.

MARCH TWELFTH

We are bound to thank God always. — II Thess. 1: 3.

OUR FATHER, we thank Thee that Thy mercies are still upon us, and that Thy love wraps us round about. We bless Thee for the joy of existence, and for every good and beautiful thing Thou hast put into our lives. Thou hast set beauty in all the world about us, and Thou dost seek us through every sense we have. We know that Thou art merciful, for there has never been a moment of our lives in which Thou hast dealt with as according to our sins. We bless Thee for the exceeding riches of Thy grace, and Thy kindness toward us through Christ Jesus.

At the close of another day we come to Thee for Thy benediction, and commit ourselves to the love that has never failed us. Look upon us in Thy tender compassion, and take away all our transgressions. Let the everlasting arms be underneath us. Give us rest in Thy love. Keep us from sin and from sorrow. Teach us to do Thy will, and lead us in the way everlasting. Quicken us by Thy Holy Spirit, and help us always to be obedient to Thy voice, submissive to Thy will, and responsive to Thy love. We ask it in the Name of Jesus Christ, our Lord. *Amen.*

David F. McGill, D.D.,
Ben Avon, Penna.

MARCH THIRTEENTH

God resisteth the proud, but giveth grace unto the humble. — James 4: 6.

OUR Gracious God and Father, we praise Thee for constant access to Thee in Jesus Christ. We bless Thee for Thy gifts day by day for spirit, soul and body. We thank Thee that Thou art ever the same in Thy unchanging love and grace and we rejoice that we may draw from Thy fulness each moment acccording to our needs. Grant to us a deep and increasing consciousness of the preciousness of Christ as our Divine Redeemer, and a growing assurance of the constant supply of Thy Holy Spirit for daily living. Teach us by that Spirit how to depend continually on Thy grace, and how to receive that grace by simple faith, and how to appropriate for our life the rich provision Thou makest for us. Then may Thy love be reflected in our daily conduct and may it constrain us to live to Thy praise, and to be the means of helping others as Thou art helping us. We desire to show "Whose we are and Whom we serve" and to be a channel of blessing at home and abroad.

Bless our relatives and friends, with all needful grace, and give to them and to us such a deepening sense of Thy love that we may do our utmost to make known the Gospel to those in far off lands. And so for our loved ones, for our friends and acquaintances and for Thy whole Church, we seek the fulness of Thy blessing, through Jesus Christ our Lord. *Amen.*

W. H. Griffith Thomas, D.D.,
Toronto, Canada.

MARCH FOURTEENTH

Ask and it shall be given you. — Luke 11: 9.

OUR Heavenly Father, accept our thanks for the re-creation of body and mind Thou hast given us in the hours of wonderful sleep.

Help us to be so attentive to the still small voice of our Teacher and Guide, the Holy Spirit, that whether we eat or drink, or whatever we do this day, all shall be done to Thy glory.

We desire that Thy Kingdom come and Thy will be done in our hearts, our home, our city, our" country, and in all the earth. We so desire this, that here and now we offer Thee our bodies, our minds, our reputations, our characters and our lives, and ask Thee to use each and all as seems best to Thee.

So relate us and all we have to Thy work in the world, that we may count for most in Thy Kingdom. So teach and train us by Thy Word and daily providences that we shall trust Thee daily for our daily needs, and witness for Thee by being as peaceful and joyous in disappointment, adversity, or affliction, as in prosperity.

We ask it in the name of Jesus, our Saviour. *Amen.*

William B. Stubbs,
Savannah, Georgia.

MARCH FIFTEENTH

I will extol Thee, my God, King; and I will bless Thy Name for ever and ever. Every day will I bless Thee; and I will praise Thy Name for ever and ever. Great is the Lord, and greatly to be praised; and His greatness is unsearchable. One generation shall praise Thy works to another, and shall declare Thy mighty acts.
— Ps. 145: 1-4.

WE thank Thee, our Father in Heaven, for life and health and home. Thou hast brought us this new day, with its new blessings and its new duties. As we go out to our new tasks and pleasures, may we carry hearts full of love to Thee and to everybody. We lay our hands in Thine, and we trust Thee to lead us in the right and safe way. We are glad to know that Thou art with us, and we are going to try to do nothing that would drive Thee away from us. Teach us to walk in the footsteps of Jesus, Who went about doing good. Bless every member of our family, bless our friends, and if we have enemies, bless them. Help our eyes to see and our ears to hear and our hearts to love that which is true and clean and good. We trust Thy care to bring us safely to our Heavenly home when the day of life is ended. Wo ask all this for Jesus' sake. *Amen.*

J. C. Armstrong, D.D.,
Kansas City, Missouri.

MARCH SIXTEENTH

When I call to remembrance the unfeigned faith that is in thee, which dwelt first in thy grandmother Lois, and thy mother Eunice, and I am persuaded that in thee also. Wherefore I put thee in remembrance that thou stir up the gift of God, which is in thee by the putting on of my hands. For God hath not given us the spirit of fear, but of power, and of love, and of a sound mind. — 2 Timothy 1: 5-7.

OUR Father, we thank Thee for binding this family together by the sacred tie of common blood. We remember with how much sacrificial love its life has been created and sustained. We bless Thee for a mother's travail and tenderness, for a father's faithful toil. Knit us together by our common joys and sorrows, so that even if we are far removed from one another, nothing may estrange our hearts. W T hen the youngest of us is old and gray-headed, may the memories of our home still be sweet and dear. May the children's children of this family still have the vigor and virtues of our best forefathers, and may the faith, too, of our fathers burn brightly in their hearts. Deal graciously with our loved ones. Give us our daily bread and strength for our daily tasks. To Thee we commit the life and destiny of each, through Jesus Christ, our Lord. *Amen.*

Prof. Walter Rauschenbusch, A.B., D.D.,
Rochester, New York.

MARCH SEVENTEENTH

Hear, O Lord, when I cry with my voice. — Ps. 27: 7.

O LORD, our Lord, how excellent is Thy Name in all the earth. Thou art our God, and the God and Father of our Lord and Saviour Jesus Christ, through Whom we, Thy children of faith, have the forgiveness of our sins. Thou art our fathers' God; and Whom they in the flesh confidently worshipped, we, their children, would also reverently worship and adore.

Humbly, yet devoutly, would we give thanks to Thee, O God, for Thy great love revealed to us in Christ; and for Thy rich and unfailing providences to us, and to all men. For Jesus' sake, receive our thanks. Continue Thy loving favors to us, and grant us pardon for sin, and life eternal.

Give us, we beseech Thee, the Holy Spirit as our Guide this day, into truth. May He ever comfort us and all Thine in times of sorrow or of trial. May He strengthen us when we are weak. May He raise us up again, if we fall. May He interpret Thy Word to us, and enable us to do Thy holy will with gladness of heart.

With us, bless also this, our nation, and the whole world with Heavenly peace, for Jesus' sake. *Amen.*

John Grant Newman, D.D.,
Philadelphia, Penna.

MARCH EIGHTEENTH

Thy face, Lord, will I seek. — Ps. 27: 8.

HEAVENLY FATHER, before entering fully upon the duties of this new day, we would bow before Thee and join our hearts and our voices in prayer. We pray Thee, that Ave may be truly conscious of Thy presence with us as we begin this day.

Help us to know, in all the work of this day, that the still small voice that speaks within us and calls us to the best things, is the voice of God; that the power that tugs at our hearts is the hand of God; and that the light that falls upon our pathway, directing us in the right way, is the light and the love of our Father, God. So may we walk this day with Thee, as Thy Holy Spirit guides us, and as we have been taught by Thy Son, our Saviour, Jesus Christ the Righteous.

We give Thee the love and gratitude of our hearts for all the blessings we enjoy. Take each one of us now, dear Father, into Thy loving care as we go forth to the duties of this day. May our lives be a benediction and blessing to all who need us. Lead us ever, we pray Thee, in the way Thou wouldst have us to go, and when the journey is done, gather us all home at last; in the name of Jesus Christ. *Amen.*

Rev. Frank G. Smith,
Kansas City, Missouri.

MARCH NINETEENTH

Therefore shall the people praise Thee. — Ps. 45: 17.

ALMIGHTY GOD, Heavenly Father, Who art the light and life of men, we give Thee humble and hearty thanks for all the blessings of Thy merciful Providence; and we commend ourselves this day, and all who are near and dear to us— our family, our friends, our neighbors — to Thy divine care and protection. Give us grace so to live that we shall not be afraid to die. Save us from all dangers of soul and body. Grant us strength for our daily work, sufficiency for our daily needs, and a right judgment in all things.

We pray for our country, that it may be exalted in righteousness; for those who exercise authority, that they may be wise and just; for all our citizens, that they may be faithful to duty and obedient to law; that our land may be a land of liberty and peace, of true religion, of mutual service, acceptable to Thee, our God, and honored throughout the world.

Finally, we beseech Thee, Father, to protect and encourage those, who, by life and doctrine, at home and abroad, are proclaiming the Gospel of Thy redeeming love. Send out Thy light and Thy truth, that all men everywhere may acknowledge themselves to be the sons of God, and that Thy Kingdom may be established in all the earth. Through Jesus Christ, our Lord. *Amen.*

Bishop Thomas F. Gailor, D.D.,
Memphis, Tennessee.

MARCH TWENTIETH

Thou forgavest the iniquity of my sin. — Ps 32: 5.

LORD JESUS, our Redeemer, be Thou ever-present with us to-day! Thou as the all-seeing Saviour art acquainted with all our ways, nothing is unknown to Thee. Thou knowest how sin endangers our lives day by day. Thou knowest how temptations beset us on all sides. Thou knowest how doubts and misgivings fill our heart with distrust. Thou knowest how the cares of life make us anxious for the morrow and forgetful of Thee and Thy glorious promises.

Lord Jesus, In Thy mercy help us, and grant us grace to look up in faith to Thee. Give us strength to withstand the many sins and temptations of to-day, help us to cast aside all our cares, and trust with child-like faith in Thee.

Above all, Lord Jesus, forgive us where we have failed in the past, and let us find in Thee our Saviour, whose Life-blood has redeemed us from sin and death. Give us faith to believe that, unworthy though we be, Thy Blood shed on the cross can save us from every sin.

Fill us, Thy pardoned children, with love to Thee and mankind. Keep us faithful in Thy all-saving Word unto our end. We ask all this of Thee, because Thou art our God and our Redeemer. *Amen.*

Rev. Alfred Doerffler,
St. Louis, Missouri.

MARCH TWENTY-FIRST

The Lord preserveth the faithful. — Ps. 31: 23.

ALMIGHTY and Most Merciful One, we humble ourselves before Thee and adore Thy power as well as Thy love; Thy bounty, as well as Thy compassion; Thy sovereign providence as well as Thy forgiving mercy. Lord, give to us — Thou knowest better what to give than we to ask. Direct graciously all the affairs of each of us this day; be in the performance of the household duties and sanctify our home life; go out with those who go out to the business of life this day, and prosper their labors and their plans. Find some blessed helpfulness for each of us to-day, and let us also find it. Encompass in like manner with Thy gracious providence all our loved ones, in their homes, in preparation for life work, in their daily avocations, in their accustomed places or on a journey, in sickness or in health. Lift our eyes above the narrow little circle of our own horizon in life, to the great work of God, and to the Kingdom of God, of which we are a part. Lord, forgive us our sins; they are many, and they humble us to the dust. Guard and guide our ways this day, that we may go to meet temptation "led of the Spirit," and so shall "find the way of escape" and go safely forward in the way of faith and hope and loving service of Thee. In Jesus' Name. *Amen.*

Melvin Grove Kyle, D.D., LL.D.,
Philadelphia, Penna.

MARCH TWENTY-SECOND

The Lord is the strength of my life. — Ps. 27: 1.

OUR Gracious Father in Heaven, we accept with thankful hearts this most wonderful privilege of entering into Thy presence through prayer. A new day stretches out before us, and we know not what shall befall us ere we come to its close. How greatly do we need a strength that is more than human. We find ourselves insufficient for the tasks of the day. Our vision is so narrow, our judgment so faulty, our wisdom so incomplete. We are becoming more and more conscious of our shortcomings and our failures, and if we

50

recognize them, how grievous must they appear in Thy sight. Forgive us and help us, we pray. Teach us that we are most strong when in weakness we 'throw ourselves upon Thee. Teach us that we shall enjoy the greatest liberty when we are in most complete bondage to Thee. Teach us that to lose self is to gain power and influence. Help us to-day to be good witnesses for Jesus Christ. May our lives ring true. May our conduct be in strict accord with the profession we make. May it be easier for others to do right to-day, because we are in the world. Make us strong in the hour of temptation, and give us grace for every trying situation that may arise. This petition we humbly offer through Jesus Christ Our Lord. *Amen.*

William S. Abernethy, D.D.,
Kansas City, Missouri.

MARCH TWENTY-THIRD

They shall prosper that love Thee. — Ps. 122: 8.

OUR Heavenly Father, we would humbly bow before Thee and in acknowledgment of Thy goodness would confess Thee to be our God. We thank Thee for Thy manifold mercies and continued love and care to us, so unworthy of any of Thy blessings.

We confess our sins, and pray that for the sake of Christ Thou wouldst forgive us and help us to so live that everywhere we may carry the Spirit and the life of the Master with us. Grant that we may have that purity of heart by which we may be always able to see Thee.

May we see our opportunities every day, and help us to use them that we may best minister to our fellow men, and bring glory to Thy great and Holy Name. Lead us day by day. May we obediently follow Thee, lovingly doing Thy will, and seek so to express the love of Christ that others will be led to accept Jesus as Saviour and Lord, while Thy believing followers may the better be established in the faith. Be gracious to all in sadness and difficulty. Help them to fully trust in Thee, and realize ever Thy presence with them.

We ask this all in the name of Jesus Christ, Thy Son, our Saviour. *Amen.*

I. G. Bowles, B.A., B.D.,
North Bay, Out., Canada.

MARCH TWENTY-FOURTH

I will give thanks unto Thee forever. — Ps. 30: 12.

ETERNAL FATHER, help us to think wise thoughts, to speak kind words, and to do good deeds through all the hours of this new day of our lives. Help us to see things as they are, and also as they ought to be. We would have a hand in making the world a better place in which to live, and, as the nearer duties are the most pressing, we would begin *at home.* To the beloved beings in this household, therefore, we will consecrate our ability to be cheerful and helpful. Enable us to lift the burdens of the weary, and to bring happiness to the sorrowful about our own fireside, and then as our strength and wisdom are increased, to impart them to others, near and far. How full of the possibilities of usefulness is a single day! How sweet to think that in a single moment of a single hour of this one, we may render some service that will increase the sum of human virtue and happiness. Help us, Lord, to do it!

Give us a new assurance of Thy love, and a new sense of the dignity and value of life. We pray Thee that we may be able to say, when our call comes, "Glad did I live and glad do I die, and I lay me down with a will." *Amen.*

Charles Frederic Goss, D.D.,
Cincinnati, Ohio.

MARCH TWENTY-FIFTH

The prayer of faith shall save. — James 5: 15.

O LORD, increase our faith. By it may we be enabled to remove mountains of difficulty from our way. May it be our shield with which to quench the darts of temptation. May it steady and encourage us as we endeavor to form our plans and assume our duties and responsibilities in accord with Thy will. May it deliver us from fearful anxiety respecting our own welfare, and that of our loved ones whom we commit to Thy care. Mav it incline us to be forgiving and patient and considerate and sympathetic. May it prompt us to gracious and kindly words and deeds. May it save us from being too much gratified by praise, and from being too much cast down by blame. May it lend zest to the day's toil, and quicken us to renewed energy and fidelity in our work. May it impel us to humility and gratitude when we are granted prosperity and happiness, and may it preserve us against bitterness and gloom of spirit if want and sorrow become our portion. May it strengthen our hold upon possessions that abide, and be unto us the evidence of things not seen, and the substance of things hoped for. May it assure us each day, as we fare on our pilgrimage, that Thou art nigh, and lead us into the blessed experience of companying with Thee as a man walketh and talketh with a friend. *Amen.*

Harry P. Dewey, D.D.
Minneapolis, Minn.

MARCH TWENTY-SIXTH

Thanks be to God for His unspeakable gift. — II Cor. 9: 15.

OUR FATHER, we offer Thee our thanks for the morning light and for all Thy goodness. We confess our faults and failures and sins, and ask Thy pardon. Give us a right judgment, that we may see what Thou wouldst have us do; a ready will, that we may do our duty with all our might; and the help of Thy Spirit, that we may be enabled this day to live according to Thy will.

Look with pity upon all who are in any need or trouble, and come and help them. Strengthen the weak, succor those who are tempted, lift up the fallen, lighten the darkness of them that doubt, give patience to all who suffer, and to them who are disheartened give courage and new interest in life.

Bless our country, and grant that righteousness, peace and good will may prevail among all nations. Bless Thy Church throughout the world, especially Thy servants who have gone forth to preach Thy Gospel in distant" lands. Take under Thy fatherly care and protection all who are near and dear to us; do more and better for them than we can ask or think, and grant that we and they may this day enter more and more into Thy joy and peace, through Jesus Christ our Lord. *Amen.*

Bishop Chauncey B. Brewster, D. D.,
Hartford, Conn.

MARCH TWENTY SEVENTH

I was brought low, and He helped me. — Ps. 31: 23.

WE thank Thee, God, that we can call Thee Father, for no parent ever loves as deeply as Thou. We acknowledge with sorrow that we have grieved Thee time and again, for even when we would do good, evil is present. But, praise God, when we sincerely confess our sins, Thou art faithful to forgive.

We thank Thee for the daily blessings of life, seen and unseen. We thank Thee that Thou art mindful of us when we least think, and dost tenderly care for us. We pray Thee to write over the door of our home, "Peace be unto this household." Help us daily to create such an atmosphere in our home as will the better tend to bring all up in the nurture and admonition of the Lord.

Keep us from temptation. Make us happy and blessed Christians, and help us in all we do, think, and say, that we may prove a blessing unto others.

When sorrow comes into our lives, may we yet praise God and trust Him. And if we should be imprisoned in grief, may the hand of God open for us the iron gate, as when Peter was liberated. And when our work is finished, take us to Thyself in Heaven, for Jesus' sake. *Amen.*

L. M. Zimmerman, D.D.,
Baltimore, Md.

MARCH TWENTY-EIGHTH

Let those that seek Thee rejoice and be glad in Thee. — Ps. 70: 4.

OUR FATHER in Heaven: We come to Thee with our deepest gratitude and love. Thou hast been a kind Father and a faithful Friend. We thank Thee for daily provision, for care and guidance and help in business affairs and in our home, for those "common mercies" which come to us so regularly that we get to receiving them thoughtlessly and we forget who gives them to us. Most of all, we thank Thee that Thou dost love us, that Thy pity and compassion are never withheld from us, that this day and every day Thy "goodness flows around our incompleteness, round our restlessness Thy rest." In Thy mercy forgive us. We are so weak and sin so easily that we must daily cast ourselves upon Thy strength and daily renew our prayer for pardon. Make us strong to resist sin and to overcome every temptation. All through this day may we be true to all that is pure and holy and Christ-like. May Thy Kingdom come! Cheer our hearts with new displays of Thy saving power, with signs and wonders as of old time, with new miracles of conversion and sanctification. We long to see Christ recognized and honored by men and by society. Heal our friends who are sick. Comfort all who are in sorrow. Where heavy burdens are to be borne, give the courage and the strength to bear them. And keep us all in the love of Jesus, and in conscious fellowship with Thee. Through Christ, our Lord. *Amen.*

W. I. Wishart, D.D.,
Pittsburgh, Penna.

MARCH TWENTY-NINTH

Whatsoever we ask, we know that we have the petitions. —I John 5: 15.

SHELTERED as we are in the peace of our own home, we pray to-day for the homeless and the lonely. The wayward souls who have broken away and are wandering restless and unsatisfied, may their hearts be turned again towards their father's house. The children, orphaned and dependent, who miss a mother's comforting touch and her good-night kiss, may they have a compensation in tender friendliness. The men and women in great cities, workers with hand or brain, separated by distance from their families; may they escape or overcome the temptations that surround them. The selfish and the cruel who have wrecked their own and others' happiness; may they be changed to a better mind. For all to whom home is only a dream, or a regret, or to whom it means remorse; we pray, Thou God of infinite compassion, that to each may come a message from Thy love that shall be an impulse to a new and higher life. It is Thy will that we be carriers of such messages!

Then fit us for this service by a broader sympathy and a readier helpfulness. This we ask in the Name of Christ. *Amen.*

Rev. A. J. Bonsall, Litt. D.
Pittsburgh, Penna.

MARCH THIRTIETH

He forgetteth not the cry of the humble. — Ps. 9: 12.

OUR Heavenly Father, we thank Thee for the watch care that was over us while we slept, and that Thou hast brought us in health and strength to see the light of this new day. But we need Thee more in the daylight than we do at midnight. Open our eyes to the opportunities and privileges of this day. As a servant would come to his master in the early morning to receive directions for the day, so we come to Thee, seeking divine guidance. Strengthen our bodies, clear our heads and warm our hearts, that we may live this day in accordance with Thy Holy Will, and that we may do nothing displeasing in Thy sight. Bless us in our home life, that by precept and example we may lead our children in the good and right way, and help us to make the atmosphere of our households so much like Heaven that it will be the natural thing for them to grow up in the "nurture and admonition of the Lord." Go with us into the larger and outer circles of life's relationships, and everywhere enable us to help and not to hinder. Bless with us all those who cry to Thee for help, and hasten the day when all mankind will join in crowning Christ "Lord of all." We offer our thanksgivings and render our petitions in the Name of Jesus. *Amen.*

Forney Hutchinson, D.D.,
Little Rock, Arkansas.

MARCH THIRTY-FIRST

Deliver me, for I do not forget Thy law. — Ps. 119: 153.

OUR Heavenly Father, with gratitude and confidence we bow together before Thee this morning after the rest of the night. We face the day, with its untried experiences, in courage and hope, claiming Thy promise, "I will in no wise fail thee nor forsake thee." We humbly place ourselves at Thy merciful disposal; forgive us, protect us, guide us, use us, and keep us in the thought of Thee all the day. Reveal Thyself to them that are dear to us, and lead them into Thy peace. Those who are in any temptation, deliver; or in any sorrow or affliction, sustain and comfort; supply every need of theirs, according to Thy riches in glory in Christ Jesus.

Give our rulers, we beseech Thee, wisdom and power to administer righteous government; save us from the covetous and proud; unite our people in the bonds of love, constraining them to justice, and mercy, and pity, that those who have may help those who have not, that oppression and poverty may cease from among us. And may we as a nation understand and fulfil our mission to the world.

Spread abroad everywhere the knowledge of Thy salvation, and bring in speedily the day of Jesus Christ, in Whose Name we ask all. *Amen.*

Rev. George Wells Ely,
Columbia, Penna.

April

APRIL FIRST

Come unto Me and I will give you rest. — Matt. 11: 28.

O GOD, our Father, and the Father of our Lord Jesus Christ, it is written in Thy Word that Thy Holy Spirit helpeth our infirmity that we may know what we should pray for as we ought; and that He maketh intercession for the saints according to the will of God.

We yield ourselves to Thee, our God and Father, that Thy Spirit may exercise this grace toward us, and work this gift in us just now; that He may cleanse our hearts from all iniquity, and lift them up in the worship and love of Thy Holy Name; that He may comfort us in our trials to-day; that He may strengthen us in every moment of temptation; that He may guide us in all our ways to do Thy will; that He may help us in our toil and enlighten us in our perplexity.

O Heavenly Father, shed abroad Thy love in our hearts and keep us loving, hopeful, patient, kind and true, thus blessing all with whom we come in contact, and glorifying Thy Great Name Who art worthy of all our heart's devotion forever and ever.

Through Jesus Christ our Saviour, Who loveth us and loosed us from our sins in His own blood. *Amen.*

James M. Gray, D.D.,
Chicago, Illinois.

APRIL SECOND

Thy prayers and thine alms are come up before God. — Acts 10: 4.

OUR Father in Heaven, we thank Thee for teaching us to value this moment of looking up to Thee at the commencement of the day — lest we forget the purpose Thou gavest it for.

We thank Thee that Thou hast placed us in a world that needs today what we can give it, and so gives dignity and meaning to our transient lives.

Teach us this day to do the thing that pleases Thee, and so through all its difficulties and all its disappointments enjoy the peace that passes understanding, that shall make us cheerful at all times.

We thank Thee for the knowledge of Thy love that forgives our sins; may we reflect it today, seeing only the best that is in others, that we may be kind all the day through. Enable us to "serve" and to "give."

Save us from the selfishness that blinds, and from the conceit that cannot walk by faith, and enable us so to let our light shine, that men may glorify Thee today for having seen us — for Thine is the power and the glory, forever. *Amen.*

Wilfred Thomason Grenfell, M. D., LL.D.,
St. Anthony, Newfoundland.

APRIL THIRD

We trust in the living God — the Saviour of all men. — Tim. 4:10.

O THOU Who art Life, and the Giver of Life, we thank Thee that Thou art also Love, and the Author of all our joys and blessings.

We bless Thee for Thy Word, for Thy Holy Day, for the church and for the wondrous sacrifice of our Lord in redemption. We rejoice for the privilege of prayer, for its fellowship with the Divine, and for the assurance that Thou dost hear and answer it.

We thank Thee for the promise of the Holy Spirit to strengthen our poor infirm spirits, to give us an internal witness that we are Thy children, and to enable us to overcome in all our temptations.

Help us to "'stand fast in the faith," and to bear witness of it to others. Enable us to do good to our fellowmen, and to serve Thee by advancing Thy Holy Kingdom over all the earth.

Bless our home; may we here rear an altar of worship to Thee, and wilt Thou send down Thy Holy Angels to guard our fireside. May peace attend all our steps through life, and may we at last depart in faith and hope of the life everlasting. *Amen.*

Junius B. Remensnyder, D.D., LL.D.,
New York City, N. Y.

APRIL FOURTH

Whoso offereth praise, glorifieth Me. — Ps. 50: 23.

O THOU Infinite Life, from Whom we have come forth and in Whom we live and move and have our being, Thou Father of our spirits Who art "closer to us than breathing; nearer than hands and feet," we would begin this new day with a deep sense of gratitude to Thee and of reverence for ourselves. Make us glad that we are alive, and that we are living in a world so full of wonder, of beauty and of inspiration. Be Thou the Great Companion of our lives this day. May we see Thee in every person we meet and find Thee in every experience that meets us. May we get the very utmost out of this day, by putting our very best of mind and heart into all its tasks. May our minds be so filled with good thoughts, and our hands so busy with kindly deeds, that there shall be no room in our lives for anything unworthy of ourselves or harmful to others. May we find happiness not in seeking it, but in bringing happiness to others, especially to those who stand closest to us. So may we live this day for its own sake, as if it were a life complete in itself, and when the day is done, may we fall asleep in the consciousness that we have honestly tried to share the spirit and follow the example of Him Who is the Master of life. In His Name. *Amen.*

J. H. Randall, D.D.,
New York City, N. Y.

APRIL FIFTH

We love Him because He first loved us. — I John 4: 19.

FOR the restful curtains of the night we thank Thee, Gracious God, our Father. Thou didst create all things in the earth for man's comfort, convenience, and contentment. When we walk with Thee every place is garden-like. We thank Thee that in Thy presence is fullness of joy.

We bless Thee for little children. We thank Thee for their prattle and laughter, their trust and purity. Freshen us with sweetening lessons from their fragrant happiness. Bless the little ones touched by our influence. Foreguard against making crooked pathways, lest they follow. Enable us to enforce all instructions with a flesh-clothed example. Deliver us from impatient speech and angry action before or to them. Fill our heart with love until it overflows, and mellows and moulds the little folk. Check arbitrary commands; hold back harsh penalties. May patient tenderness have the mastership in our lives. Saturate us with sympathy, grace us with gentleness, control us with considerateness, and honor us with the beauty of holiness. Give us an obedience as prompt and as confident as that of a loveled child. Command us until we shall conform to the image of our Elder Brother, and so be worthy disciples and helpers of humanity everywhere. In Jesus' Name. *Amen.*

Christian F. Reisner, D.D.,
New York City, N. Y.

APRIL SIXTH

The faithful God which keepeth covenant. — Deut. 7: 9.

OUR Heavenly Father, Whose life is within us and Whose love is ever about us, make Thy life manifest in our lives this day, as with gladness of heart, without haste or confusion of thought, we go about our daily tasks, conscious of ability to meet every rightful demand, seeing the larger meaning of little things, and finding beauty everywhere.

In the sense of Thy presence may we move through the hours, breathing the atmosphere of love, and seeking by love, rather than by anxious striving, to quicken and bless the lives of others. Knowing that we are laborers together with Thee, may we live above all the influences that depress and discourage, and come into that assurance of faith which is itself the victory that overcometh the world.

And now we would enter into the secret place of Thy presence, that, hidden with Thee, our souls may be filled with a sense of Thy sheltering care and all our energies quickened into newness of life. Lay Thy hand of love upon each one of us as in silence we seek Thy blessing.

(A moment of silent prayer.)

This blessing we ask in the Name of Jesus Christ, our Lord. *Amen.*

Andrew V. V. Raymond. D.D., LL.D.,
Buffalo, New York.

APRIL SEVENTH

For the love of Christ constraineth us. — II Cor. 5: 14.

My Prayer Today.

Psalm 51: 10-12.   Luke 22: 39-46.   Luke 11: 1-4.

LORD, search our hearts, and make them clean. Renew continually a right spirit within us. Make us willing to do Thy will. Teach us how to pray and how to work.

Help us to go where Thou dost send us. Give us courage to speak for Thee, and loving patience in trying to help others. Bless every member of our church and Sunday school. Help us soon to win some soul for Thee. Make us to see whom we might help, and to be eager to go to them.

Fill our hearts with deeper and truer love for Thee. Forgive our sins, and make us better Christians every day. For Jesus' sake. *Amen.*

Ernest Bourner Allen, D.D.,
Toledo, Ohio.

APRIL EIGHTH

Then shall we know, if we follow on to know the Lord: His going forth is prepared as the morning; and He shall come unto us as the rain, as the latter and former rain unto the earth. — Hosea 6: 3.

O GOD, Father, Saviour, and Revealer, sanctify all those who in the midst of truth seek more truth. As they question the authority of the past, increase their loyalty to the things which are eternal. May liberty of thought leave unsullied the simplicity of their trust in Thee. As the steep ascent of truth reveals the ever-widening horizon of Thy thought, lead them in the narrow path of humble and sacrificial service. Enable them to share the joy of their emancipation without weakening other men's faith in the God of their own experience. May pride of learning never chill the warmth of prayer. May opposition and misinterpretation arouse within them no bitterness or plans for retaliation. As by Thy grace they are led into deeper sympathy with their Lord, may they give to the world their new assurance of the triumph of His Kingdom, rather than the agony of their struggle with doubt. And ever amid the clash of argument may they find the peace that passeth understanding in Jesus Christ our Lord. *Amen.*

Shailer Mathews, D.D.,
Chicago, Illinois.

APRIL NINTH

God is faithful by Whom you were called. — I Cor. 1: 9.

OUR FATHER, Who art in Heaven, Thou hast graciously answered our petition for safe keeping through the darkness and dangers of another night. For these mercies we now thank Thee, Father, and lift our refreshed hearts and minds to Thee in thanksgiving, and in an appeal for guidance as we start out into the duties and privileges of a new and unknown day. Graciously cause Thy Holy Spirit to dwell in us richly, and to make real unto us a Father's omniscience, love and power. Help Thou us to realize what it really is to have the very hairs of our head all numbered. Show us anew the deep concern of the Good Shepherd as He feedeth His flock and nourisheth it for the Father's service. Cause Thy Kingdom to come, and Thy will to be done in and through us each moment of the day. Bring to our remembrance, Oh Spirit of God, such portions of the Divine Word as will give us the vision, the inspiration, and the faithfulness that will make us profitable — profitable to Thee by being helpful to those about us in real need of the knowledge of a Saviour's love and grace. These favors, together with the forgiveness of our own sins, we ask in the Name of Jesus — Thy Son and our Saviour. *Amen.*

S. J. McDowell, D.D.,
Baltimore, Md.

APRIL TENTH

Be ye therefore followers of God, as dear children: And walk in love, as Christ also hath loved us, and hath given himself for us an offering and a sacrifice to God for a sweet-smelling savour. — Ephes 5:1-2

OUR FATHER, Who dost so deeply care about all that we have to do this day, help us to do everything as in Thy sight. Make us faithful in all our work, and help us always to do our best. May we be ashamed to shirk or neglect any task that is set before us to-day, at home, in business, or at school, and may we have Thy guidance as we face it. In all our work and play, help us to be fair and honest, considerate of our mates, and even more anxious to play squarely and well than to win. Keep us thoughtful of others and friendly toward them. Guard us from the quick word, the unworthy thought, the selfish deed. Bind us more firmly to our dear ones and our friends this day, and to Thee, the Friend that sticketh closer than a brother. So bring us to the end of the day wiser and stronger, and more able to serve Thee better to-morrow. In Jesus' Name. *Amen.*

Charles W. Gilkey, D.D.,
Chicago, Ill.

APRIL ELEVENTH

For the Father Himself loveth you. — John 17: 27.

OUR Heavenly Father, we thank Thee for the peace, the rest, the comfort of the night through which we have come. We surely have reason to be grateful for Thy increasing care. Thou art ever thinking of us, and we sleep in safety under the shadow of Thy protecting presence. Now we enter upon the light and blessing of another day. May it be a clean day, a glad day, an undefiled day! May no dark, impure thoughts obtain possession of our hearts! May we have the grace to put away everything that is sinful and selfish and unworthy of Thee! Enable us to overcome every form of temptation. If moments of weakness, or weariness, or doubt come to us, may we have gracious help from Thee. In our business life, our home life, with our associates, with our friends, may we be thoughtful, tender, loving, generous, ever bearing in mind that we are to have the Spirit of our Divine Master "Who went about doing good." Teach us to be pitiful, to be kindly affectioned, to speak words of gentleness, and to remember especially the poor, the wayward, the unfortunate, the sorrow-stricken. So fill us with Thy Spirit as to make us joyous, radiant, eager for service, anxious only to do Thy Will. We ask all these favors in the Name of Thy Son, our Saviour, Jesus Christ. *Amen.*

Rev. J. Wesley Johnston, Litt. D.
Brooklyn, New York.

61

Thou Lord art good and ready to forgive. — Ps. 86: 5.

OUR FATHER Who art in Heaven, we come before Thee in the Name of Jesus Christ, Thy Son, our Lord and Saviour. For His sake bow Thine ear and hear our prayer. We bring Thee our offering of thanksgiving for all Thy loving kindness and tender mercy toward us. Thy goodness has never failed us. We humbly pray for the forgiveness of our sins. We confess that in many things we have offended and come short of Thy Holy Will. But there is forgiveness with Thee, that Thou mayest be feared. Deliver us from the power of evil. Let not any sin have dominion over us. Shield us from all that would hurt us in body or spirit. Order our future, make our plans, choose our changes. Suffer us not to live selfish or useless lives. May we do good as we have opportunity, and serve our generation according to Thy Will. We commend to Thy fatherly care our loved ones who are absent from us in the flesh. Protect them from evil, and do them all the good that they need, both for this life and for that which is to come. We pray for the coming of Thy Kingdom! Pour out Thy Holy Spirit upon all Thy churches. May they bear faithful witness for Thee, and through their testimony may multitudes be brought to know Thee, and accept Thy great salvation. We humbly ask all in the Name of Jesus Christ, our Lord. *Amen.*

John F. Cannon, D.D.,
St. Louis, Missouri.

APRIL THIRTEENTH

Mine eyes shall be upon the faithful of the land. — Ps. 101: 6.

ALMIGHTY GOD, our Heavenly Father, in Whom we live and move and have our being, we. Thine unworthy children, come to Thee with humble minds and hearts to offer our prayer and thanksgiving. Pardon, we beseech Thee, the sins we have committed against Thee in thought, word and deed, and make us truly sorry for them with the godly sorrow that worketh repentance unto Salvation.

Bless us and our relations, friends and neighbors, and give us all things necessary both for soul and body. May Thy Holy Spirit guide Thy church, and all who minister therein, that Thy Kingdom may come, and all may do their duty in their vocation and ministry.

Have pity on the sick and dying, and on all sinners. May Thy Holy Angels dwell within this place to preserve us in peace. Into Thy hands, God, we commend our bodies, souls,' and spirits. May we enjoy such refreshing sleep as will fit us on the morrow to go forth to our duties and responsibilities with vigor of mind and body. Our Heavenly Father, we thank Thee for all Thy many and great blessings and mercies to us and to all mankind.

Through Jesus Christ our Lord, Who with the Father and the Holy Ghost
livest and reignest, ever one God, world without end. *Amen.*

Bishop Harry S. Longley,
Des Moines, Iowa.

APRIL FOURTEENTH

The just shall live by faith. — Hab. 2: 4

GRACIOUS and most merciful Father, we to Thee in His hallowed
Name Who loved us and gave Himself for us. We thank Thee that Thou didst
guard our home and keep us in safety while slept. We thank Thee for the
promises of Thy Wind, and for the assurance of their fulfilment to all who
trust and obey Thee. We thank Thee for all the blessings of opportunity and
service which have come to us with the morning. Help us to be faithful to Thy
Word in all duty and opportunity, and to be kind to all in word and service. In
every task or trial, may Thy presence attend us. Make obedience to Thy will
our joy. Help us in all things to follow the example of our Lord, and thus to
become like Him. Help us to be kind to the poor, and to all in need. Give comfort and healing to the sick, to the tired and lonely everywhere, and help
them to look to Him whence cometh help. Come to the sinful in gracious
compassion, and bless every effort to win them to Thyself. Remember our
pastor, and all who preach the Gospel in our own and in heathen lands. Put
away the hurt of the sinful and the erring everywhere, and hasten the coming
and triumph of our Lord, And to Thy Name. Father, and Holy Spirit, be all the
praise. *Amen.*

M. Rhodes, D.D..
St. Louis, Mo.

APRIL FIFTEENTH

Thou answeredst them, Lord our God. — Ps. 99: 8.

OUR Heavenly Father, we bow before Thee to thank Thee this morning
for Thy mercy and love that has brought us again into Thy holy presence.
We have sinned. Wilt Thou forgive us?
We thank Thee for the food Thou hast given us. Wilt Thou also feed our
souls with that bread that cometh down from Heaven. We bless Thee for our
home. We are thankful for our loved ones. As Thou art present with us here,
wilt Thou also abide with those who are bound to us by kindred ties, but are
separated from us by distance. We thank Thee for our friends and neighbors,
and ask a blessing on them. We thank Thee for the church, and its influence.
Give it spiritual power for its tasks in this community and in all the land.

Supply Thy limitless grace to the missionaries who in answer to prayer, Thou hast thrust into the dark places of the earth. May their message be so used by the Holy Spirit, that Thou, Oh Christ, may be known in all the world, and the coming of Thy Kingdom may be hastened!

We ask this, our Heavenly Father, in the Name of Thy Son, our Lord Jesus. *Amen.*

George Innes,
Philadelphia, Penna.

APRIL SIXTEENTH

So will we sing and praise Thy power. — Ps. 21: 13.

OUR Divine Father, Who in holy love hast created and art sustaining us, Thy children, we invoke Thy gracious blessing upon us at the threshold of this day. Bless Thou us in our going out and our coming in. May our lives be precious in Thy sight. Fill our hearts with love, and our minds with all high and worthy purposes. In our vocations assist us to see the divinity of labor, the expansive power of sympathy, the eternal might of righteousness and integrity. May we do good to all men as we have opportunity.

Prompt us to the relief of suffering; fill us with pity for the needy; gird us with might to oppose the aggressions of evil men; supply unto us courage to bear adversity and pain. Establish Thou the labors of our hands and hearts upon us. Encourage us to defeat temptation. Bring us from toil to our firesides in tranquillity, and bathe us with the peace which floweth like a river, even that which the world cannot supply.

Teach us how greatly to live and greatly to love, and at the evening time of life may there be light. In that hour may we be worthy to stand before Thee and before the Son of Man, in whose name we seek from Thee these benefits. *Amen.*

Clarence M. Gallup, D.D.,
Providence, R.I.

APRIL SEVENTEENTH

Great is the Lord, and greatly to be praised. — Ps. 145:3.

WE rejoice, gracious Lord, that Thou art willing to hear Thy children call upon Thee. No earthly ruler is as open to his subjects as Thou art to us.

From any place, not merely from a temple or a church; at any time, not only upon sacred days set apart for Thy worship; with any need or desire, Thou dost bid us open our hearts to Thee, and never dost Thou send us away without an answer.

Therefore, made bold by Thy promise and by our own experience of Thy blessings, we come to Thee once again. We praise Thee for Thy mercies, so great and numberless. We beseech Thee, O Lord, to forgive our sins, for Thou delightest to pardon; whether sins of wrong-doing, of evil passion, or of duties left undone. Forgive them all, we pray, and stamp the assurance of pardon,, of peace, and of acceptance upon our hearts.

Bless us in making us more like Thyself, conformed to the image of Thy Son. Stand beside us in the hour of temptation to give us victory, and at last bring us to Thyself, to dwell with Thee forever. *Amen.*

Jesse L. Hurlbut, D.D.
Newark, New Jersey.

APRIL EIGHTEENTH

He will love thee and bless thee. — Deut. 7: 13.

OUR Heavenly Father, Thou hast been good to us, and we come to Thee in love and gratitude to thank Thee for the right use of our minds, for health of body, and for opportunities of development and service. Help us to show our gratitude by the obedience of our lives. May we labor in joy and trust, by Thy grace, to make this world a brighter, happier, and better place for men and women to live, and for children to play and grow. May all fathers and mothers have a sacred sense of privilege and responsibility, and may the God of all grace be merciful to the multitudes of mothers and fathers, brothers and sisters, wives and little children, who suffer from the curse of strong drink. Lord, destroy that which would destroy those for whom Christ died. Keep all little children, all boys and girls, all young men and women, unscarred and unstained by sin, and remember in great tenderness the aged, the lonely, the sick, the tempted, the discouraged, and those who suffer for the sins of others. May joy and peace and harmony and holiness alone reign in our hearts. Bind us closer to each other, and closer to Thee. Help us to be happy, and useful, and good.

These things, with the forgiveness of sin and the baptism of the Holy Spirit, we ask in the Name of the Blessed Christ, Who loved us and gave Himself for us. We can ask nothing more; we dare ask nothing less. *Amen.*

Prof. Charles Scanlon, A.M.,
Pittsburgh, Penna.

APRIL NINETEENTH

Let the people praise Thee, O God; let all the people praise Thee. Then shall the earth yield her increase; and God, even our own God, shall bless us. God shall bless us; and all the ends of the earth shall fear Him. — Ps. 67:5-7.

OUR FATHER in Heaven, we thank Thee for this day and all its opportunities. Help us to show our gratitude by the use we make of it. May Jesus

Christ so dwell in our hearts that we shall be kept from sin. Wilt Thou rule and bless our home this day. We pray Thy blessing on friends and neighbors. May we so live before them that we may honor Thy Name. Bless, we pray, the poor and sick and suffering. May their need be to us a call to service.

We pray for Thy blessing on our church. May we strive to win men to Jesus Christ. We pray for town and state and country, that righteousness may prevail. We pray that the Gospel message may speedily go into all the world; that wars may cease; that sin and greed may no longer rule. To this end may we give as Thou hast blessed us. May the peace of God dwell in our hearts this day. We ask it all in the name of Jesus Christ, our Saviour. *Amen.*

Roger Leavitt,
Cedar Falls, Iowa.

APRIL TWENTIETH

He hath set His lave upon me. — Ps. 91: 14.

THOU God of our fathers — our Father which art in Heaven, Thou art good to all, and Thy tender mercies are over all Thy works. We thank Thee for the night and for the day; for quietness and rest and sleep, for life and light and love. We confess that we sin against Thee even in our lying down and rising up. We shield ourselves in Thy Fatherhood, and believe that for Christ's sake Thou dost forgive our sins. We commit ourselves to Thy covenant keeping for this day. Give Thine angels charge over us, and keep each one of us from harm. Guide us with Thine eye. Preserve our going out and our coming in. Keep us in health and safety in body and soul. Help us to live together in peace and love. Give us rule over our own spirits. Fit us for all Thou hast appointed to us, that we hear and do Thy holy will. May our Elder Brother walk with us all the way, and may His presence help and comfort us.

Bless our friends and neighbors, and all whom we love, especially those who may be sick or in any trouble. Comfort and speedily relieve them. Be with the great multitude that "go out this morning to toil and weariness, and give them good cheer and rest, and the salvation that is of Thee. For Christ's sake. *Amen.*

Wallace Radcliffe, D.D., LL.D.,
Washington, D. C.

APRIL TWENTY-FIRST

One thing have I desired of the Lord, that will I seek after. — Ps. 27: 4.

WE need Thee, loving God. We are lonesome, discontented, helpless, defeated, without Thee. How shall we know ourselves aright unless Thou

66

teach us? How shall we love goodness and strive after holiness, and know the deep joys of the soul unless Thy Spirit abide in us? How shall we be able to meet Thy just expectations unless we companion with the Most High God? How shall we bear our burdens and overcome our temptations, or be unselfish in service, or turn away from our sins, or grow into the beauty and majesty of the character of Christ, unless Thou take possession of us?

Thankful we are, then, that Thou dost not withhold Thyself from any eager, hungry, obedient heart. We know that Thou art willing to give Thyself to us. Teach us how to open our natures to Thee. Help us to be obedient to Thy will, joyous in our allegiance, co-operative in all of Thy plans.

Disturb us when we go astray; discipline us when we are wilful; hearten us when discouraged; strengthen us when perplexed.

Through all the experiences of our lives, fashion us into the likeness of our exalted Christ, so that we may be Thy true sons and daughters. *Amen.*

Philip L. Frick, Ph.D.,
Buffalo, New York.

APRIL TWENTY-SECOND

My lips shall utter praise. — Ps. 119: 171.

OUR Heavenly Father, help us to be thankful for our home with all of its blessings and privileges. Give each of us eyes to see, and grace and strength for the duties and privileges that are ours. Help us to be home-lovers and home-makers. Grant that we may bless every home coming within the radius of our influence.

Give us the eye of pity and the hand of help for all whose needs have claims upon us. Save us from "the snare of the fowler" and from pestilence, that we may in purity and strength serve Thee.

Bless our church — Thy church— -O, our God, and him who ministers to us in spiritual things, and Thy servants the world over. May our religion be real and satisfying to us, and appetizing to others. Let our love to Thee be voiced in our efforts, gifts, and prayers, in behalf of a lost world.

Help us to live in constant readiness for whatever Thy providence hath in store for us, and to say ever in word, thought and deed, "Thy Kingdom come, Thy will be done in earth as it is Heaven." *Amen.*

Rev. M. P. Hunt,
Fayetteville, Ark.

APRIL TWENTY-THIRD

Casting all your care upon Him; for He careth for you. — I Peter 5:7.

OUR FATHER, we know not what a day may bring forth, but our help is in Thee. We thank Thee for Thy promised watchfulness. And so we pray for a faith that will send us forth trusting ourselves to Him Who neither slumbers nor sleeps.

Keep us, we pray Thee, true to our responsibilities as followers of Thy Son, Jesus Christ. As we, day by day, succeed in making a living, may we not fail in making a life. We would learn of Him Who intermingled heaven's glory with earth's common toil. Our tasks are too often made heavy through our forgetfulness of Thee.

May we so hunger and thirst after righteousness as to enter into the full assurance of Thy protection and help, and thus when other voices entice us, saying, "All these things will I give Thee if Thou wilt fall down and worship me," may we find our refuge in Thee, and hear Thee say, "The Lord shall preserve Thee from all evil: He shall preserve Thy soul."

May our hearts be freed from fret and care this day, and may the peace of God which passeth all understanding be ours from this time forth, and even forevermore. *Amen.*

Rev. F. A. Robinson, B.A..
Toronto, Ont. Canada.

APRIL TWENTY-FOURTH

Rest in the Lord, and wait patiently for Him. — Ps. 37: 7.

HOLY FATHER, we thank Thee for the gift of life, the gift of reason, the gift of love. We are little, but Thou art great; yet it is great to be but little for Thee.

With single span Thou measurest the heavens Thou hast made, but Thine whole arm Thou takest to bear one lamb. We are confident of Thy love; grant us faith, forgiveness, and Thy Spirit of power, that our assurance may be based on Thee.

Give us this day a sound mind in a sound body, health, knowledge and wisdom grant us, self-control, and a right attitude to Thee, to all men, and to all things good. Help us to know that the majestic deed is the deed of service. May we do kind, brave, beautiful things not to be seen, but to be serviceable. May we not be seeking to do great things, but to do simple things greatly. Help us know our Saviour-friend, Who bears the other end of the yoke, and makes the burden light. Let us find our happiness in our service. Comfort us in believing that angels of sorrow always heal the wounds they make. Give us noble aspirations, and pure satisfactions. In Thy wisdom and power, help us. *Amen.*

Prof. M. Coover, D.D.
Gettysburg, Penna.

Thou art my God, arid I will praise Thee. — Ps. 118: 28.

OUR FATHER! We thank Thee for the tenderness enwrapped in the very name by which Thou art known to us. If Thou art a Father, then we are little children. Grant to us this day the filial heart, and help us ever to trust all Thy good ways with us. We do not even know our wants, and sometimes we ask for stones, mistaking them for bread. Help us henceforth, we pray Thee, to trust ourselves to Thee, O Lord! to Thy wise counsel and Thy Father heart, and to accept with gladness whatever Thou dost give, because we are sure that Thy gifts are always best. Keep our souls, we pray Thee, in the peaceful faith that all things work together for our good.

Let our words be true this day, we pray, and let our deeds be upright. Give to us a heart for all conditions of men, and soften our spirits with the sympathies of Jesus. And if, in the secret recesses of our souls, there yet lurk some remnants of our hated sin, let the tides of forgiveness descend upon us from the heights of Thy holiness, and lo! we shall be clean. All this we know is according to Thy will, through Jesus Christ our Lord. And to Thee shall be the glory forever and ever. *Amen.*

A. H. Chipman Morse, D.D.,
Denver, Colo.

APRIL TWENTY-SIXTH

If thou seek Him, He will be found of thee. — I Chr. 28: 9.

O THOU Who art Infinite Wisdom, we, Thy short-sighted children, desire Thy guidance throughout this day.

We know not what of joy or sorrow it may hold for us, but we believe Thy grace to be sufficient for its needs, and so we pray that we may appreciate and appropriate that grace so freely given. If sorrow be our lot, let that grace comfort us and make us strong to bear it. If joy be ours, let that grace keep us in_ humbleness and dependence upon Thee.

In the midst of the uncertainties among which we must make our way, hold us by the hand and keep us in Thy paths. Help us to put down that desire we so frequently find taking possession of us, to make explorations here and there, beyond the boundaries Thou hast marked off, and to be content to follow Thee in paths that are safe.

We are depending upon Thee. Thou hast never failed us in the past, and we trust Thee for this day. We do not know the way, but it is plain to Thee. Guide us safely, through Him Who has loved us and given Himself for us. *Amen.*

J. Stewart French, D.D.
Bristol, Tenn.

Let the people praise Thee, O God. — Ps. 67: 3.

BLESSED GOD, this day uphold us by Thy gracious omnipotent Hand. Give to us whatever measure of blessing seems best in Thy sight, and if disappointment or difficulty of any kind awaits us, help us to brace ourselves and play the part of a man, and cause us not to forget that our sorest trials are ofttimes blessings in disguise. So may we always give thanks, being persuaded that if we love Thee, all things work together for our good.

Give us at all times holy ideals, O God, and may our daily endeavor be commensurate with them. That which is dark within us, do Thou illumine by Thy Holy Spirit, and cleanse us from all unrighteousness. May we be truly penitent for our sins, and may we be strengthened with might in the inner man to do Thy blessed will. Let not this day's low descending sun be unprivileged to shine upon some small deed of kindness done, or some spoken word of Christian love. May those with whom we walk and commune along life's way take knowledge that we have been with Jesus Christ, and may this day's life and every other day which in Thy goodness Thou art yet to vouchsafe unto us, make us increasingly fit for the endless and the perfect day through which we are to live in Thy presence. For Christ's sake. *Amen.*

William E. Biederwolf, D.D.,
Chicago, Illinois.

APRIL TWENTY-EIGHTH

Rejoice evermore. Pray without ceasing. In every thing give thanks, for this is the will of God in Christ Jesus concerning you. Quench not the Spirit. Despise not prophesyings. Prove all things; hold, fast that which is good. Abstain from all appearance of evil. And the very God of peace sanctify you wholly; and I pray God your whole spirit and soul and body be preserved blameless of our Lord Jesus Christ. — I Thess. o; 16-20.

CREATE in us a clean heart, O God; and renew a right spirit within us. Cast us not away from Thy presence, and take not Thy Holy Spirit from us. We commend to Thy loving protection all those for whom we long to pray (especially those whom we now name in our hearts before Thee * * *). Give to them all their heart's desire, we pray Thee in as far as Thou seest it best, for Jesus' sake! Bring each of us, O Father, to the close of this day in peace and honor. For all those who love us so much better than we deserve, we thank Thee. For their sakes, help us to sanctify ourselves this day. And do Thou, O Lord, grant that we may abide steadfast in this purpose, and by Thy continual aid be fully master of all the desires and emotions of our hearts.

For Jesus' sake. *Amen.*

Rev. John Edgar Park,
West Newton, Mass.

APRIL TWENTY-NINTH

My prayer is unto Thee, Lord. — Ps. 59: 13.

O GOD, our Father, give us Thy blessing in these moments of spiritual communion with Thee. We come before Thee in a deep sense of our own unworthiness. We have sinned in thought and word and deed. Yet hear us, as we turn to Thee again with penitent hearts. Forgive us our sins; grant us again Thy peace. And give us grace to serve Thee in newness of life, to the glory of Thy Holy Name. We thank Thee for Thy constant goodness; for the bounty which has supplied our wants; for the providence which has kept us from harm; for the love which has redeemed us from sin; for the grace which has helped us to serve Thee on earth; and for the promise of an inheritance in Heaven.

Keep us from the evil in ourselves; from the evil in the world about us; from all selfish, unkind, and impure thoughts; from all hard and bitter words; from doing that which we ought not to do, and from leaving undone that which we ought to do. Keep us in the constant sense of our membership in Christ; in the thought that we are His disciples and followers; in the love of our Father's house, and in the hope of our eternal home. We ask all in the name of Jesus Christ, our Lord. *Amen.*

Compiled and adapted by permission from A Book of Common Order, in use at St. Giles' Church, Edinburgh, Scotland.

Bishop Boyd Vincent, D.D.,
Cincinnati, Ohio.

APRIL THIRTIETH

O, sing unto the Lord a new song; for He hath done marvellous things: His right hand, and His holy arm. hath gotten Him the victory. — Ps. 98: 1.

OUR kind Heavenly Father, it would be presumption for us to thus address Thee were it not for the cross upon which the Prince of Life opened the way. In His dear Name we come, confessing our sins, which are too numerous for us to mention, and too grievous for us to understand; and seeking Thy gracious forgiveness and Thy Spirit's power in our full restoration to Thy rich favor.

As we attempt in our weakness to lift our eyes to the celestial sources of righteousness, may Thy merciful providences protect our vision from the influence of the flesh, the allurements of the world, and the illusions of the wicked one.

71

In all our thoughts, words, plans, impulses, and associations let Thy gracious Spirit have control, that when the day is ended, the memories that would otherwise bring remorse and bitter regret, may be sanctified by a calm and holy peace.

Sanctify the world with Thy truth. Lead all human genius with Thy light. Center and keep the affections of men upon Jesus Christ, our Saviour, that the strength of nations may be set in alignment with the issues of His Kingdom, to Whom we gladly ascribe glory, majesty, and power, for evermore. *Amen.*

William E. Crouser, D.D.,
San Jose, California.

May

MAY FIRST

We thank Thee, and praise Thy glorious Name. — I Chr. 29: 13.

OUR FATHER Who art in Heaven, we are Thy children, created in Thy image, redeemed by the blood of Thy Son, and dependent on Thy grace for all that we enjoy. Our health, our happiness, our food, our clothing, and many other good gifts are the evidence of Thy gracious care, and we pray that we may have grace and strength to honor Thee for what Thou hast done for us, by loving one another, and doing good unto all men, as we have opportunity. Come Thou, blessed Saviour, and dwell within us by Thy Spirit, and teach us in all things to do Thy will. We have often been forgetful of Thee, and disobedient to Thy commands, and we pray that our sins may all be forgiven for Thine own Name's sake. As we enter upon each new day, remind us of the fact that we can only hope to attain to the best success by Thy favor and blessing, and we would seek to make ourselves worthy of these, by so performing the common tasks of life, as to honor Thy Name. If we have difficult duties to perform, or dangerous temptations to meet, help us to realize that our sufficiency is in Christ, and that all things are possible to him that believeth.

And all we ask is in the Name of Christ, our Saviour. *Amen.*

W. B. Smiley, D.D.,
Oneonta, N. Y.

MAY SECOND

Knock and it shall be opened unto you. — Luke 11: 9.

OUR FATHER Who art in Heaven, help us to start this new day with Thee. May its first moments be laid on Thy altar, and may the dew of refreshing sleep irradiate the sacrifice. Thou hast taught us that prayer is incense; may the fragrance of our morning petition be detected in Thy holy place. The path that leads to sunset is unknown. There may be swollen streams, dangerous ravines, dense thickets, and unseen foes on Thy plan for this day. Clouds may darken the sky which laughed at sunrise, and noon on our journey may witness a severe moral struggle. We would choose to walk where the flowers bloom, the birds sing, the brook ripples, and clouds vanish into thin air. But our choices we would submit to Thine approval, for we covet Thy presence when the darkness falls. In loving, generous, and prompt obedience to Thy will may we find a new zest in our waking hours. May new vistas of beauty and new visions of service stir our hearts. May souls where our path winds be glad that we travelled their way. And when the stars shine out, invisible by day, may they beckon the best that is in us to worship at the Throne of Him Who has promised to make wise souls to shine as the stars. We proffer our petition in the Name of Him Who taught us to pray. Amen!

Rev. James E. Norcross,
Pittsburgh, Penna.

MAY THIRD

For we know that all things work together for good. — Romans 8: 28.

O LORD, how slow we are to recognize Thee when Thou comest in disguise! We know Thee when Thou comest in robes of light, but not when Thou art clothed in clouds. Help us to learn Thy ways, and to thank Thee for all that Thou doest. We would thank Thee when Thou puttest us into the fires of affliction, knowing that there Thou revealed Thyself as the gracious Sanctifier and great Deliverer. How often Thou hast come to us in lowly ways, and we have not seen Thee because we did not expect to see Thee there. Sometimes Thou comest to us in heaven's glowing chariots, and we do not mistake Thee then; but more often Thou comest through earth's common places, and like Mary, we suppose Thee to be the Gardener and not the Lord. But, O, may we, as she, enquire of the gardener about Him Whom, we love, and Thou mayest reveal Thyself to us as Thou didst to her. Thou hast been doing for each ot us all that Thou didst for Thy saints of old, but the blight of unbelief has been upon us, and that which Thou didst design for blessing has been a curse. O, Lord, forgive! O Lord, forget! O Lord, prevent! To Thy wounds we flee, and in Thy merits we hide. Wilt Thou Who hast given us life give us also spiritual sensibility, hearing, and sight, and taste for all that is divine. And now unto Thee, Father, Son, and Spirit, be glory and praise. *Amen.*

Rev. W. Graham Scroggie,
Sunderland, England.

MAY FOURTH

The Lord is my light and my salvation. — Ps. 27: 1.

OUR Heavenly Father, Thine we are, and Thee we desire to serve. We thank Thee that Thou hast made us Thine in Christ.

We thank Thee also that Thou hast made it our privilege to serve Thee. Help us, we pray, to serve Thee this day — each in the sphere and under the conditions in which Thy providence has placed us. May each of us let our light shine for Thee just where we are. May the same mind be in each of us that was in Christ Jesus, our Lord, Who, though He was Lord of all, yet pleased not Himself.

Make us strong to do the right and to resist the wrong. Give us filial love for and confidence in Thee. Give us a spirit of brotherly interest and kindness towards our fellowmen. Incline us, as we have opportunity, to do good to all men, especially to them that are of the household of faith.

Forgive our sins, and grant that we may more and more die unto sin and live unto righteousness. Bless to us the discipline of life. May we be more concerned to profit by that discipline than to escape its pain. For Jesus' sake. *Amen.*

W. M. McPheeters, D.D.,
Columbia, S. C.

MAY FIFTH

Therefore we ought to give the more earnest heed to the things which we have heard, lest at any time we should let them slip. For if the word spoken by angels was steadfast, and every transgression and disobedience received a just recompense of reward; How shall we escape, if we neglect so great salvation; which at the first began to be spoken by the Lord, and was confirmed unto us by them that heard him. — Hebrews 2: 1-3.

OUR Heavenly Father, we thank Thee for all the gifts that come from Thy liberal hand; for life, and health, and friends, and home. We thank Thee for Thy protection and care while we slept; and for the new morning with its call to work; for the food and raiment so freely provided, and for the shelter and peace of this house. Guide and direct us this day in all we do, that we may do Thy will in all our relationships with other people. Help us to be patient, faithful, considerate, and kind, and may we not be drawn into temptation and sin. Be with all our absent dear ones, and may their lives and health be precious in Thy sight. May Thy Kingdom come in all the earth, so that all men may be brothers. We ask in the Name of Jesus Christ, our Lord. *Amen.*

Dan Freeman Bradley, A.B., D.D.,
Cleveland, Ohio.

MAY SIXTH

The Hand of our God is upon all them for good that seek Him. — Ezra 8: 22.

IN the Name of the Father, the Son, and the Holy Ghost, *Amen.*
We thank Thee, blessed Lord, for the loving care which has guarded us through the watches of the night, bringing us safely to the light of another morning. Fill our hearts with gratitude, which we would express "not only with our lips, but in our lives, by giving up ourselves to Thy service." May we appreciate all the blessings of this life — our health, reason, and love of those who are about us, and above all, may we be grateful for Thy love.

Send Thy blessing upon our dear ones, wherever they may be; keep them from accident of body, and sin of soul. Be merciful to the sick, the sorrowing, and the dying, and grant to them the "peace which passeth understanding." We pray Thee, send benedictions upon Thy church; grant that Thy Kingdom may be enlarged, and Thy people inspired to earnest duty.

And now we commend ourselves unto Thee; may the angels of God watch over us this day; keep us in our going out and our coming in; preserve us from all evil; sanctify us by Thy Spirit dwelling in us, and save us at last for Jesus Christ's sake. *Amen.*

Bishop William Andrew Leonard, D.D.,
Cleveland, Ohio.

MAY SEVENTH

Let us lay aside .... the sin which doth so easily beset us. — Heb. 12: 1.

OUR dear Heavenly Father, 'tis Thy hand that opens for us the gates of the morning and draws about us the curtains of the night. We thank Thee for all the blessings that enrich our days, for the watchful care that shields us from evil, for the strength of body and mind with which to perform daily tasks and duties. Truly Thy compassions fail not, and there is no measure to Thy love. Thou dost care for each of us as if each were Thine only child.

To all Thy love and grace may we respond with a life dedicated wholly to Thee. Help us to glorify Thee by consecrating to Thee every affection of our hearts and every work of our hands.

May we do nothing which Thou canst not approve, ask nothing that we cannot receive from Thee, nor go where we cannot go with Thee. Blot out from the book of Thy remembrance our many transgressions. Strengthen us that we may shun every allurement of sin, and grow daily in the knowledge and love of our Saviour, so that when we nightly pitch our moving tents we may be a day's march nearer home. We ask it in the Name of Jesus. *Amen.*

Rev. G. Arthur Fry,
Pittsburgh, Penna.

If ye forgive .... your Father will forgive you. — Matt. 6: 14.

OUR FATHER, we praise Thee for the blessings that crown us morning and evening, for the love that abides with us through the darkness and the light.

With contrite hearts we confess our sins, pleading for the cleansing that God gives through the atoning blood of the Cross, and for the sanctifying power that causes us to grow into the beauty and strength of the Christ life.

Master, we dedicate ourselves to Thee for service. Wherever we may be and whatever the task that may be laid upon us, help us to be Christ-like. May we touch other lives with blessing, communicating the Spirit that cheers the depressed, comforts the sorrowful, supplies the needy, encourages the weak, and leads the unredeemed soul to the Saviour. Thou hast honored us by calling us to be co-laborers with Thyself, the God Who works. May we toil in the fulness of our powers, to the end that earth may become like Heaven.

Father, keep us true to the highest ideals. Give us, in ever increasing measure, the peace that passeth understanding, and in life's evening hour may the light of the Glory Land be upon our faces.

Our prayer is in Jesus' Name. *Amen.*

W. E. McCulloch, D.D.,
Pittsburgh, Penna.

MAY NINTH

Incline my heart unto Thy testimonies. — Ps. 119: 36.

OUR FATHER, we thank Thee for the gift of life, for soundness of body and sanity of mind, for keenness of conscience and strength of will, for power of choice and privilege of service. We thank Thee that Thou settest the solitary in families, for membership in the great family circle where Thou art our Father. We lift our hearts to Thee in thanksgiving for all the gifts that make life so rich and worth living — for love of father, mother, brother, sister. We thank Thee for friends, for education, for our country.

We ask Thee for power to live as we ought, to serve as we should. We ask Thee to bless our family, our neighborhood, our city, our state, our nation. Grant Thy grace upon those that Thou hast placed to govern and lead us. Grant Thy wisdom to our teachers, Thy blessing upon our schools, hospitals, prisons, that out of sorrow and suffering we may gain strength and patience. Make and keep the nations of the earth righteous, that we may have peace. Lead us through the valley of the shadow of death to the city where there is no night, no sin, no sorrow, no death.

All these favors we ask through Jesus Christ our Saviour. *Amen.*

Orrin Philip Gifford, D.D.,
Brookline, Mass.

MAY TENTH

Faith which worketh by love. — Gal. 5: 6.

O THOU great and eternal God, Creator, Redeemer, and bountiful Bene-factor — the one from whom every good and perfect gift descends, we are assembled as a family to engage in worship of Thee. Breathe into our hearts the spirit of true devotion. Give to us repentance for our sins. Thou hast taught us that there is but one thing that can come between our souls and Thee — one thing that can exclude us from the Kingdom of Grace and from the Kingdom of Glory; the one and only thing that Thou dost hate — sin. We rejoice that we may be delivered from sin; that we may have our fruit unto holiness, and in the end everlasting life. We are taught in Thy Holy Word that if we confess our sins, Thou art faithful and just to forgive us our sins, and to cleanse us from all unrighteousness. Give to us faith — faith in Jesus as our present personal, all-sufficient Saviour. Give to us hope — the hope that is an anchor to the soul, sure and steadfast, that entereth into that within the veil, and that will securely hold us in the midst of life's storms and trials. Give to us love — that perfect love that casteth out fear. O, give to us these and all other graces that the Holy Spirit imparts. We ask all in the Name of Jesus Christ. *Amen.*

Adna B. Leonard, D.D.,
Brooklyn, N. Y.

MAY ELEVENTH

But the fruit of the spirit is love. — Gal. 5: 22.

GOD of love and of infinite compassion, Who hath taught us to call Thee "Our Father which art in Heaven," and hath revealed that "like as a father pitieth his children, so the Lord pitieth them that fear Him," we approach Thy Throne with reverence and humility.

We have sinned and come short of Thy glory. When we would do good, evil is present with us. Yet, Lord, we never can be satisfied until we awake with Thy likeness. Have mercy upon us, O God, according to Thy loving kind-ness. According unto the multitude of Thy tender mercies, blot out our trans-gressions.

May Christ dwell in our hearts by faith, that we being rooted and grounded in love, may be able to apprehend with all saints what is the breadth and length and depth and height; and to know the love of Christ which passeth knowledge, that we may be filled with all the fulness of God. Yea, Lord, may we grow up into Him in all things, Who is our living Head, and daily bear the fruits of the Spirit, that men may take knowledge of us that we have been with Jesus.

In His Name, *Amen.*

Rev. Marshall P. Talling, Ph.D.
Toronto, Ont., Canada.

MAY TWELFTH

Thou Lord hast not forsaken them that seek Thee. — Ps. 9:10.

O GOD, Our Heavenly Father, we thank Thee for all the gracious gifts Thy love bestows. In whatsoever ill we suffer, teach us submission to Thy holy will. Forgive us our transgressions for His sake, Who is the propitiation for our sins. With hearts softened by Thy boundless mercy, may we forgive all who have offended against us.

For every one whom we should remember before Thy Throne of Grace, we beg the special blessings needed. Advance the interests of Thy Kingdom throughout the world. By Thy Holy Spirit prompt and enable us to be workers together with Thee for the salvation of all men. Make those in authority over us to be capable and honest; and may we honor them as ruling by Thy ordinance. Pity all who are in adversity. May Christ so dwell in our hearts that we shall seek to minister, rather than to be ministered unto.

For our tasks make us sufficient, and for our burdens, strong; and, when Thou art ready for us, call us home, O Father, to the joy of Thy eternal presence.

All these things we ask in the Name of Jesus Christ, our Lord and Saviour. *Amen.*

Bishop Lewis W. Burton, D.D.,
Lexington, Kentucky.

MAY THIRTEENTH

I waited patiently for the Lord; and he inclined unto me, and heard my cry. He brought me up also out of an horrible pit, out of the miry clay, and set my feet upon a rock, and established my goings. And he hath put a new song in my mouth, even praise unto our God: many shall see it, and fear, and shall trust in the Lord. Blessed is that man that maketh the Lord his trust. — Ps. 40; 1-4.

OUR FATHER, in Thee every family in Heaven and earth is named. We thank Thee for our own home and fireside. We thank Thee for the great family of mankind. For ourselves and for all our brothers and sisters in all the world we pray Thee this day. Send us forth to our own work with willing hearts and ready hands, and fit us and all men for the burdens we must bear this day. Bring us to our home this night at the end of fruitful toil, and at the day's end grant us rest, and quiet sleep. Accept our thanks for all Thy mercies to us and to all men, and give to us the added blessing of grateful hearts. We ask in the Name, as we seek to pray in the Spirit, of our Lord Jesus Christ. *Amen.*

William E. Barton, D.D., LL.D.,
Oak Park, Illinois.

MAY FOURTEENTH

Blessed is the man that walketh not in the counsel of the ungodly, nor standeth in the way of sinners, nor sitteth in the seat of the scornful. But his delight is in the law of the Lord; and in his law doth he meditate day and night. And he shall be like a tree planted by the rivers of water, that bringeth forth his fruit in his season; his leaf also shall not wither; and; whatsoever he doeth shall prosper. — Ps. 1: 1-3.

OUR FATHER Who art in Heaven and in earth, enter, we pray Thee, and be the centre of our family love and peace. We differ in our wants, our tempers and tastes. Selfishness and egotism spoil our perfect union. Only as Thou dost dwell in us, and we in Thee, can we realize that unity of life and action which makes for true happiness and strength. As we go forth this day to our toil and our pleasures, help us to keep Thee and one another in our minds and hearts. Help each of us to efface our self-centered desires, and to make mutual surrenders for the comfort and good of all our household. Help us to remember that larger unity of Christian life which Thou hast planned in Jesus, our Saviour and Lord. May Thy revelation of Fatherhood fashion our nation and the peoples of other lands into that one family wherein righteousness, peace and joy shall dwell forever. *Amen.*

Edwin Heyl Delk, D.D.,
Philadelphia, Pa.

MAY FIFTEENTH

Yet will I not forget thee. — Isaiah 49: 15.

OUR Heavenly Father, with grateful hearts we offer Thee our thanks this morning. Thou hast caused us to dwell in safety during the night; refreshing sleep has invigorated us, and we look forward courageously to the duties of this new day. Were it not for the assurance we have that whatever the trial, perplexity, or difficulty which the coming hours may bring, they bring no surprises to Thee, we should hesitate to step out into the unknown future.

We pray that as we separate from one another to engage in our daily vocations, there may be no separation from Thee. As we work for others, may our service be given faithfully, as unto Thee, O Lord, rather than unto men. If our labors be those of the common round of the home, with many irritating interruptions, enable us to triumph by the display of a calm, unruffled temper, and thus witness to Thine own indwelling power in our lives. Let not the enemy of our souls gain advantage over any of us this day. Thou art stronger than he. Help us to be on our guard against him. Lord Jesus, may we have Thy mind to-day, that we may exhibit unselfishness, and be concerned about the needs and the sufferings of others. We make these requests in the name of our Lord Jesus. *Amen.*

George M. Paden,
Pittsburgh, Penna.

MAY SIXTEENTH

Believe in the Lord your God. — 2 Chr. 20: 20.

OUR Heavenly Father, a new day opens before us — grant that we may enter its portals with gratitude for every mercy of the past, and with a melody of praise in our hearts. We are deeply conscious of our sin, and are unworthy of Thy loving kindness. We realize our dependence upon Thee, and we beg Thee for Thy presence with us during the coming day. Forbid that we should shirk any duty, or murmur at any trial. Keep us sweet and hopeful; make us kind in word and thought; and save us from "the rashness of unguarded moments." We pray for those whom we love, and for all who do not love us. We pray for the stranger, the poor, the sick, the lonely, the sorrowing, and the wayward. Grant Thy presence to all who labor in Thy Name the world over, and send forth more workers into the vineyard. For our own home circle we pray, and for that larger circle of the world. Bless little children everywhere, and the helpless aged. Let wars cease upon the earth, and the Prince of Peace rule in all lands. Make us unselfish in our dealings with each one, and help us so to serve Thee this day, that at its close we may go to our rest conscious of Thy presence and Thy approval; we ask in our Saviour's Name. *Amen.*

Rev. George W. McDaniel,
Richmond, Va.

MAY SEVENTEENTH

Your sins are forgiven you for His Name's sake. —I John 2: 12.

ALMIGHTY GOD, Our Heavenly Father, as we begin the life of another day we would, humbly and sincerely seek Thee as our guide, our protector, and merciful Saviour. All our strength comes from Thee; in Thy wisdom we find light and truth; in Thy presence, joy and comfort. We know not what snares may be laid for our feet, what sudden trials we may have to meet, or what burdens we may have to bear during the coming day. Make us wise to see where temptation lies; make us strong to resist. May we be brave and patient under trial; unselfish and cheerful in burden bearing. Give us consciences tender and quick to recognize sin; breathe into our hearts the spirit of fervent prayer and perfect trust. Enable us to consider the needs of each other. By helpful word and deed may we make it easier for some one to be strong and faithful. May this day not pass until we have done some good in the Master's Name to such as have need. Grant, our Father, the forgiveness of all our sins, and enable us to forgive one another as Christ commanded us. We pray for a holier life through Jesus Christ, Who gave Himself that we, through Him, might become children of God. Grant these, and all other blessings that Thou seest we need, to the glory of Thy most Holy Name, through Jesus Christ our Lord. *Amen.*

Frank N. Parker, D.D.,
Atlanta, Georgia.

MAY EIGHTEENTH

To know the love of Christ which passeth knowledge. — Eph. 3: 19.

OUR FATHER in Heaven, we praise Thee, the God and Father of our Lord Jesus Christ, Who is the great Shepherd of the sheep, that when all we, like sheep, had gone astray, Thou didst lay upon Him the iniquity of us all. Forgive us our sins, we pray Thee, in His Name.

Show us our need of Thee, how great it is; not only for deliverance, but also for daily grace and guidance. Lead us into the green pastures of Thy love and mercy, and give us to drink of the water of everlasting life.

Make plain before us the path of duty and privilege, and help us to walk in it, that it may be for us the path of the just which shineth more and more unto the perfect day.

Help us to be kind, tender-hearted and true in our dealing with others, and filled with the power of the Holy Spirit, that we may be faithful witnesses for Christ in the world. Thus may we live that when the Chief Shepherd shall appear, we may receive the crown of life that fadeth not away. For Christ's sake. *Amen.*

Russell Cecil, D.D.,
Richmond, Virginia.

O, sing unto the Lord a new song; sing unto the Lord, all the earth. Sing unto the Lord, bless His Name; shew forth His salvation from day to day. Declare His glory among the heathen, His wonders among all people. For the Lord is great, and greatly to be praised. — Ps. 96: 1-4.

FATHER of us all, we thank Thee for life and that we live now; that our eyes have been opened to the beauties of today; that our hands have been filled with the tasks of the present. Nor do we despise the past, into whose labors we have entered; its errors warn us, its successes inform us, its sacrifices inspire us, and to its brave souls we are forever debtors. We are thankful for the moral leadership of the world, for the women and men who are the road breakers of liberty, for those prophets of the humanities who hear first the call of life, to whom bodies are more than gold, and the soul of a little child of greater value than the buildings of a city. We are thankful for the friends whose faith in us makes us better than we are; for the children who call us by the holiest name men may ever know; for the tasks we are unworthy of, but rejoice in; and for Jesus of Nazareth, Thy Son and our only Saviour, in Whose Name are all our prayers and supplications. *Amen.*

Rev. Daniel A. Poling,
Boston, Mass.

MAY TWENTIETH

Incline your heart to the Lord God of Israel. — Josh. 24: 23.

OUR Heavenly Father, we pray Thee to accept this, our morning prayer and praise. We praise Thee for Thy goodness in having brought us safely to the beginning of another day; for Thy preservation of us during our past lives; for all the mercies Thou hast bestowed upon us, notwithstanding our repeated transgressions; but especially for Jesus Christ, our Saviour, and in Him, all our means of grace and hopes of glory.

Give us grace that, amidst all our worldly cares and occupations, we may never forget Thee, but remember that we are ever walking in Thy sight. Enable us to subdue all unholy desires, and, denying all ungodliness and unholy lusts, to live wholly righteously and godly in this present world. Preserve us from idleness in the concerns both of our souls and bodies, that we may not be slothful in business, but fervent in spirit, serving the Lord. Be pleased, Lord, to comfort and succor the poor and the afflicted, and dispose us to do good unto all men.

Spread the knowledge of Thy Word, and make Thy Church the instrument of diffusing and upholding true religion. Preserve us all in the unity of the faith, in the bond of peace, and in righteousness of life, and finally bring us to Thy Kingdom in Heaven, through Jesus Christ, our Lord. *Amen.*

Bishop James Steptoe Johnston, D.D.,
Kerrville, Texas.

MAY TWENTY-FIRST

Lord increase our faith. — Luke 17: 5.

OUR FATHER in Heaven, it is fitting that we acknowledge Thee every day; Thou dost not forget us. Teach us to set Thee before our eyes continually.

Our reasons for thanksgiving are new every morning; give us grateful hearts. Keep us from sin; cleanse us from its pollution; save us from its guilt. Grant us true repentance for our sins; help us to overcome evil with good.

Give us eyes to see, and ears to hear, and hearts to understand. May we value our time, see our opportunities, and hear and understand Thy voice. Help us to love Thee supremely, and our neighbors as ourselves.

Give us our daily bread, and something for those who lack. Keep our eyes lifted up to the white fields, and to the Lord of the Harvest, Who is able to send the needed laborers. Grant to us some share in the labor and some sheaves to bring with rejoicing.

Hasten the coming of Thy Kingdom, and the doing of Thy will among men. May our days end in peace, and may the House of the Lord be our dwelling-place for evermore. *Amen.*

Rev. Thomas M. Huston,
Whitinsville, Mass.

MAY TWENTY-SECOND

If thou canst believe, all things are possible. — Mark 9: 23.

OUR FATHER, we bless Thee for the privilege we have, through Jesus our Lord and Saviour, to call Thee Father. In this new day we would put our hands in Thine and ask Thee to lead us. The future is all dark to us, except as it is lighted up with hope of Thy presence to go with us. Thou knowest the end from the beginning — not a temptation will lurk in our way, not a danger will beset our feet, not an opportunity will cross our path, but that Thou knowest beforehand. When we think of Thy servants of old, how Thou didst lead them and give them the victory over every weakness and every foe, we are encouraged to trust Thee. Make each of us to-day helpers to the ongoing Kingdom of our Christ. Our neighbors we would remember. Make plain to us our duty to them. May our sympathies flow out to all the sorrowing of earth.

Help us by our efforts to give wings to the Gospel of our Lord, which made life here sweeter to us and filled our hearts with hope of a life to come. To this may the best thoughts of our minds, the best efforts of our lives, and the most liberal offering of our means be given. For the sake of Thy Son, our Saviour, we ask these blessings this day.

Rev. W. B. Crumpton,
Montgomery, Alabama.

MAY TWENTY-THIRD

Unto Thee, O Lord, do I lift up my soul. — Ps. 86: 2.

OUR Heavenly Father, as we close our eyes we would open our hearts to Thee. Thou knowest us altogether; the very thoughts of our hearts, our innermost ambitions and desires, our secret ways — "all things are naked and open unto the eyes of Him with Whom we have to do." Thee we cannot deceive. Keep us from trying to deceive others or to deceive ourselves. May we be sincere, without guile or hypocrisy, genuine — our lives of one piece, like the seamless garment of our Lord.

Keep us from the folly and wickedness of a divided life, that is one thing within and another without; that is humble and reverent on the day of worship, but hard and cold and selfish on the days of work and of pleasure.

May we be thoughtful for those who serve us, and faithful to those whom we serve. May our daily task be consecrated to Thee, that not only the fruit of our labor, but the toil itself of hands and heart and brain, may be used for Thy Kingdom.

Make all our lives of friendship and books and rest and love and laughter and service sacred to Thee, that Thine may be the glory, through Jesus Christ, our Lord and Master. *Amen.*

Herbert Welch, D.D., LL.D.,
Delaware, Ohio.

MAY TWENTY-FOURTH

The love of God is shed abroad in our hearts. — Rom. 5: 5.

LIVING and loving God, our Father and our Friend, Thou hast in Thy wisdom created all things; for Thy pleasure they are and were created. To know Thee is life; to serve Thee is freedom; to praise Thee is our chiefest joy. As Thou hast created us in Thine own image, so, in the light of this new day of opportunity and duty, re-create us in the likeness of Him Who is the unchanging Light of life, and the unfailing source of strength and comfort. Help us in childlike faith anew to accept Him, and to faithfully follow in His steps. In Him may our sins be forgiven, our affections purified, our wills controlled, and our labors blessed.

Sanctify by the indwelling of Thy Spirit our worship in the home and in the church, hallow our holy relationships, make useful and joyful our lives, for the sake of Him Who has taught us to pray, saying:

"Our Father, W T ho art in Heaven, hallowed be Thy Name. Thy Kingdom come. Thy will be done on earth, as it is in Heaven. Give us this day our daily bread, and forgive us our trespasses as we forgive those who trespass against us. And lead us not into temptation, but deliver us from evil, for Thine is the Kingdom, the power, and the glory, forever and ever." *Amen.*

W. H. Wray Boyle, D.D.,
Detroit, Michigan.

MAY TWENTY-FIFTH

The Lord is my Shepherd; I shall not want. He maketh me to lie down in green pastures: He leadeth me beside the still waters. He restoreth my soul; He leadeth me in the paths of righteousness for His Name's sake. Yea, though I walk through the valley of the shadow of death, I will fear no evil; for Thou art with me; Thy rod and Thy staff they comfort me. Thou preparest a table before me in the presence of mine enemies: Thou anointest my head with oil; my cup runneth over. Surely goodness and mercy shall follow me all the days of my life; and I will dwell in the house of the Lord for ever. — Ps. 23. (Complete.)

OUR Heavenly Father, give us renewed power to overcome all our faults. Give us a renewed spirit of good will toward all our fellow beings. Give us a firmer faith in Thee, and in all the promises of Thy Holy Word. Help us to follow those lines of action which bring peace, honor and prosperity. And, by the guidance of Thy Holy Spirit, guide us ever in the way that goeth upward, through Jesus Christ our Lord. *Amen.*

Dean Charles R. Brown,
New Haven, Conn.

MAY TWENTY-SIXTH

Without faith it is impossible to please God. — Heb. 11: 6.

OUR FATHER, which art in Heaven, with praise on our lips and thanksgiving in our hearts, we, Thy children, worship Thee. From Thy hand we have been fed; by Thy bounty we have been clothed; and day and night under the shelter of Thy love we have dwelt in safety. In the poverty of our service of Thee we have freely received all things.

Forgive, we beseech of Thee, all our ingratitude. Cast away all remembrance of our sins, for with sorrow do we repent of them before Thee. Stir up within a compelling desire to love Thee above all else, and to do in our living all Thy will concerning us.

Grant us Thy Grace that in word and thought and deed we may show that we have been with Christ and learned of Him. May, in some measure, Thy Kingdom come through our living, and so Thy Name be glorified. By the indwelling of the Holy Spirit make us fitted for Thy service in all our days here, and bring us in Thine' own good time to Thyself, for the sake of Jesus Christ, our Lord. *Amen.*

John Gribbel,
Philadelphia, Penna.

MAY TWENTY-SEVENTH

Therefore I say unto you, Take no thought for your life, what ye shall eat, or what ye shall drink; nor yet for your body, what ye shall put on. Is not the life more than meat, and the body than raiment? Behold the fowls of the air: for they sow not, neither do they reap, nor gather into barns; yet your Heavenly Father feedeth them. Are ye not much better than they? — Matt. 6: 25-26.

ALMIGHTY GOD, Thou Who art the Creator, the Preserver, and the Beneficent Ruler of the universe — God the Father, God the Son, and God the Holy Ghost, we praise and magnify Thy Great and Excellent Name, not only because of Thy Majesty and Glory, but also because of Thy Divine Love and Compassion. We thank Thee for Thy goodness, and all the blessing of life, and we most humbly beseech Thee to forgive our sins, to increase our faith, and to make us love Thee more and serve Thee better. We pray for the peace of the world, for the spread of Thy Gospel, and the salvation of mankind. Do Thou most graciously grant us in this life food, raiment, shelter, home, friends, and happiness, and in the world to come, life everlasting.

We ask it all in the Name and for the sake of Thy Beloved Son, Jesus Christ, our Saviour and Redeemer. *Amen.*

Judge Henry W. Harter,
Canton, Ohio.

MAY TWENTY-EIGHTH

I will instruct thee and teach thee in the way that thou shalt go. I will guide thee with Mine eye. — Ps. 32: 8.

FATHER in Heaven, we turn our hearts to Thee as the source of life, and truth, and love. We do not claim Thy constant bounty because of merits we possess, but in Christ, the Saviour's name, we seek Thy favor.

Give us our daily fare today — the food from heaven for bodies spent; manna for the mind; and more than all, we crave the Bread of Life to make us strong of heart and pure of soul.

Teach us to love our fellow-men as Thou dost love, forgiving those who treat us ill, and giving help and hope to those who need our aid. Let not temptation come too great to bear. Give us abundant grace to do the appointed task with cheerful heart and ever ready hand.

And when the shadows of the night have come, grant that Thy presence we may feel, as One Who in the day has walked with us. In Thy dear name we pray. *Amen.*

Prof. Edward B. Pollard, D.D.,
Chester, Penna.

MAY TWENTY-NINTH

Let your requests be made known unto God. — Phil. 4: 6.

OUR FATHER, Who art in Heaven, we draw near to Thee in glad and grateful recognition of our dependence upon Thee. We thank Thee for the blessings of the night — for refreshing sleep, for freedom from sickness, accident, or sudden alarm, and for the restoration of our powers with the coming of the new day.

We would begin this day with Thee, for we would fain receive Thy blessing ere we venture upon its untrodden paths. Continue with us, Lord, throughout its hours, lest amid busy cares and thronging duties we meet the onslaught of sudden temptation, and, missing Thee, we fall.

Help us to do our duty. Keep us from the shame of the slurred task. May we have no occasion to blush over our appointed work neglected or ill done. Grant us the spirit of comradeship; give us to speak the word of cheer. May our lives radiate joy. Let the evening find hope and happiness where we shall have passed by.

Then, dear Father, through the blood of the everlasting covenant, when life's evening shall have come, gather Thy children home, and let us find a refuge, fearless and unashamed, in Thine arms of love.

In Jesus' Name. *Amen.*

Rev. H. Edgar Allen,
Brockville, Canada.

MAY THIRTIETH

Now therefore ye are no more strangers and foreigners, but fellow-citizens with the saints, and of the household of God. And are built upon the foundation of the apostles and prophets, Jesus Christ Himself being the chief corner Stone; In Whom all the building fitly framed together groweth unto an holy temple in the Lord: In Whom ye also are builded together for an habitation of God through the Spirit. — Ephes. 2: 19-22.

DEAR FATHER, the privileges are so exceedingly great that we can hardly conceive that they are ours — to come to Thee, the King of kings and Lord of lords, at any time and any place, and commandingly invited to ask and seek and knock, with the Divine assurance that everyone that asketh receiveth, ana he that seeketh findeth, and to him that knocketh it shall be opened — for these unspeakable privileges, dear Father, we thank Thee. The day is before us, and soon it will be behind us forever; only this once can we live through it.

Father, cleanse us of all sin with the blood of the Lamb, and occupy our bodies, making them temples of the Holy Ghost. Use us so that we shall not leave one thing undone that we should do, nor do one thing we should leave undone. Keep us happy in Thee. Give us a faith that will not waver, worry nor whine, nor wrangle, but a faith that will wait, watch, work, wrestle, and always win. *Amen.*

S. P. Long, D.D.,
Mansfield, Ohio.

MAY THIRTY-FIRST

The Lord is nigh unto all them that call upon Him. — Ps. 145: 18.

O THOU, God and Father of us all, Thou art over all Thy children — over all their joys and sorrows, God blessed forever. Thou art the light of the living, the refuge of the dying, and our eternal home. Thou hast placed us here in families, and dost unite the hearts that make the happiest homes. Thou hast led us most graciously in the past. Our yesterdays are luminous with Thy mercies. Through dangers seen and unseen; through doors which have opened as strangely as by an angel's hand, Thou hast led us, and always safely. On the smiling surface of life Thou hast wafted us by favoring breezes, and when the surges of trouble arise, we trust that we shall not be borne away from Thee, but nearer to Thee, and into closer fellowship with the only real and abiding world — the spiritual. Comfort the mourners. Walk with them all their life's journey. Strengthen them as Thou alone canst, and light "the shadows of earth's little while." Thou art the Lord of life and death. If we are united to Thee by a living faith, nothing can separate us from Thee and Thy gracious guidance. As the distance shortens, and the flesh fails, may mind and heart become more and more stayed upon Thee; may every duty become more joyous because done unto Thee, and a part of our high calling in Christ Jesus. *Amen.*

Rev. Daniel Dorchester, A.M., Ph.D.,
Lexington, Mass.

June

He heareth the prayer of the righteous. — Prov. 15: 29.

GRACIOUS and loving Father, with what tenderness Thou hast guarded and guided us! Gratefully we acknowledge Thy goodness.

We crave a closer fellowship with Thee. Show us the plan and program of life marked out for us in Thy loving kindness and infinite wisdom. The struggle up is hard. empower us for life's tasks and temptations. Grant us trustful resignation where mystery surrounds the way Home. Keep us calm while all about us is turbulent. Keep us patient when conditions are most trying. May the Redemptive Passion of Jesus Christ be in reality imparted to us, so that we shall delight to render humble service to Thee. Help us to love our fellowmen. Make us willing to undertake hard and apparently impossible tasks when we are impressed that it is Thy will. We would know the truth. Reward us with revelations which will build us and bless us. We pray for those in deep affliction. Teach us how to bear comfort to the sad, hope to the discouraged, peace to the troubled, confidence to the belated and overwhelmed. On every child of humanity may the healing rays from the Sun of Righteousness fall. Make us ready for service and sacrifice. Protect us, and provide for all our needs, and grant the forgiveness of all sin, through Jesus Christ, our Lord. *Amen.*

A. Z. Conrad, D.D.,
Boston, Mass.

JUNE SECOND

He that trusteth in the Lord, mercy shall compass him about. — Ps. 32: 10.

OUR Father, in Whom we live and move and have our being, we thank Thee for Thy care, for our home, for our parents, and our friends. We thank Thee for the joy of salvation, for the health of body and vigor of mind, for the joy and delights of social intercourse. We thank Thee for Jesus Christ, for His sacrifice for us, and for the promise of eternal life through faith in Him.

Teach us, our Father, how to appreciate Thy love to us, Thy boundless care and Thy constant watchfulness. Indicate to us the things which Thou wouldst have us to do. Teach us how to be helpful and kind one to another. Teach us how to live so as to bring joy and blessing into the lives of others. Give unto us the Holy Spirit, that we may know the true meaning of Thy Word, and how to do Thy will. Help us to watch and pray as we walk in the midst of temptation. Make us to abhor evil and to cleave only to what is good. Strengthen us in the day of adversity. Protect us from the snares of prosperity. Help us to do only the things which are pleasing to Thee. Hear us, O God, in this our prayer, for Jesus' sake. *Amen.*

Rev. R. R. Butterwick,
Mountville, Penna.

JUNE THIRD

Let the poor and needy praise Thy Name. — Ps. 74: 21.

OUR Father in Heaven, we kneel together to thank Thee for Thy goodness and mercy, which have been so manifest in our lives. Thy good gifts have not failed, morning nor evening. When we have forgotten Thee in the absorption of work and play, when we have neglected Thee through lack of gratitude and love, Thou hast continually looked upon us to bless and keep us.

We beseech Thee, blessed Lord, to keep us from all unholy desires and practices, and to inspire within us a love for Thee, for all our fellowmen, and all good work. We ask Thee to open doors of opportunity to us, that we may in some way each day honor Thy Name and establish Thy will in the world. Give us the highest privilege of hourly fellowship with Thee, that we may be confident of Thy nearness to us and Thy interest in our affairs.

Forgive the many things that have marred our lives and stained our souls. We are ashamed of them, and turn from them in sincere repentance, blessing Thee that there is forgiveness and cleansing in Jesus Christ, our Lord and Saviour.

In His Name we ask all these good and precious gifts. *Amen.*

W. Courtland Robinson, D.D.,
Philadelphia, Penna.

JUNE FOURTH

Make confession unto the Lord God of your fathers. — Ezra 10: 11.

OUR Father in Heaven, we bow before Thee in gratitude for the care of the night, and for the light and hope of the new day. Grant that we may enter upon it in the joy of forgiven sin. Bring us to its close with souls unstained by conscious disobedience. Give us wisdom through the indwelling of Thy Holy Spirit that the choices of the day may be right. Keep us from the follies into which we shall be tempted to fall; preserve us from harm and danger of every kind. Bestow upon us the grace of love. Help us to love Thee and Thy Kingdom, and our fellowmen. Let Thy gracious presence today attend all with whom our lives are linked. Give them every blessing we ask for ourselves. Be in the hearts and homes especially present to our daily thoughts.

Keep from sin and shame and harm all who are dear to us. Have mercy upon Thy people of all creeds and tongues. Build up a holy Church throughout the world. Give victory to those who in hard places witness for Christ. Deal tenderly with men everywhere who have missed the way. Minister to the poor and the sick, the prisoner, and the oppressed. Rebuke and save those who plot evil against their neighbor. Win victory for Thyself in the affairs of our nation, and the nations of the earth. We offer these our morning prayers in the Name of Thy Son, our Lord and Saviour, Jesus Christ. *Amen.*

Rev. Hubert C. Herring,
Boston, Mass.

JUNE FIFTH

They that wait upon the Lord shall renew their strength. — Isa. 40:31.

O GOD, our Heavenly Father, Who hast declared Thy love for Thy children by sending Thy Son Jesus Christ into the world to be our Redeemer, we beseech Thee to enable us to live today and every day in thankfulness to Thee for what Thou hast done and art doing for us. In all our temptations and trials, in all the duties that are to be performed, teach us to seek Thy grace, which is sufficient for us and seeking it, to use it so that we may not fall into sin, nor fail to fulfil the work that Thou hast given us to do. Grant us ever to keep in the forefront of our remembrance the fact that as Christ has enlightened us, so we are to be a light unto the world.

Preserve us from the sin of denying Thee by our lives while we confess Thee with our lips, and from bringing harm to others by our inconsistency and neglect. Increase our faith, our hope, and our love, and use us "just as Thou wilt, and when, and where," as instruments for the promotion of Thy glory, and for the salvation of the world.

We ask it in the Name of Thy Son, Jesus Christ, our Lord. *Amen.*

Bishop Joseph M. Francis, D.D.,
Indianapolis, Indiana.

JUNE SIXTH

That at the name of Jesus every knee should bow, of things in Heaven, and things in earth, and things under the earth. And that every tongue should confess that Jesus Christ is Lord, to the glory of God the Father. Wherefore, my beloved, as ye have always obeyed, not as in my presence only, but now much more in my absence, work out your own salvation with fear and trembling. For it is God which worketh in you both to will and to do of His good pleasure. - Phil. 2: 10-13.

MERCIFUL GOD, our Father, we thank Thee for health, and life, and every good gift. Thou hast created us in Thine own image, and highly endowed us as thinking creatures. We recognize Thy divine right to rule over us, and we pray that we may be kept true and right before Thee. Give us grace for this day's duties, and make us kindly disposed toward our fellow-men. Support Thy people everywhere in the midst of difficulties, and bring this world to Thyself. Regard with much mercy the poor and unfortunate. Redeem men from the sins that beset them. For ourselves, our loved ones, our community, and our nation, we make our humble prayer.

Mercifully grant unto us all those blessings Thou seest we need, through the merits of Jesus Christ, our adorable Saviour. *Amen.*

Prof. Charles G. Heckert, D.D.
Springfield, Ohio.

JUNE SEVENTH

The prayer of faith shall save the sick. — James 5: 15.

OUR FATHER who art in Heaven, we kneel before Thee in this home which Thou hast given us, and in which Thou hast blessed us. As we rejoice in the good things of this earthly home, help us not to forget the better home on high, which Thou hast prepared for them that love Thee, and in which we shall some day dwell with Thee and with loved ones gone before.

Provide us today our daily bread, and feed not only our bodies, but feed also our souls with the "bread of life," even Jesus Christ.

Keep Thou our feet today, that they may not go into evil places; keep Thou also the door of our lips, that no unkind or unclean word may pass them; create within us clean hearts, for "out of them are the issues of life;" and whatsoever our hands find to do, may we do it "heartily, as unto the Lord."

Bless with Thy healing touch all sick and troubled ones. May Thy grace abound unto them and be sufficient for them. Hide all our loved ones, as under the shadow of Thy wings, that no evil or harm may befall them. Lead us all in the good and perfect way. Through Jesus Christ our Lord. *Amen.*

Rev. John W. Springer,
Pittsburgh, Pa.

JUNE EIGHTH

Then will I hear from Heaven, and forgive their sins. — II Chr. 7: 14.

ALMIGHTY GOD, our Heavenly Father, we thank Thee for the way of approach to Thyself through the rent veil of the flesh of Jesus Christ, our Lord; for the efficacy of His most precious blood, which cleanseth from all sin; for the promise of help through the Holy Spirit, when we know not what we should pray for; for the assurance that Thou hearest us, and dost delight to answer our prayers when they are in accord with Thy Holy Will. We bless

Thee for Thine unspeakable Gift, for the matchless expression of Thy love in the sacrifice of Christ, and for the grace so freely bestowed upon the sinful sons of men. Accept the homage of our hearts, the surrender of our wills, the consecration of our powers, and help us in all circumstances to be true to Thee. Deliver us in the time of temptation. Keep our feet so that our steps may not slide, and help us not to sin against Thee. Enable us to realize that sin is our enemy, that it hides Thee from us, and will, if indulged in, ruin us in time and eternity. Fill us with the spirit of Jesus, that all our speech and conduct may reveal His life in us, and that we may constantly glorify Thee, our adorable God. Graciously accept us and our petitions in the name of Jesus our Lord. *Amen.*

Rev. James H. Boyd,
London, Canada.

JUNE NINTH

Thou shalt love the Lord thy God with all thy heart. — Deut. 6: 5.

GRACIOUS Father in Heaven, admit us as a family into the secret of Thy presence, that we may worship Thee in spirit and in truth.

Accept our grateful praise for all that Thou art, and for all that Thou hast done for us and our fellowmen. Especially do we thank Thee for our redemption and salvation through Thy Son, Jesus Christ.

Father, reveal to us our sins and faults, that we may repent and forsake them, and that Thou mayest forgive us and cleanse us from all unrighteousness. And let Thy Holy Spirit dwell within us today, restraining us from all wrong-doing, and directing us into paths of truth and peace.

Guard us in those points of our characters that are most weak. Keep us from vanity and pride, from evil thoughts, and from unkind speech. Help us to love Thee with all our hearts, and to cordially love one another. Aid us as we try to serve Thee by ministering to our fellowmen. And grant us at last a home with Thee in Heaven, through our Saviour, Christ. *Amen.*

Jesse Thompson Whitley, D.D.,
Norfolk, Virginia.

JUNE TENTH

Let them praise Thy great and terrible Name. — Ps. 99: 3.

OUR dear Lord and Master, Thou hast set each family apart, and Thou dealest with them each according to duties well done, and faith well founded. We come, humbly imploring Thy forgiveness for the errors and mistakes of the past, and we beseech Thy guidance for the days to follow. Well and truly do we need Thee every hour, and therefore we entreat Thy guidance, without which we would be led astray, or fall into danger. Guard us from the terror by night, and the arrow that flieth at noon-day.

We have our trials, our necessities, and our distresses. All these we put into Thy hands, asking that Thou wouldst deal with us as little children. We have no fear of Thee, Almighty Father, for we have the assurance of Thy love.

Watch over all our business matters; help us to be honest and square in attending to them, and do Thou so guide us that we shall always do what is right in Thy sight. Lead us safely along the journey of life, and at last give to us all the Eternal Life, which we long for more than for the hidden treasures of earth.

Save all whom we love from passion, pride, and discontent, and finally bring us into Thy presence, through Jesus Christ our Lord. *Amen.*

William P. Jacobs, D.D.,
Clinton, South Carolina.

JUNE ELEVENTH

Bless the Lord, O my soul. — Ps. 103: 2.

OH GOD, our Heavenly Father, through Thy mercy we have been brought to the saving knowledge of our Lord Jesus Christ; and by Thy goodness we are permitted to enter upon the duties of another day. We thank Thee for Thy loving kindness, and humbly beseech Thee that we may this day show forth Thy praise with our lips and in our lives. Banish all doubt from our minds, and drive away all shadows from our souls, and enable us to realize Thy presence in our going out and our coming in, in our down-sitting and our uprising. May we have grace to think those things that are right, and courage to speak the words that may set forward Thy Kingdom! We pray that our dear ones may be kept both outwardly in their bodies, and inwardly in their souls, and be defended from all adversities which may happen to the body, and from all evil thoughts which may assault and hurt the soul. Keep Thy Church in continual godliness; and grant that through the consecrated work of Christian people everywhere, the whole world may be brought to Jesus Christ, and be saved. And oh, blessed Lord, when the busy day of our little life on earth is over, may we with all our loved ones, enter the service of eternal praise in Thy Heavenly Home, through the sole merits of our Lord and Saviour, Jesus Christ. *Amen.*

Bishop James R. Winchester, D.D.,
Little Rock, Arkansas.

JUNE TWELFTH

Let us draw near with a pure heart in full assurance of faith. — Heb. 10: 22.

OUR GOD and Father, we come to Thee with grateful hearts for all Thy mercy and goodness toward us. We know we are unworthy of the least of Thy favors. We have nothing in ourselves to commend us to Thee, except our weakness and need; but we rejoice that, notwithstanding our unworthiness, Thou dost bid us come to Thee and tell Thee all that is in our hearts. We confess before Thee our sins, and beseech Thy forgiveness. We plead for Thy grace, and the strength Thou alone canst give, for every experience of life. We pray that Thou wilt draw us nearer to Thyself. May we ever be conscious of Thy presence, and be uplifted by the assurance of Thy guidance and fellowship. Make the better and nobler life of the Spirit more real to us day by day. Take Thou possession of all our thoughts, and fill us with Thy Holy Spirit. Enable us to overcome every temptation, and to know and to do Thy holy will. Lead us by Thy mighty and loving hand always, and make our lives a blessing to other souls. When Thou art done with us here, receive us, we pray, to Thyself, in the upper and better world.

We ask all this in the name of and for the sake of Jesus Christ, our Lord and Saviour. *Amen.*

A. Judson Rowland, D.D.,
Philadelphia, Penna.

JUNE THIRTEENTH

They that know Thy Name will put their trust In Thee. — Ps. 9: 10.

O GOD, Thou art our Father and our Mother too, and under no circumstances can we get beyond the tireless search of Thy love. Ever since we were born Thou hast cared for us as though Thou hadst no other children, and still Thou dost follow us with ten thousand loving persuasions and infinite solicitude.

Grant, we beseech Thee, that Thy goodness may lead us to deeper consecration and to more heroic endeavor to extend Thy Kingdom. May we prove our love for God, Whom we have not seen, by self-denying service in behalf of our brother who is ever before our eyes. Save us from selfishness, from Pharisaism and bigotry, from pride and vain glory, and all narrow mindedness and uncharitableness.

May we make our Master visible to some who have not yet beheld Him, and may we help our neighbors and associates to think of Him Who came not to be ministered unto but to minister; Who would not save Himself, but saved others, and gave His blessed life that we might live a life of Christ-like courage and sacrifice. Hear us, Father, for all sorts and conditions of men. Make wars throughout the world to cease, and bring this poor little sin-cursed planet back into Thy bosom! *Amen.*

Dillon Bronson, D.D.,
Boston, Mass.

JUNE FOURTEENTH

The living shall praise Thee. — Isaiah 38: 19.

HEAVENLY Father, we thank Thee for the refreshing sleep of last night, for sparing us to see another day, for our loved ones, and for this family altar, for the gift of Thy Son, Jesus Christ, and for His love and self-sacrifice.

We sincerely repent of all wrong-doing. Pardon all our sins, and give to us a forgiving spirit. Help us to trust in Thy Word, and may we find in it medicine for the mind, and food for the soul.

We pray for our beloved country, and for all in authority, in our own and other nations. Bless the poor and needy, the sick and dying, the bereaved and all who are in distress. We plead with Thee for any who are wrongfully treated, until "justice roll on like water, and righteousness as a perennial stream."

Abundantly reward the preaching of Thy Gospel everywhere, and bless our church and minister with an outpouring of Thy Holy Spirit, until one shall not have to say to another — "Know the Lord, — for all shall know Him from the least even unto the greatest."

And to Thee will we give the glory forever and ever. *Amen.*

Capt. (Rev.) H. S. Mullowney, M.A., B.D.,
Owen Sound, Ont., Canada.

JUNE FIFTEENTH

He shall call upon Me, and I will answer him: I will be with him in trouble; I will deliver him, and honor him. — Ps. 91: 15.

LOVING Father, may we realize what a great privilege it is for us to come directly into Thy very presence, in the name, and by the close relationship of Thy Son as our Saviour and Elder Brother, and to really be Thy children. Help us today to be able to call Thee "our Father." Help us to realize that Thy great loving heart turns towards us as the heart of a loving parent turns towards his child. Each day may this relationship mean more and more, and become very precious to us.

As we take up the duties of the day, may we take shelter under the wonderful promises of the Ninety-first Psalm, and may they be fulfilled to us and our loved ones. May we in some way be a help and blessing to someone who may need us this day. Help us to be careful about our example before others.

May we "walk, stand, and sit" in such places as may be pleasing in Thy sight, and be safe for others to follow us in.

May we, by our faith in the Lord Jesus Christ as our personal Saviour, be clothed with His righteousness, and have a part in His resurrection. Guide us and help us as the days pass, we ask in His name. *Amen.*

E. K. Warren,
Three Oaks, Mich.

JUNE SIXTEENTH

The Lord hear thee in the day of trouble; the Name of the God of Jacob defend thee; Send thee help from the sanctuary, and strengthen thee out of Zion; Remember all thy offerings, and accept thy burnt sacrifice; Grant thee according to thine own heart, and fulfil all thy counsel. We will rejoice in thy salvation, and in the Name of our God we will set up our banners: the Lord fulfill all thy petitions. — Ps. 20: 1-5.

ALMIGHTY GOD, our Heavenly Father, we pray Thee to bless this family and household, and all "who are dear to them, wherever they may be. Bless them with all best blessings, both temporal and spiritual.

Bless them in the basket and in the store, bless them in their rising up and lying down, their going out, and coming in, and in all that they put their hands unto.

But above all, bless them with all best spiritual blessings; increase in them true religion, nourish them with all goodness, and of Thy great mercy keep them in the same, and help them to bring up their children in the nurture and admonition of the Lord, that as they grow in age, they may grow in grace, and be truly members of Christ, children of God, and inheritors of the Kingdom of Heaven, that they may be faithful even unto death, and finally attain unto everlasting life, through Jesus Christ, our Lord. *Amen.*

Bishop William Crane Gray, D.D.,
Orlando, Florida.

JUNE SEVENTEENTH

I prayed unto the Lord, my God, and made my confession. — Dan. 9: 4.

EVER-LIVING, ever-loving God, our Heavenly Father, we bless and praise Thee, that Thou didst set the human race in families for its higher development and its greater influence. This morning we bless Thy holy name that we have been called into this family now before Thee in prayer.

May we gratefully recognize our duty and our responsibility to Thee, and to one another, and to this community.

Keep us this day from sin, as we do the tasks of the day. Watch Thou over us and guard us from danger. Teach us how to live unselfishly, each for the other, in all the little things of the home.

May we, as father and mother, as brothers and sisters, fulfill our tasks to each and to all, with the blessed example of our Elder Brother always before our minds.

Prosper the work of each one of us, and the labors and business of all our neighbors. Grant, above all, to our family the real and abiding prosperity of a rich and helpful faith in our Lord and Master, to Whom be praise, and glory, now and forever. *Amen.*

L. B. Wolf, D.D.,
Baltimore, Maryland.

JUNE EIGHTEENTH

Men ought always to pray and not to faint. — Luke 18: 1.

OUR Heavenly Father, we come to Thee in humble worship this morning. We thank Thee for Thy loving care while we slept, and for the sleep and rest of the night. We thank Thee that, refreshed in body and mind, Thou hast brought us to see the beginning of a new day. Lord abide with us still.

We ever need Thee. Protect us from harm, and guide us in all the duties of this day. Deliver us from evil, and make us strong to do Thy will.

Be pleased to remember with Thy blessing all our loved ones. Some of them are far distant from us, but Thou art everywhere present. Be pleased to bless Thine own work. Let great grace be given to ministers of the Gospel, and all Christian workers everywhere, that Thy Name may be glorified through their efforts.

And now, blessed Lord, we commit our loved ones and ourselves to Thy care. Pardon our sins, and guide us by Thy Spirit in the way pleasing to Thyself this day, and all we ask in the Name of Jesus our Saviour. *Amen.*

Rev. Douglas Laing,
Kingston, Ont., Canada.

JUNE NINETEENTH

The Lord knoweth them that trust Him. — Nahum 1: 7.

OUR Heavenly Father, we lift up our hearts to Thee in adoring praise for Thy love and grace made known unto us in Jesus Christ, our Saviour, Who died for our sins.

We thank Thee for Thy blessed Book, which is able to make us wise unto salvation. Help us to read, and inwardly digest it. We thank Thee for the Holy Spirit, Who takes of the things of Christ and shows them unto us, and Who is promised to guide us into all truth, and to comfort us all the days of our life. Help us to recognize Him in all we think, or say, or do, and never vex, grieve, nor sin against Him. But help us to follow Him and to realize His presence with us.

We need Thee for the little things of life as well as the big things. Help us to control our tongues, so that we may not speak unadvisedly with our lips. Help us to live daily in expectation of our Lord's coming, and be ready when He comes. Bless all the families of the earth, and graciously give success to all ministers, missionaries, and Christian workers who are humbly seeking to glorify Jesus, and to win the nations to Him.

We ask it all in His Name. *Amen.*

Rev. Lewis Powell, D.D.,
Hopkinsville, Kentucky.

JUNE TWENTIETH

The Lord loveth the righteous. — Ps. 146: 8.

O LORD, our God! We present ourselves to Thee in the Name of Jesus Christ Thy Son, our [Saviour. Give us a joyous sense of our acceptance with Thee in Him. May the Spirit of Thy Son in us now cry "Abba: Father."

We would know Thee more and more. Reveal Thyself to U3 increasingly in Thy Word, and in the Spirit of Jesus, our Lord. We would love Thee; show us Thy love. We will then trust Thee always, and we will serve Thee in all we think and say and do. Accept and seal us in all this, our Heavenly Father. Loving and serving Thee, we will love and serve all Thy creatures, and especially our fellow men as members of the great family of God on earth. We will regard none of our powers or possessions as our own. We will seek every one the other's good, and "thus fulfil the law of Christ." Every day fulfil Thy Will and accomplish Thy purpose in and through us, and thus prepare us to meet Thee, and be with Thee, and be filled with Thee, and made Thy instruments in ever higher, richer, and more blessed service, through eternity.

We ask this not for ourselves alone, but for all Thy people, and finally for all mankind, through Jesus Christ, our Lord. *Amen.*

Rev. J. R. Johnston,
Preston, Ontario, Canada.

JUNE TWENTY-FIRST

The Lord is merciful and gracious, slow to anger, and plenteous in mercy. He will not always chide: neither will he keep His anger for ever. He hath not dealt with us after our sins; nor rewarded us according to our iniquities. For as the Heaven is high above the earth, so great is His mercy toward them that fear Him. As far as the east is from the west, so far hath He removed our transgressions from us. Like as a father pitieth his children, so the Lord pitieth them that fear Him. — Ps. 103; 8-13.

O ALMIGHTY GOD and gracious Father, we beseech Thee, hear our prayer today. Bless us with all health and happiness. Give us sane minds, light hearts, unsullied vision of our duties and responsibilities, and, above all, a right judgment in all things. Guard our inexperience; keep us from all self-conceit; make us become as little children, that we may be wise; to become gentle, that we may be strong; to become humble, that we may become divine.

Prepare us to fulfil our course in life with honor; and grant that we may so live in this world that, in the world to come, we may have life everlasting; through Jesus Christ our Lord. *Amen.*

David M. Steele, D.D.,
Philadelphia, Penna.

JUNE TWENTY-SECOND

My peace I give unto you. — John 14: 27.

O THOU Who art the giver of every good and perfect gift, in Whose unfailing love we live and move and have our being, and without Whom we should be poor indeed, enable us, we beseech Thee, to discern even more clearly Thine abounding goodness to us, and as Thou hast made us rich in blessings, make us also rich in gratitude. We praise Thee, our Father, for those revelations of Thy love with which we are most familiar, and which we are all too prone to forget; for rising and setting suns, and the stars; for clouds and winds and passing seasons; for the outer light in which we walk serenely and dwell securely; and the light within, the true light which witnesses to our oneness with Thee. Wilt Thou help us reverently to interpret all our blessings in terms of Thy love. We thank Thee for our friends and all that friendship has meant to us, and that we may think of ourselves as friends of Jesus Christ. Wilt Thou help us also to understand what high obligations such friendship lays upon us. We praise Thee for Thy gift of peace — that peace which the world cannot give nor take away, the peace of those who have found their sanctuary in the love and goodness of God. Evermore give us this peace. In His name, who came to bring us peace. *Amen.*

G. Glenn Atkins, D.D., LL.B.,
Providence, R. I.

JUNE TWENTY-THIRD

Ye believe in God, believe also in Me. — John 14: 1.

ALMIGHTY GOD, in Whom we live and move and have our being, we adore Thee as the God and Father of our Lord Jesus Christ, in Whose name we present our adoration, our thanksgiving, our praise, and our supplication. We thank Thee for the gift of Thy Son, through Whom we have our redemption, and in Whose name we ask for the pardon of all our sins. We beseech Thee, Lord, to keep us this day, in all joy, health, and safety from the perils that may beset us. Grant that from day to day we may walk in all reverence and godly fear in the way of Him Who hath called us into His Church and Kingdom. Deliver us, we pray Thee, from all envy, and fear, and temptation. Grant unto us that which is good and profitable, and forgive us those things wherein we have sinned against Thee. Deliver us from all those things which estrange men one from another, from such things as cause men to stumble and err from the truth as it is in Christ. Keep us from the dominion of selfishness, and grant us willingness to bear one another's burdens. These, and all other needed blessings, we ask in the adorable name of our Saviour, to Whom with the Father and the Spirit shall be the praise and power and dominion now and forevermore. *Amen.*

David H. Bauslin, D.D.,
Springfield, Ohio.

JUNE TWENTY-FOURTH

My God, unto Thee will I pray. — Ps. 5: 2.

HOLY Father, we thank Thee for the privilege of prayer. It is of Thine amazing goodness that we are permitted to pray, and of Thine infinite wisdom that our prayers are answered. Our gratitude goes out to God for life and health, and all the blessings which come to us. Above all other blessings, we are grateful to Thee for the Saviour. In thinking of the blessings so graciously bestowed upon us, our hearts adopt the words of Scripture — "Thanks be unto God for His unspeakable Gift." We lay ourselves at Thy feet, most Holy One; we adore Thy Great and Holy Name. Thou alone art God, and beside Thee there is none else. Do Thou bless our home, and guide us, to make it such a home as Thou wouldst have it be. Sanctify our relations one to another, to become all that God has planned for our lives. Bless, we pray Thee, all other families, our neighbors and friends, together with the stranger afar off; though an enemy, hear us for them, most gracious Father, and give to them every good thing we would ask for ourselves. Bless our country. Give the spirit of wisdom and sound judgment to all civil officers and those in authority. So overrule, that peace shall be maintained among all nations. Let Thy Kingdom come. Speed the glad day when every knee shall bow and every tongue confess Him Lord to the glory of God the Father. *Amen.*

Rev. F. C. McConnell,
Atlanta, Georgia.

101

JUNE TWENTY-FIFTH

The Lord is worthy to be praised. — II Sam. 22: 23.

O THOU Who art the same yesterday, today, and forever, as we think back over life, we think how many revelations we have had of Thee. Some days we were very sure that Thou art infinitely kind; some days we have groaned in bitterness. On some of the bright mornings of life our hearts have sung in spite of us; and on the black midnights our hearts have sunk to despair. Yet, Thou art the same Lord; God over all, blessed forever, "Whose property is always to have mercy," and Who hast never requited us according to our sins, but in wrath "hast remembered mercy." Father, we are daring to say to our hearts that what Jesus was, Thou art; that He unveiled Thee for us. As men, tempted and defeated could trust Him, we may trust Thee. As women scorned, trusted Him, nor were disappointed, women today may trust Thee. As little children held out their arms to Him, with the unerring response of childhood to goodness, so the children of our homes and hearts may hold out their hands to Thee, Who art the Father of our Lord, Jesus Christ, and of us all.

Accept our thanks for the days past, and our praises for this day, and our heart-full trust for the days to be. In the Name of Christ. *Amen.*

George Clarke Peck, D.D.,
Baltimore, Maryland.
JUNE TWENTY-SIXTH

I pray that thy faith fail not. — Luke 22: 32.

O LORD, our Lord, how excellent is Thy name in all the earth! Who hast set Thy glory above the heavens. How glorious art Thou in all Thy attributes; how gracious in all Thy acts! Thou openest Thine hand and satisfiest the desire of every living thing. Accept our worship and adoration and thanksgiving. We make confession of our unworthiness and unfaithfulness, and humbly beseech Thy fatherly forgiveness. We bear before Thee in supplication the needs of a lost world, lying in wickedness. Pour out upon all people Thy Holy Spirit, that His gracious influence may deepen the spiritual life, and change the character of those who are without God and without hope in the world, transforming them into the likeness of the Son of God. Remember this family in Thy infinite mercy, that it may be a household of faith, and that this may be a home in which Thou wilt delight to dwell; and when Thou makest up Thy jewels, gather them all without a missing one, a whole family in heaven, saved by grace. Hear us in this our supplication, and do for us not according to our merit, but according to Thy mercy, exceeding abundantly, above all that we ask or think, according to the power that worketh in us, to whom be glory in the Church by Christ Jesus, throughout all ages, world without end. *Amen.*

Samuel L. Morris, D.D.,
Atlanta, Ga.

JUNE TWENTY-SEVENTH

I believe God, that it shall be even as it was told me. —Acts 27:25.

THE night has brought us rest and refreshment and renewal of strength and hope, Father. The day opens to us its opportunities, and brings us its manifold tasks and, it may be, its trials and burdens and cares.

We thank Thee, our Father for the restoration of power and courage while we have slept. We trustingly pray for guidance and enabling for the undertakings and employments of the day.

We seek the direction which shall set us forward along right ways, the wisdom which shall cause us rightly to choose in every issue, the integrity which shall keep us wholly loyal to the truth.

May no burden be laid upon us beyond our strength, and if the trials of the day are to be many, grant unto us great patience, constant self-control, and the power to keep our tempers and our judgment.

Grant that we may suffer no loss of faith in our fellowmen, no lessening in our belief of purity and goodness, no dimming of our vision of the ideal. And bring us at the end of a day of useful labor and helpful living to the joy of an unbroken home. *Amen.*

Rev. J. Percival Huget,
Detroit, Michigan.

JUNE TWENTY-EIGHTH

The Lord hath made known His salvation: His righteousness hath He openly shewed in the sight of the heathen. He hath remembered His mercy and His truth toward the house of Israel: all the ends of the earth have seen the salvation of our God. — Ps. 98: 2-3.

ALMIGHTY GOD and Heavenly Father, Who, through Thine only-begotten Son didst sanctify the ties of marriage and home, we heartily thank Thee for Thy loving care and watchful providence over us from the beginning of our lives to this day. We praise Thee for all our happinesses and joys; for the gifts of affection and sympathy towards one another; for any chastening of sorrow or tribulation with which Thou hast seen fit to visit us. And we beseech Thee to continue Thy gracious goodness towards us. Give us grace to do our daily duties faithfully, as parents or children, as members of Thy Church, and as citizens of the nation. Pardon all our offences, and make us sorry for them with the godly sorrow that worketh repentance unto salvation. Comfort the distressed; bless the work of the clergy and all other servants of Thy Kingdom. Bring the nations into Thy fold, and add the heathen to Thy inheritance, so that righteousness and peace, truth and justice, fellowship and good-will may prevail among men, to the honor and glory of Thy Name; through Jesus Christ our Lord. *Amen.*

Bishop Frederick B. Howden, D.D.,
Albuquerque, New Mexico.
JUNE TWENTY-NINTH

His faith is counted for righteousness. — Rom. 4: 5.

ALMIGHTY Father, Shepherd and Bishop of our souls, lift upon us the Light of Thy countenance. We thank Thee that it is possible for us to approach the unveiled mercy seat. We come not in our own name, nor do we plead any merit in ourselves. Our hope is in Christ, Thy beloved Son, crucified for us. He bore our sins in His own body on the tree, and by His stripes we are healed. Let Thy benediction rest upon this family circle. Help us to keep the fire of gratitude and devotion burning on Thine altar. Give us grace to overcome evil in the day of temptation. Give us courage in the hour of adversity, and humility in prosperity. Help us to live as in Thy sight; doing Thy will with alacrity and cheerfulness. Give wisdom and integrity of purpose, we pray Thee, to all those in authority over us, that in the administration of public affairs they may "do justly, and love mercy." We invoke Thy special blessing upon the household under this roof, that we may not disappoint Thy gracious will concerning us. Bestow Thy heavenly grace upon father, mother, and children, so that we may be worthy to have a place in the Great Family of God, which shall, by and by, enter upon their eternal inheritance. Thanks to Thee for victory through our Lord Jesus Christ. Amen, and *Amen.*

Thomas F. Dornblaser, D.D.,
Chicago, Illinois.
JUNE THIRTIETH

Holding the mystery of the faith in a pure conscience. — I Tim. 3: 9.

WE extol Thee, Lord, our King, as we present ourselves before Thee, through the merits of Jesus Christ, Who by His cross and precious blood, hath redeemed us from our sin. We humbly beseech Thee, O merciful Father, to pardon our offences against Thee and Thy Holy Law; to create within us a clean heart and a right spirit; to cause the words of our mouths and the meditations of our hearts to be acceptable in Thy sight, Lord, our Rock and our Redeemer. We bless Thy Holy Name, our Father, for Thy manifold and unceasing goodness unto us. "We owe to Thee the temporal blessings of our lives, and all the opportunities we have for usefulness and happiness. Enable us, by Thy Holy Spirit, that we may enjoy and use these, and all Thy good gifts, in a worthy and acceptable manner. Be compassionate, O God, toward all the suffering, sorrowing, and sinning ones. Be the comforter of the aged, the guide of the young, the wisdom of all who teach, the ruler of all who govern, the light of all who are in darkness — the Saviour of all mankind. Hasten, Lord, Thy glorious appearing, and number us among those who shall receive at Thy right hand the crown of glory that fadeth not away. Through Jesus Christ our Lord. *Amen.*

Rev. M. C. MacLean, B.A.
Toronto, Ont., Canada.

July

JULY FIRST

O, praise the Lord, all ye nations: praise Him, all ye people. For His merciful kindness is great toward us: and the truth of the Lord endureth for ever. Praise ye the Lord. — Ps. 117 (complete).

ALMIGHTY GOD, our Father, do Thou accept such acknowledgment, devotion, and worship as we, with all our limitations are able to bring to Thee. Thou knowest that some of us, with the utmost willingness, cannot apprehend Thee at all according to accepted standards. Thou knowest that some of Thy most devoted children do most fearfully misapprehend Thee. The best of Thy children the world over do but see Thee as in a mirror darkly. Therefore, we pray that Thou wilt save us all from any pride of spiritual aristocracy, and help us to help each other toward the light. Save us from contempt and bitterness toward those whose eye of faith is not focused like ours, and save those of us who cannot see at all from misjudging those who can see. Thou hast compelled no man to acknowledge Thee, but by Thy good providences and gracious mercies Thou art drawing all men unto Thyself. May we, Thy children, go and do likewise; compelling no man, by sneer or by fear, and winning all men by love and by sincerity. *Amen.*

George W. Coleman.
Boston, Mass.

JULY SECOND

Faithful is He that called you. — I Thess. 5: 24.

O GOD, our hope is in Thee. We lift our eyes to the hills whence cometh

105

our help. We are in the valley where there is darkness; but looking up we can see the light of Thy glory on the hill-tops above us, and the vision dispels our fears and fills us with hope and courage. Fill our hearts with a longing for Thee, greater than the longing of those who wait for the morning, and grant us that knowledge of Thyself, through Jesus Christ our Lord, that Thy presence may be constantly real to us.

Grant us strength for our tasks, and may we do all of our work as in Thy sight, and for Thy glory. Make the way of duty and service very plain to us. Quicken us in faith and hope and love, and strengthen us in all our worthy purposes and desires, and make us a blessing to others.

Keep us from all mistakes or blunders in word or act that might bring reproach upon Thy Name and Thy cause. Make us quick to see every opportunity for service, and faithful to improve it. Cleanse us from all sin, perfect us in all goodness, give us victory in time of temptation, and make our lives to be beautiful with the beauty of God. All of which mercies and blessings we ask in the Name and for the sake of Jesus Christ, our Lord. *Amen.*

William Wirt King, D.D.,
St. Louis, Missouri.

JULY THIRD

As Jesus prayed the heavens were opened. — Luke 3: 21.

O LORD our Heavenly Father, as Thou hast graciously spared us to the light of another morning, accept Thou our glad thanksgiving for this and all Thy countless mercies to us.

Pardon us wherein we have grieved Thee in the past. Grant unto us, we humbly beseech Thee, all such benefits for body, mind and spirit as Thou seest best for us this day. Show us Thy will, and may it be our pleasure.

Impart unto us such faith in Thee that we may successfully meet all the testings that await us. May ours be the patience, the courage, and the joy of those who know Thy love and have learned the secret of the Lord. Make Thy blessings to us to be, through us, Thy gifts to our world.

Remember in Thy mercy, our loved ones in their especial needs. Comfort and heal the afflicted. Bless all who toil.

Give through Thy Church, salvation to our Nation and to all people, and speed the time when earth shall be done with evil and over all shall be established the sceptre of Thy Son, our blessed Saviour. *Amen.*

John Edward Bushnell, D.D.,
Minneapolis, Minnesota.

I praise and extol the King of Heaven. — Dan. 4:37.

O GOD, our Father, we turn to Thee with the light of the morning, thankful for Thy mercies and trusting in Thy care. We thank Thee for the rest of the night, and for the fresh gift of daily bread from Thy bounty. We thank Thee for the renewal of strength, and for the opportunities of service that await us. We thank Thee for the dear bonds of family affection and for the counsel and comfort of Thy word. Help us, O Lord, this day to bear each other's burdens, and to serve Thee by serving our fellowmen. Grant us grace for the duties of the day. May the spirit of our toil bear witness to our faith. Especially we commend to Thee all our dear absent ones, wherever they may be. Though we see them not, we rejoice that Thine eye is upon them, and Thy care enfolds them. May our church be a true Household of the Faith. Bless our nation. May it uphold the banner of righteousness. Bless all who labor for the poor and the suffering. Be with those who in distant lands proclaim Thy love, and hasten the day when all shall know and serve Thee.

Keep us, Father, through the day, and bring us to its close in peace. We ask it all in the name of Jesus Christ, our Lord. *Amen.*

Charles S. Mills, D.D., A.B.,
Montclair, N. J.

JULY FIFTH

Then He said unto them, O fools, and slow of heart to believe all that the prophets have spoken: Ought not Christ to have suffered these things, and to enter into His glory? And beginning at Moses and all the prophets, He expounded unto them in all the scriptures the things concerning Himself. And they drew nigh unto the village, whither they went: and He made as though He would have gone further. But they constrained Him, saying, Abide with us: for it is toward evening, and the day is far spent. And He went in to tarry with them. — Luke 24: 25-29.

GRANT rest, dear Lord, to the weary; comfort to the sorrowing; shelter to the homeless; and pillow the head of every sufferer upon Thy everlasting arms, and gather, Heavenly Father, within the shelter of those loving arms the lonely who stand in need of Thee, and shed the brightness of Thy countenance upon them that in their darkness they may see Thy face and so obtain that peace that remaineth for the people of God.

We Thy children ask it for His sake, Jesus Christ, our Lord. *Amen.*

Rev. Henry C. Stone,
Philadelphia, Penna.

JULY SIXTH

Jesus answered them, do ye now believe? — John 16: 31.

OUR Father, God, we know Thee through Jesus Christ our Lord, and we praise Thee for all Thy loving kindness and tender mercies. With the assurance that Thou wilt never leave nor forsake us, we enter upon the duties of a new day. We lift our eyes unto the hills, from whence cometh our help.

Direct us in all the way that we should take, in view of our great responsibilities and opportunities. Help us to earn our bread honestly, but not to be so busy as to let the King pass by. May we live our day before Thee in all reverence, quietness, love, and usefulness.

Remember our loved ones everywhere. Bless all for whom we ought to pray — the sick, the suffering, the sinful, God pity them and minister to their needs. Let Thy grace be upon every heart lifted up in true and simple desire for a better life.

Bless our nation in all her crises. Give wisdom unto our counsellors, and direction to those who lead our affairs.

Bless especially the Church of Jesus Christ, her missionaries and ministers, and bring us all to the redeemed in glory, through Jesus Christ. *Amen.*

J. M. Francis, D.D.
Sunbury, Pa.

JULY SEVENTH

Great is Thy faithfulness. — Lam. 3: 23.

MAY we never forget to be thankful to Thee, our Father. Thou dost daily load us with benefits. Thou art continually planning for our welfare; yet we are indifferent to Thy great goodness. We pray, and our prayers are answered, but we forget often to say, "Thank you."

Make us more mindful of Thee, of our dependence upon Thee, and of Thy readiness to supply all our needs. Then may we do more than speak our praise; may we live our praise, and show our love to Thee by our acts.

Be present with us in our home. Teach us to trust Thee, to listen to Thy Word, to do Thy will. Teach us the joy of serving Thee. When doubt disturbs us, may we have a vision of Thee that will take away all distress. Forbid it that we should darken the days of others by doubting words.

Forgive our sins, and make us more earnest in prayers, in gifts, in service. Let our home be a center from which blessings go out to neighbors near and far. And show us how to live always to the praise of Thy Holy Name. *Amen.*

John T. Faris, D.D.,
Philadelphia, Pa.

JULY EIGHTH

And this is the confidence that we have in Him, that, if we ask anything according to His will, He heareth us: And if we know that He hear us, whatsoever we ask, we know that we have the petitions that we desired of Him. - 2 John 5: 14-15.

OUR Father, it is with reverence we bow to Thee. We thank Thee for every blessing of life, for we realize that Thou art the Giver of every good and perfect gift. We pray that every member of this household may realize that God hath a purpose in every individual life; may it be the highest ambition of our lives to know what God would have us do. May the Holy Spirit ever abide with us and direct us in all the things Thou hast made it possible for us to do. May Thy love for us, as manifested in so many ways, constrain us to serve and honor Thee our Father.

Dear Lord, we commit ourselves with all we have and are, into Thy loving care, and would ask Thee to bless us, keep us, guide us, forgive our sins, and finally take us to Thyself with all the redeemed. We ask it in Jesus' Name and for His sake. *Amen.*

Rev. C. Stubblefield,
Miami, Oklahoma.

JULY NINTH

Jesus said, I thank Thee and Praise Thee, O Lord of Heaven. — Matt. 11: 25.

OUR, Father, we thank Thee for all Thy gracious care, new every morning and continued every evening: for life and health; for food and raiment and home; for Thy presence which sanctifies and blesses all our human relationships.

May we spend this day as in Thy sight. Keep us, we pray, pure in heart and clean in life. Make us strong in temptation, brave in danger, patient and courageous in sorrow or trial, faithful in every trust. Preserve undimmed the light that glows on our home altar. Guard our lips, that we may speak no unkind or thoughtless word; our hearts, that we may think unselfish and generous thoughts; and our hands, that we may help one another.

If it be best for us, keep us from sickness and death, that in gladness we may serve Thee; but if misfortune befall us, do Thou draw us close to Thyself and comfort us, that our faith may not fail.

Bless all homes. Have compassion on the homeless. Through human kindness make Thy love known to all men, and in mercy grant us a place at length in Thy Heavenly home, through Jesus Christ, our Lord. *Amen.*

Charles W. McCormick, D.D., Ph.D.,
Brooklyn, N. Y.

JULY TENTH

According to your faith, be it done unto you. — Matt 9: 29.

ALMIGHTY GOD, our Heavenly Father, we thank Thee for Thy great goodness unto the sons of men. We realize that it is in Thee we live and move and have our being. We give Thee thanks for Thy love which sent into this world One Who is its Master — Jesus Christ our Lord. We not only thank Thee for Thy Fatherhood, but also for Thy Motherhood, for we know that as one whom his mother comforteth, so wilt Thou comfort us. We look to Thee for strength in our weakness; hope in our time of despondency; courage in the fearful hour.

Day after day we are bidden to get us to Cherith, only to find the brook is drying up! Continue to try our faith, and lend us of that spirit of trust and patience that we may hear Thy words, "Get thee to Zarephath," where we come face to face with Thy availing mercy. Feed us with the bread of Heaven, that we may be strong of mind, pure of heart, and unselfish in our service, and may the love of Jesus Christ so fill our hearts that others will take knowledge of us that we have been with Thee. Help Thou us to attain to the character of Thy Son, to in. corporate His spirit, and live His life. *Amen.*

James A. Fraser, Ph.D.,
Pittsburgh, Penna.

JULY ELEVENTH

I thank God. Whom I serve. — II Tim. 1: 3.

O GOD, Whose paternal goodness is unfailingly tender and constant, we unite as a family to yield Thee glad and earnest praise and to invoke upon our home and all its interests Thy gracious and heavenly blessing. Cause us so to realize our utter dependence upon Thee and our profound obligation toward Thee, that we may submit ourselves anew to Thy sovereign sway, live our lives henceforth as in Thine all-searching sight, and consistently show ourselves Thine. We bring to Thee at this time all who are in any wise related to our home, and any who may be attempting to live their lives apart from Thee. Suffer none of us to be enticed from the path of simplicity, purity, or honor. Keep us from every form of secularity and avarice, defend us from the seductive snares of vanity and pride, and enable us to serve Thee with such undivided fidelity in this life that in the life to come we may all receive Thine exceeding great reward. And with this prayer for ourselves, we beseech of Thee in behalf of those without — our neighbors, our friends, and all classes and conditions of men — that it may please Thee to give them likewise of Thy fatherly favor, to further them in all their undertakings and relationships, and to bring them with us at length into Thine Heavenly household, where we may praise Thee ever, world without end. *Amen.*

John Bai.com Shaw, D.D.,
Elmira, New York.

JULY TWELFTH

The joy of the Lord is your strength. — Neh. 8: 10.

OUR Father, help us to find the secret of the Master's joy, that we may no longer dwell in the outer courts where our happiness comes and goes as the flowers bloom and fade. May we enter into the secret place of the Most High where He lived, until our joy, like His cannot be taken away from us.

Teach us the joy of discovering the tokens of Thy presence always — in the song of birds, the fragrance of flowers, the marvelous beauty of sunrise and sunset, but more in the ringing laughter and plaintive cry of little children, in the deep hunger in the hearts of our brothers and sisters, and in our own souls, so that we are never alone.

Teach us the joy of a friendship that leaves no hurt nor sting. Help us to enter into the deep joy of sympathy with our brother's need, the sympathy that gives insight, and knits heart to heart, until we are able to help where help is needed, and able to receive help when it is offered. Save us, our Father, from the darkness of selfishness, and unite us with wise and tender love to those who need us, and those whom we need. All of this, and more which we cannot express, we ask in the Master's name. *Amen.*

Rev. Raymond C. Brooks,
Berkeley, California.

JULY THIRTEENTH

Nay, in all these things we are more than conquerors through Him that loved us. For I am persuaded, that neither death, nor life, nor angels, nor principalities, nor powers, nor things present, nor things to come, nor height, nor depth, nor any other creature, shall be able to separate us from the love of God, which is in Christ Jesus our Lord. — Romans 8: 37-39.

ALMIGHTY GOD, our Heavenly Father, in Whom we live and move and have our being, we render Thee our humble praises for Thy preservation of us from the beginning of our lives to this day; for Thy many mercies we bless and magnify Thy glorious Name. And since it is of Thy mercy, gracious Father, that another day is added to our lives, we here dedicate both our souls and our bodies to Thee and Thy service.

We would remember before Thy Throne of Grace all those who are near and dear to us, and all for whom we are bound to pray.

Be merciful to all who are in any trouble, and be graciously pleased to take us and all things belonging to us under Thy Fatherly care and protection this day, and forevermore.

We ask it for Christ's sake. *Amen.*

Bishop Ethelbert Talbot,
South Bethlehem, Pa.

JULY FOURTEENTH

I will praise Thee, for Thou hast heard me. — Ps. 118: 21.

OUR dear Heavenly Father, reverently do we approach Thee, the giver of all good and perfect gifts. We give thanks to Thee for all the blessings Thou hast so graciously bestowed upon us. Thou hast kept us day by day unto this hour. We must say that goodness and mercy have followed us. We have sinned, and come short of the glory of God. For the sake of Jesus do Thou forgive all our sins. Wash us in the blood of the Lamb.

Give us grace to perform every duty in life conscientiously, and in Thy fear, Lord. May we not be slothful in business, but fervent in spirit, serving the Lord. May our lives be fully consecrated to Thy service. Help us to love our neighbors as ourselves. Give us the mind of Christ. May we crucify the old Adam with all his affections and lusts, so that the new man may daily arise within us to live before Thee in righteousness and purity. Give us grace, dear Lord, to live such lives day by day, that when our end shall come we may be prepared to enter upon the rest that remaineth for the people of God. Grant these blessings unto us, and to all our fellowmen, out of the fulness of Thine infinite love and mercy, in Christ Jesus our Lord and Saviour, and for His sake alone. *Amen.*

Conrad Huber, D.D.,
Richmond, Ind.

JULY FIFTEENTH

I will praise Thee, O Lord my God, with all my heart: and I will glorify Thy Name for evermore. For great is Thy mercy toward me: and Thou hc.ot delivered my soul from the lowest hell. But Thou, O Lord, art a God full of compassion, and gracious, long-suffering, and plenteous in mercy and truth. O turn unto me, and have mercy upon me; give Thy strength unto Thy servant, and save the son of Thine handmaid. — Ps. 86: 12-13; 15-16.

OUR Heavenly Father, we bow before Thee humbly, reverently, and thankfully, for Thou art great and holy and good. Forgive our sins for Jesus' sake, and by Thy Holy Spirit take away our love of sinning that we may be willing and able to do Thy will. Make our home life strong in truth and righteousness, and beautiful with love, and courtesy, and cheerfulness. May these children, like Jesus, increase in wisdom and in favor with God and man. We thank Thee for the gift of life. May we all lay hold on eternal life, which also is Thy gift. Show us our work, and make us faithful. Make us unselfish, and so helpful to the weak, the tempted, the sorrowing, the discouraged, and the lost. Bless our country with righteousness. Bring men to the new brotherhood in Christ, and clothe Thy Church with power, that the Gospel may be preached, and Thy Kingdom hastened, through Jesus Christ, our Lord. *Amen.*

Prof. J. H. Farmer, LL.D.,
Toronto, Canada.

JULY SIXTEENTH

Let God be magnified, — Ps. 70: 4.

O GOD our Father, we earnestly desire in these brief moments, to give Thee thanks for all the blessings which enter into our lives, and enable us thus to come to Thee. According to Thy knowledge of us commune with us, and grant us comfort in sadness, guidance in our perplexities, strength for all duty, and preservation from all evil. If in anything — in thought, or word, or deed, we have grieved Thee, forgive us, for His sake Who gave Himself for us; and wherein we have failed, grant us sufficient grace that we may fail no more. May Thy Good Spirit make Thee so real to us this day, and reveal Thee to us as so consciously near, in all that lies before us, that when its hours shall have passed away forever, there may be left no saddening memory of failure. In all these things hear us, O Father, for others as well as for ourselves; especially for all who are dearest to us, whether close at hand or far away. May there come special blessing to them, even according to all their real need. We beseech Thee to guide and strengthen all who are fighting the good fight on behalf of righteousness, and have pity on all who seem to be content with evil. So do Thou now and ever hear and answer us, beyond all our thought, and abide with us even to the uttermost, for our Saviour's sake. *Amen.*

Frank Ballard, D.D., M.A.,
Sheffield, England.

JULY SEVENTEENTH

Evening, morning and noon will I pray. — Ps. 55: 17.

ABBA, FATHER, trusting in the merits and saving grace of Thy Son, our Saviour and Redeemer, Jesus Christ, we come before Thee to ask grace and loving mercy during the hours of this day. Should temptations assail us, we ask for strength to resist them successfully. Should evil attack us, may Thy grace strengthen us to fight a bold fight for the right.

May we hold ourselves as valiant soldiers of the Cross, thoroughly furnished to all good works. May our ears be open to the cry of the weak and suffering, and our hearts be ready to respond to every appeal from one of Thy suffering ones, and may we be enabled to minister to others in Thy Name, as Thy servants.

Let the close of this day find us in the path of duty, and grant that in rendering loving service to others we may realize a blessing as having rendered the service to Thee.

View with compassion our many weaknesses and faults, and touch us with a consecrating power that we may be able to stand in the evil day, and to render worthy and acceptable service as faithful servants of Jesus Christ, in Whose Name we ask all these blessings. *Amen.*

Clarkson Clothier,
Philadelphia, Pa.

JULY EIGHTEENTH

Let the word of Christ dwell in you richly in all wisdom, teaching and admonishing one another in psalms and hymns and spiritual songs, singing with grace in your hearts to the Lord. And whatsoever ye do in word or deed, do all in the Name of the Lord Jesus, giving thanks to God and the Father by Him. — Coloss. 3: 16-17.

OUR gracious Lord, we thank Thee for those who have helped us to know Thee. We bless Thee for the revelation of Thy love in eyes of affection and arms of tenderness to which our baby hearts willingly responded, and for the knowledge of Thy law in persuasive suggestion and stern command, to which we gave obedience.

We praise Thee for lips that taught ours to speak Thy name in reverence; for love that believed in us, and would not let us go; for arms that sheltered and sustained us in time of testing; for eyes of vision that enabled us to see things invisible, but eternal.

We magnify Thee for lives shining with the glory of rectitude and winsomeness; for shoulders divinely strengthened to bear another's burden; for hands beckoning to the blessedness of sacrificial service. Grant unto all these, whether on earth or in the Glory Land, to know the joy of our gratitude and love, and vouchsafe unto us that it may be ours to bless others as we have been so greatly blessed. *Amen.*

Rev. Frank Otis Erb, Ph.D.,
Portland, Maine.

But the fruit of the Spirit is love, joy, peace, long-Spirit. — Gal. 5: 22-25.

HEAVENLY Father, we thank Thee for having kept us through the death of sleep and brought us to the life of another day. Be with us during the hours of this day, and grant us grace to spend them profitably. Give us wisdom to know Thy will for us and patience and perseverance to fulfil it.

Grant us the grace of love, and help us with purity and discretion to show it forth to our kindred and friends and neighbors. Help us to be industrious, and so to do our duty as to merit Thy approval.

We ask Thy care of all the members of this home, and Thy blessing upon all for whom we ought to pray (especially.........). Guard, and grant our rulers and spiritual pastors wisdom from above. Keep us under Thy watchful providence, that the day may be spent in Thy presence, without sin, and in the service of Him through Whom all blessings come, our Blessed Lord and Saviour, Jesus Christ. *Amen.*

Bishop Theodore DuBose Bratton,
Jackson, Mississippi.

JULY TWENTIETH

Give ear to my words, O Lord, consider my meditation. Hearken unto the voice of my cry, my King, and my God: for unto Thee will I pray. My voice shalt Thou hear in the morning, O Lord; in the morning will I direct my prayer unto Thee, and will look up. — Ps. 5: 1-3.

GRACIOUS GOD, our Heavenly Father! To call Thee by this glorious title is at once to give Thee praise, and place ourselves in right relation to Thee. To know that Thou art God, and to know that the Great God is our loving Father, is to have all prayers heard before they are asked. "Before they call upon Me, I will answer them"; this is Thy promise to us. "I am more willing to hear, than they to call," is Thy lament and challenge. Thus entreated, we turn trustingly to Thee in every time of trouble. Guide us by Thine eye. Build us up into Thy likeness. Feed us on Thy love, and keep us pure in life and love. Be patient with us in our ignorance. Be our knowledge and wisdom, for there is none else to whom to go.

Forgive us all our faults and follies. Help us to forgive others as graciously as Thou dost us. We place ourselves in Thy care, in Jesus' Name. *Amen.*

August Pohlman, M.D., D.D.
Philadelphia, Penna.

Who shall ascend into the hill of the Lord? or who shall stand in His holy place? He that hath clean hands, and a pure heart; who hath not lifted up his soul unto vanity, nor sworn deceitfully. He shall receive the blessing from the Lord, and righteousness from, the God of his salvation. — Ps. 24; 3-5.

HEAVENLY Father, for all the blessings of the night past and for this new day that Thou hast given us, we desire now to thank Thee, and we pray that as Thou hast given us rest in sleep, so now may we serve Thee this day with all the strength of the life Thou hast given back to us again. Direct us, we pray Thee, in all the work of our hands this day, so that in all things we may please Thee. Help us to be kind, loving, forgiving, and ever watchful lest we offend against Thee in word, thought, or deed.

And while we pray for ourselves, we would not forget to pray for those near and dear to us — our fathers and mothers, brothers and sisters, kindred and friends. Bless each and all toward whom our hearts turn with a great love, and finally bring us, unbroken family circles, to our Father's house above, from which we shall go out no more, but shall ever be at home with Thee. *Amen.*

Llewellyn Brown, M.A.,
Brantford, Ont., Canada.

JULY TWENTY-SECOND

This is My blood of the new testament, which is shed for many. - Mark 14: 24.

(For Communion Sunday.)

WE sing our eucharistic hymn this day, God, with voices from which all tones of mortal sadness have vanished away. We sing the song of new-born life, and not of death. In the beginning was the Word and the Word was made flesh, and men beheld the glory of Thy love in the face of Jesus Christ.

Come, Creator Spirit blest, and impart anew Thy marvelous gifts. May Christ be born again in every heart. Purge our ears from the rattling noises of the world, until they are quick to hear the heavenly song of Thy peace and good-will for men. Lead all seekers to some spiritual Bethlehem and help them to find the Holy Child. May the nations come to His light, and rulers behold the brightness of His rising.

May the kingdoms of the world become the kingdoms of our Lord and of His Christ, that He may reign forever and ever. *Amen.*

Oscar Edward Maurer, D.D.,
New Haven, Connecticut.

JULY TWENTY-THIRD

O, how love I Thy law! it is my meditation all the day. Thou through Thy commandments hast made me wiser than mine enemies: for they are ever with me. I have refrained my feet from every evil way, that I might keep Thy word. I have not departed from Thy judgments: for Thou hast taught me. — Ps. 119: 97-98; 101-102.

OUR Father in Heaven, we thank Thee for the blessings of another day. Thy mercy is great toward us. May the sense of Thy presence be realized in each hour, and in the performance of every duty. We thank Thee for Thy word, a lamp to our feet, a guide to our path. Reveal Thy will to us through it, and enlighten us by Thy Holy Spirit, we pray Thee in Jesus' Name Almighty God! before Whom every knee must bow, we pray Thee on behalf of those who in Christian countries, are living without Thee, in rebellion against Thee, and bowing down their lives to worship according to the work of man, or any temptation of the evil one. Prosper, we pray Thee, the efforts of Thy servants who are "set apart" for the "ministry of the Word", and especially of those who are being used to let the light shine in the darkness of heathenism. Hear us as we pray on behalf of suffering humanity! Bless the innocent who suffer with the guilty, and grant us all Thy peace this day. In Jesus' Name. *Amen.*

Rev. H. W. Weight, B.A.,
Smith Falls, Ont., Canada.

JULY TWENTY-FOURTH

Seek the Lord and His strength. — Ps. 105: 4.

MOST gracious God, our Heavenly Father, source of every blessing, giver of every good and perfect gift, we adore Thee; we praise Thee; we magnify Thy Holy Name. Every day we receive new proofs of Thy care over us, new pledges of Thy love and favor. Thou hast made bountiful provision for all our physical needs; the seasons come and go, the sun shines, the rain falls, the harvests never fail: we have homes and friends; for all these things help us to be truly grateful. Help us to be no less thankful for that "bread which came down out of heaven" for the ever-flowing fountains of living water, for that home not made with hands, for that Friend that sticketh closer than a brother. We remember with affectionate sympathy all kinds and conditions of men — the poor, the destitute, and him that hath no helper.

Do Thou bless our home. May it ever be Thy dwelling place. Be Thou in our midst, O Lord. May Thy angels encamp round and about us, and keep us in all Thy ways. And when our race has been run, and our work done, receive us into the everlasting habitations. Our sins have been many; we confess them; we repent of there; do Thou forgive them all. In the Name of Him Who loved us and gave His life for us. *Amen.*

P. W. Snyder, D.D.,
Pittsburgh, Pa.

JULY TWENTY-FIFTH

Whatsoever we ask, we receive of Him. — I John 3: 22.

O GOD, our Heavenly Father, by Whose good hand upon us we are brought to see the light of a new day, and to enter upon its duties, we lift up our hearts to Thee, praising Thee for Thy continued goodness. We humble ourselves before Thee, Holy Majesty, confessing that we are unworthy to receive anything from Thee. We have sinned against Thee daily, in thought, word, and deed, yet Thou hast been long-suffering to us, and hast borne with our shortcomings. Grant unto us true repentance, and Thy Holy Spirit, that we may perfectly love Thee and worthily magnify Thy Holy Name, through Jesus Christ our Lord.

As we address ourselves to the responsibilities of another day, we beseech Thee for the wisdom that is profitable to direct. Hold up our goings that our footsteps slip not, and bestow upon us needful energy of body and mind for the efficient discharge of the duties of our calling. While diligent in business, may we be fervent in spirit, serving the Lord. Doing justly, loving mercy, may we walk humbly with Thee, our God.

These mercies we ask. with the forgiveness of our sins, for the sake of Jesus Christ, our only Lord and Saviour. *Amen.*

Robert Campbell, D.D.,
Montreal, Canada.

JULY TWENTY-SIXTH

Thou wast a God that forgavest them. — Ps. 99: 8.

FATHER, Thou forgivest us, so far as we are truly penitent. May we likewise forgive all who sin against us; all who sin against society; all who sin against Thee; even as Thou forgivest us and them. May we count no sin too heinous to pardon; no man too hardened to reclaim; no woman too fallen to uplift. When we forgive the penitent, help us to stand by him against a hard and unforgiving world. Thus may we make our forgiveness a reality in the world, and open the door of genuine social restoration to those who have gone astray.

Help us to find our chief delight in work, wherein we join our hands, our brains, our hearts, to Thy power, Thy laws, Thy love. May we choose that task which most taxes our highest powers, and best serves the world's deepest need. May we do it with such skill, such thoroughness, such joy, that it shall have about it the strength of the mountains, the freedom of the streams, the gladness of the sunshine, the fertility of the fields, the beauty of the stars and flowers. Thus may we become not mere creatures, but creators; not one of Thy works, but Thy coworkers. *Amen.*

William DeWitt Hyde, D.D., LL.D.,
Brunswick, Maine.

JULY TWENTY-SEVENTH

The Lord upholdeth all that fall, and raiseth up all those that be bowed down. The eyes of all wait upon Thee; and Thou givest them their meat in due season Thou openest Thine hand, and satisfiest the desire of every living thing. The Lord is nigh unto all them that call upon Him, to all that call upon Him in truth.
— Ps. 145: 14-16, 18.

O LORD, Heavenly Father, Who knowest our proneness to forget Thee in the busy rush of life, and while health and success attend us, but who art our ever prompt refuge and defence in times of illness, bitter grief and failure, we ask Thy forgiveness for our want of gratitude, and selfish lack of filial affection. We are of the earth, earthy, unworthy of our Heavenly parentage, and yet we are Thy children. We do not mean to be disobedient or unmindful of Thy mercies. It is only because Thy care and oversight has been constant from our earliest childhood that we sometimes presume on it, and fail to remember Thy tenderness. As we recall the past, make us braver for the future. May we trust even when we cannot trace the reason of Thy Providence. Give us godliness with contentment, and in all the chances and changes of mortal life make us patient and prayerful, and may the peace of God which passeth human understanding be ours in such measure as we can receive it. We ask it all for the sake of Jesus Christ, our Lord. *Amen.*

Bishop James Henry Darlington, D.D.,
Harrisburg, Penna.

JULY TWENTY-EIGHTH

I will praise Thee with my whole heart: before the gods will I sing praise unto Thee. I will worship toward Thy holy temple, and praise Thy Name for Thy loving kindness and for Thy truth: for Thou hast magnified Thy word above all Thy Name. — Ps. 138: 1-2.

DEAR Father, we thank Thee for a restful night, for sleep, and for Thy care. Now we look to Thee for a blessing as we begin a new day. May we pass through it without hurt, or sickness or death.

May we not fail in doing our work; in everything may we remember Thee, and honor Thee in our words as well as our acts. Give us love for Thee in our hearts, and perfect trust that Thou wilt direct us, and bring to pass what is for our good. Supply as with everything needful, and make us happy in Thy love. Bless Thy people everywhere, and help the missionaries and ministers in their work, that all who dwell upon this earth may soon learn of Jesus Christ and His love and desire to save them. Give help to those in want, and strength to the weak. Remember all who are dear to us, according to their needs. And forgive all our sins for the sake of Jesus Christ, our Saviour. *Amen.*

William C. Stoever,
Philadelphia, Pa.

JULY TWENTY-NINTH

Lay not up for yourselves treasures upon earth, where moth and rust doth corrupt, and where thieves break through and steal: But lay up for yourselves treasures in Heaven, where neither moth nor rust doth corrupt, and where thieves do not break through nor steal: For where your treasure is, there will your heart be also. — Matt. 6: 19-21.

OUR gracious Father, we would take account of this day in Thy presence. It is Thy gift to us — new, and speaking of Thine unfailing care; clean, and may we keep it so, and return it to Thee so filled that the day may be pleasing to Thee, an honor to our living Lord, and a help to those with whom we live and work. Grant us some new manifestation of Thyself today; some deeper experience of Thy grace; a clearer vision of our field of service, and more joy in its work. May we have a real inclination to our duty, and an honest preference for Thy will. So may our fellowship with Thee be unbroken today. We commit ourselves and friends, with our needs and anxieties, to Thy faithful keeping. Therefore may we be glad and free from care. May the day come soon when all the earth shall seek its 'refuge in Thee. Forgive our sins, and make us more like our Master— sensitive and strong, unselfish and true, for His Name's sake. *Amen.*

Rev. Emory W. Hunt,
Newton Centre, Mass.

JULY THIRTIETH

God hath dealt to every man the measure of faith. — Rom. 12: 3.

OUR Father, Ave thank Thee that Christ hath led us to Thee, and now in His name we pray for Thy perfect blessing.

Refresh us with Thy joyous strength. We humbly await Thy Spirit's work in us and through us. Cleanse our hearts and free our lives from every defiling and hindering thing. Fashion us into the Master's mind and habit. Lift our thoughts from self to the needs of ethers. Give us to see the fields of humanity white to harvest. Lay heavy burdens of toil upon us, and give us the joy of the reaper in the sure wages of the Kingdom.

May we give in running-over measures, so that those who receive shall become generous also. May we so rebuke ourselves without mercy — and others in love — that we and they shall be glad to correct our ways. Provide for our real needs out of Thy unwasted fulness. Keep us so near to Thee that we may know the joyful sound and walk in the light of Thy countenance. And whenever we are allowed to choose our topic, may we triumphantly present Jesus to those with whom we walk and talk. And now as we go forth or stay in, may we have the grace of God from the God of Peace, through Jesus Christ our Lord and Saviour. *Amen.*

Herbert Judson White, D.D.,
Hartford, Connecticut.

JULY THIRTY-FIRST

Jesus saith, have faith in God. — Mark 11: 22.

OUR Father Who art in Heaven, we come into Thy presence with full hearts to thank Thee for Thy many mercies: first of all, that Thou dost permit us to call Thee "Father," and that out of Thy tender compassion Thou art ever ready to receive us in love, and to help us to overcome the evil in our natures. We thank Thee for Thy wonderful provision — "Whosoever will may come and take of the water of life freely," and that the "whosoever" includes us, and that we know that when we approach Thee in a spirit of repentance, we are not turned away. Father, may we catch a clearer vision of what Thou art willing to do for us. Grant that we may ever be ready to respond to Thy call to bear Thy message to others, and may we be able to bring to someone a definite conception of Thee and Thy love. May each of us be a willing instrument in Thy hands for the advancement of Thy Kingdom, and we pray Thee to grant us an open mind toward the daily opportunities for helping our fellowmen. May the love of self be withdrawn from our hearts, to be replaced by a full portion of love to Thee. May the time soon come when all the world shall know Thee in the forgiveness of sin. *Amen.*

Edwin R. Graham,
Chicago, Illinois.

August

AUGUST FIRST

Save with Thy right hand and hear me. — Ps. 60: 5.

THE All-Wise and Ever-Living Father: We have been called to the consciousness of another day. The sunshine and the flowers and the singing of the birds summon us to worship at Thy footstool. Thou hast placed us in a beautiful world where we are refreshed by the songs of the winged messengers and the fragrance of the flowers. "The heavens declare the glory of God, and the firmament showeth forth Thy handiwork." We come, with all our shortcomings and unworthiness. We have sinned against much light, and deserve to be cast from Thy presence, but thank Thee for Thy love and long-suffering toward us. Help us to realize that religion is not a mere cloak that may be worn and laid aside at will. Grant that we may be spared the idle wasting of God's time, but that we may engage in worthy enterprise, with an eye single to Thy glory. Have mercy, Lord, upon those who are rejecting Thy Word, and may the Christ find a place in their hearts and lives, may they come to know Him as their personal Saviour. Let Thy truth, like a sharp two-edged sword, cut its way home to the inner nature, and arouse the slumbering conscience and stir the will to action. Grant Thy forgiveness for our transgressions. Blessed be the God and Father of our Lord Jesus Christ, Who hath blessed us with all spiritual blessings in heavenly places in Christ, Who rules and reigns forevermore. *Amen.*

Rev. John J. Ross,
Cincinnati. Ohio.

AUGUST SECOND

Pray to thy Father, which seeth in secret.— Matt. 6: 6.

OUR Heavenly Father, we bow ourselves before Thee and humbly pray Thee that Thou wilt help us to remember all this day our dependence upon Thee Give unto us a vision of the upward pathway. Make us conscious of Thy holy presence.

Guard us from all enticements to do wrong Enliven our consciences with Christian truth, that we be not deceived by error. Fill us with love and give unto us a disposition like that of our Master. Help us in all our toil to serve Thee.

Bear Thou our burdens with us. By Thy grace teach us to seek first Thy kingdom and righteous ness. Work Thou in us the courage of faith, and the peace of trust. Through Thy Holy Spirit pervade our home with gracious kindness.

Abundantly bless our friends, our minister, and our Church And "whether we eat or drink or whatsoever we do, may we do it all to the glory of Thy

This we ask with the forgiveness of our sins of which we repent, through our Lord and Saviour, Jesus Christ. *Amen.*

Ralph W. Brokaw, D.D.,
Utica, N. Y.

AUGUST THIRD

It is better to trust in the Lord than to put confidence in man. — Ps. 118: 8.

GREAT God of Hosts, Who reigns above and in our hearts, for all the gracious favors of today which bless and strengthen us, we give Thee thanks. Let not our gratitude be limited to words, but be expressed in every impulse, thought and deed, and serve to draw us nearer to Thee; for we desire to praise Thee with our lives and not alone with suppliant words.

Our weakness and faults, which ofttimes grow to errors and misdeeds, forgive — nay, cover them with Thine eternal love. Restore our wills, too prone to bend to sinful things which we give place to in our lives. Cleanse all our thoughts and plant the seeds of righteousness within our minds. Uproot from in our hearts the tendency toward wrong or selfish interest or pride, and put instead the love of truth and a yearning for a Christlike life with knowledge to attain it.

Should trials come, Jesus, be Thou near; encourage with Thy presence, strengthen with Thy power. If temptations come, fill our hearts with holy and heroic resolution that we will yield ourselves to Thee and not to them; and may tomorrow find us still drawing nearer, Lord, to Thee. This we ask for Jesus' sake. *Amen.*

Rev. S. Clark Riker,
Cincinnati, Ohio.

AUGUST FOURTH

Whatsoever ye shall ask in My name, that will I do. — John 14: 13.

THOU, God, art our Father. We are the children of eternal love. Help us, we pray Thee, to live our lives in Thy sight. Let nothing unworthy claim our hearts, and may we find in Thy will our peace.

We pray that Thy likeness may be formed in us, and that our lives may abound in the love and peace and joy of Thy Holy Spirit. Help us to love Thee with a pure heart fervently, and to love those who love Thee and are loved by Thee.

Bless, we pray Thee, all for whom we should pray. We name their names in the silence of our hearts. Pity the ungrateful, the wayward, the wanderer. Comfort the lonely and the desolate. Let Thy peace rule in our hearts and in our home. Whom have we in heaven but Thee, and there is none upon the earth that we desire but Thee.

When we stumble, may Thy strength support us, Thy wisdom lead us, Thy love redeem us. Open our hearts to receive Thee, the Divine Gue3t, into the home of our souls, and may we hold fellowship with Thee as we walk the path of life. We ask all in Jesus' name. *Amen.*

Hugh Thomson Kerr, D.D.,
Pittsburgh, Penna.

AUGUST FIFTH

I will not leave you comfortless. — John 14: 18.

O GOD, our Heavenly Father, we thank Thee for Thy love and wisdom and power and grace and mercy. Thou hast put an infinite longing for Thee in our hearts. In Thy absence we feel our orphanage. We have aspirations which Thou alone can satisfy. We have sins which Thou alone can cleanse. We have infirmities which burden and shame us without Thy help and strength and forgiveness. We thank Thee for Thy forgiving love, Thy protecting care, Thy comforting presence. We beseech Thee to direct us in all the ways of life; give us guidance in our perplexities, strength in weakness, comfort in sorrows, inspiration in despondencies, and courage in our battles of life. Give us patience in hard labor. May we not become weary in w r ell-doing. May we be real representatives of the Christ we confess and profess. Thou knowest our sorrows and bereavements and trials. Sanctify them to our highest spiritual good. Put into our souls the psalm of love. May it dominate our lives, and express itself in every Christlike attitude and spirit in all the relations of life. Let the Holy Spirit dwell within us. In the midst of the sorrows that tend to embitter and the burdens that oppress, get under us with the mighty arms of Thy love, and lift us up into conscious communion with Thee. Help us, lather, to be willing to enter doors of usefulness that open daily. May we be faithful to Thee and our fellows. Through Jesus Christ, our Lord and Saviour. *Amen.*

G. M. Matthews, D.D.,
Dayton, Ohio.

AUGUST SIXTH

And very early in the morning the first day of the -week, they came unto the sepulchre at the rising of the sun. And they said among themselves, Who shall roll us away the stone from the door of the sepulchre? * * * He is risen. — Mark 16: 2-3.

(For Sunday Morning.)

FOR the light of this Holy Sabbath Day, with its recurring privileges and blessings, our God, we thank Thee. For the gracious memories that it stirs within our hearts that on the first day of the week Christ Jesus arose from the dead, we give Thee praise. For the gracious hope that it revives within our spirit that there remaineth a rest, keeping of the Sabbath, for people of God, we would call upon our souls and all that is within us to praise and bless and magnify Thy Holy Name. We pray Thee that Thou wilt make straight paths for our feet this day, and help us to walk therein. Do Thou bless us in the worship of Thy house and in the quiet meditation of our homes. Make this a day of rest and gladness to our hearts. Grant that it may be a great day in Thy Zion, a day marked by the ingathering of many precious souls out of darkness into the marvelous light and liberty of the Gospel of Christ. And now unto Him Who is able to keep us from falling and to present us faultless before the presence of His glory, with exceeding joy, to the only wise God, our Saviour, be glory and majesty, dominion and power, both now and ever. *Amen.*

Henry H. Sweets, D.D.,
Louisville, Kentucky.

AUGUST SEVENTH

Like as a father pitieth His children, so the Lord pitieth them that fear Him. For He knoweth our frame: He remembereth that we are dust. * * * But the mercy of the Lord is from everlasting to everlasting upon them that fear him.— Ps. 103: 13, 14, 17.

DEAR Father, Thou hast given us the great gift of a new day. May it be unto us a Father's house of love where we shall serve, not as slaves, but as freemen; not as strangers, but as friends; not as aliens, but as sons and heirs.

As children come to their mothers when wearied, or conscience-smitten, or grieved by their fellows, so may we come to Thee in any hour of need. As the confidence and love of our parents gives us strength for duty, much more may the knowledge of Thy confidence and Thy love for us enable us to bear each burden and trample each temptation under foot.

And may we have such intimate companionship this day with Thy Son, our Saviour, that truth and cleanness and gentleness and hope shall abide in us until the twilight falls, and we lie down to sleep again beneath the shadow of Thy wings. *Amen.*

Daniel Russell, D.D.,
New York City, N. Y.

AUGUST EIGHTH

He is their help and their shield. — Ps. 115: 9.

O LORD, our Father in Heaven, we thank Thee for our home, its mercies, its joys, its shelter, and its peace. Help us to be Thy children in our home, and make it like the home in Bethany, where Christ loved to go. Help us this day to bear one another's burdens. May we be burden-bearers, and not burden makers. Help us to practice the Golden Rule, to do unto others as we would have them do unto us. Give us Thy grace that we may control our tempers and our tongues. May Thy blessing, Lord and Master, be with those who stay at home to work today, and may they glorify their tasks by cheerful spirits. Bless those of our home who go out for business, and help and prosper them. Keep them from temptation, and may they always remember that a good name is better than great riches. Let integrity and uprightness preserve them. Bless the children at school; give them diligence, application and ambition in their studies; keep them from evil communications and comradeships. Bless the children who are at home. May their play be innocent and bright. May the love of Christ which moved Him to die for our sin3 crucify in every one of us worldliness of life, and may we all be faithful, spiritual members of the Church. May this home honor God in public worship, and claim the promise, "Them that honor Me, I will honor." Forgive us for our sins, and give us the forgiving spirit, for Jesus' sake. *Amen.*

John Van Lear, D.D.,
Little Rock, Arkansas.

AUGUST NINTH

I have laid help upon One that is mighty. — Ps. 89: 19.

O GOD, our Father, we believe in Thee; we believe that Thou art, and that Thou art a rewarder of all them that diligently seek Thee. Therefore we venture confidently to come before Thee in prayer, through Jesus Christ our Redeemer. We but dimly comprehend and but partly understand Thy greatness, Thy perfection of being and character, and are keenly conscious of our limitations, imperfections and sins. But we feel the need of Thee; Thou art a necessity to us. Without Thee we cannot live, and without Thee we dare not die. Therefore we turn to Thee as the flowers in springtime turn toward the sun, as the rivers carve their courses through the hills to find their home in the sea, for "Thou hast made us for Thyself, God, and our spirits cannot rest until they rest in Thee." We pray Thee, pour the treasures of Thy love and life into our poor souls. We search for Thee in a dry and thirsty land where no water is. We are glad with unending joy if we may but be near Thee. Steady Thou our staggering faith, clarify our vision, intensify our desire to be free from all that is sin in Thy sight. Bring us into harmony with Thyself, Thy purpose, Thy life. Create in us a clean heart, God, and renew a right spirit within us. Save us from narrowness and selfishness. Bless us and make us a blessing. May we not be reservoirs, but channels through which Thy grace may flow into other lives that pant for Thee. All this we humbly ask in the name of Jesus. *Amen.*

Bishop Samuel P. Spreng,
Naperville, Illinois.

O taste and see that the Lord is good. — Ps. 34: 8.

O LORD, our Father, help us to begin this day with worthy thoughts of Thee. Thy mercies are new unto us every morning, and call for new expressions of gratitude. We slept, and awoke, and lo! Thou art still with us. Let the same power and goodness which have been over us during the night attend us during this day. We are weak and ignorant, and given to thoughtlessness and vanity. Be Thou our light and our guide, our shield and our protector.

Bless our home and family, and make love and peace and kindness dwell in our midst. Visit us, we pray Thee, with Thy salvation, and grant us whatever is necessary for body and soul.

Defend us from all harm and evil this day. Help us to overcome the power of sin in our own lives, and to subdue the unlawful desires of body and mind.

Remember with Thy grace and favor the sick and the hungry, the helpless and the homeless. Have mercy upon the prisoner and the criminal, the heathen and the unbeliever.

Encourage and support by Thy wisdom and power Thy holy Church, that she may bring in speedily the full victory of Thy Kingdom, through Jesus Christ our Lord. *Amen.*

C. E. Creitz, D.D.,
Reading, Penna.

AUGUST ELEVENTH

Forgive, and ye shall be forgiven. — Luke 6: 37.

WITH grateful hearts, our Father, we humbly bow around this family altar. We are Thy children. We confess our sins and acknowledge Thy loving kindness and tender mercies. Forgive us our sins and create in us forgiving hearts. Make us as willing to forgive as we are to be forgiven. Enlarge upon us Thy loving kindness and encircle us with Thy unwearied compassion.

Broaden our sympathies, and save us from selfishness. Open our ears to the cry of our next door neighbor and to the call of the man of Macedonia. Multiply our opportunities for doing good and consecrate our energies to Thy service. Warm our hearts to respond to the needs of our fellow-man, and make us messengers of strength and comfort to the discouraged and broken-hearted. Fill us with Thy Spirit, energize us with Thy love, and use us to Thy glory. Continue to beautify our lives with Thy blessings, strengthen us in the hour of our temptation, and sustain us when we pass through the valley of deep darkness. And now, Father, we thank Thee for everything that makes us better children of Thine; for everything that makes us more beloved of Thee, and more useful in the world; for our home, our family and the Church. But above all, we thank Thee for Thy Son, our Saviour, in Whose name we pray. *Amen.*

Rev. Ira M. Boswell,
Georgetown, Kentucky.

AUGUST TWELFTH

I will instruct thee and teach thee in the -way which thou shalt go.— Ps. 32: 8.

WE praise Thy name, our Father, that Thou hast again brought us to the sweet consciousness of life and to a realization of Thy divine grace and loving favor. We are grateful to Thee for all the mercies so abundantly bestowed upon us through Thy Son. Grant unto us this day Thy watch-care and guidance, that we may in nothing offend Thee or bring reproach upon Thy name.

May we, by the inspiration of Thy Holy Spirit, be led into that truth which will enable us to glorify Thee in our lives. Keep our minds from error and our hearts from sin. May all our thoughts be true, our loves be pure, and our actions right before Thee. Give unto us and ours the things necessary for our temporal comfort and our spiritual good. Bless Thou the toil of our hands and make it abound to the welfare of our fellow-men and to Thine own glory. Help us to be ever conscious of the presence and fellowship of Thy dear Son, our Saviour and our Friend.

Comfort, we pray Thee, those who are in sorrow. Strengthen those who are weak. Be Thou beside the beds of suffering, to ease pain, strengthen courage and inspire hope. We ask all in the name of Him Who dwelleth in our hearts through faith. *Amen.*

Rev. Daniel McGurk,
Cincinnati, Ohio.

AUGUST THIRTEENTH

And they continued steadfastly * * * in prayer. — Acts 2: 42.

GRACIOUS Lord, we bring Thee anew this day the praise of our lips and the worship of our hearts. We bless Thee for the care of our bodies, for the guarding of our minds, and for the delight of our awakened spirits in Thyself. We confess we have not merited even the least of Thy mercies, and yet our lives are crowned each day with unnumbered tokens of Thine infinite love. Wilt Thou beget within us a new humility, a deepened sense of our dependence, and a fuller surrender to Thy will.

Give us the peace which springs from a constant sense of Christ's infinite sacrifice; give us the sanctity of a life which is the fruit of His indwelling; give us the power through Thy Holy Spirit to serve and honor Thee.

Help us to walk in a spirit of constant prayer, to increasingly delight in Thy Holy Word, to love one another, and to have some part in bringing the light of the Gospel to those in darkness. In the midst of the confusion and stress of earth, may our souls rest in Thine own perfect calm, and may we be able to comfort those in trouble with the comfort wherewith we are comforted of God. We ask all in Jesus' name. *Amen.*

Hugh R. Munro,
New York City, N. Y.

AUGUST FOURTEENTH

Here are they that keep the commandments of God, and the faith of Jesus.
— Rev. 14: 12.

O GOD, our Heavenly Father, Thou hast been good and gracious to us. In the morning Thou gavest us a day, each minute to be used in service to Thee and to humanity. Help us to use each of these minutes, O Lord, to Thy name's honor and glory and to the advancement of Thy cause and kingdom. At the close of the day may we return all of the hours just as sacred and holy as they were when given to us at early dawn.

We thank Thee for Thy love and protection. Thy gracious love is so boundless and unlimited that it has overshadowed us and sheltered us from all harm and danger. Thy heart of love includes us in its beatings, and so we are grateful to Thee.

Thou art our Friend, Jehovah of hosts. Thou hast been with us through thick and thin. When other supposed friends were deserting us, Thou didst abide with us as a Friend that sticketh closer than a brother. We seem to hear Thee speaking to us now. Yes, Thou art so very near and Thou wilt surely keep and protect us through the night. Accept these our petitions this hour, we pray, in Jesus' name. *Amen.*

Rev. G. Frank Burns,
Cincinnati, Ohio.

AUGUST FIFTEENTH

Look not every man on his own things, but every man also on the things of others. Let this mind be in you, which was also in Christ Jesus: Who being in the form of God, thought it not robbery to be equal with God. — Phil. 2: 4-6.

O GOD, we come to Thee because Thou art in Thyself all that we desire to become in ourselves. We are weak, but Thou art strong; we come seeking Thy strength. We are sinful but Thou art holy, and we come seeking Thy holiness. We are ignorant but Thou art wise, and we come seeking Thy wisdom.

Bless us, that we may be in our characters what Thou art in Thine, pure and holy. Aid us, that we may be in our hearts what Thou art in Thine, good and righteous. Help us, that we may in our lives be what Thou art in Thine, kind and generous. All that Thou art, we pray that thus we may become, so that we can think Thy thoughts after Thee, walk in the steps of the One Who went about doing good, and so live that our wills may be brought into harmony with Thy divine purpose, and our lives conformed to Thy eternal righteousness.

W. W. Bustard, D.D.,
Cleveland, Ohio.

AUGUST SIXTEENTH

This is the victory that overcometh the world, even our faith. — I John 5: 4.

ALMIGHTY and most merciful Jehovah, the Father of our Lord Jesus Christ, Who art worthy of the praises of all the children of men, be pleased to hear our prayers this day. Holy art Thou, and may all Thy creatures worship and adore Thee. May we who dwell in this house truly fear and love and trust in Thee above all things. We bless Thee for all Thy goodness and tender mercies, especially for the gift of Thy dear Son and for the Bible, the revelation of Thy will and grace.

Our lives, though unworthy, have been precious in Thy sight. Thou hast provided for our bodies every needed blessing. Thou dost feed our souls upon the Bread of Life so long as we humbly seek salvation through Jesus the Messiah. Continue Thy blessings to us.

Overshadow us with Thy mercy. Empty us of all pride. Forgive our sins. Implant Thy Word in us that we may bring forth fruit by patient continuance in well doing.

Graciously deliver us from sickness, fire, want and trouble. Help us to lay to heart Thy Fatherly chastenings that we may judge ourselves and amend our ways. These and all needed benefits we ask only through the merits of Jesus Christ our Lord. *Amen.*

Rev. H. F. Obenauf,
Pitcairn, Penna.

AUGUST SEVENTEENTH

For the Lord God is a sun and shield; the Lord will give grace and glory; no good thing will He withhold from them that walk uprightly. — Ps. 84: 11.

LORD, we thank Thee for the blessings of the day that is gone. We were guarded and guided at every step, and not a single good thing was withheld from us. We pray Thy forgiving mercy as we begin the duties and face the dangers of this new day. Cleanse us in Thy blood; comfort us with Thy presence; strengthen us with Thy power, and help us like little children to put our hand in Thine and be led by Thee all the day through.

Deepen the gratitude of our hearts, and help us to lean upon Thy bosom as John leaned upon the bosom of his Lord.

May we be busy today that we may be blessed of Thee, and become a blessing to others. We pray for all the world, every man and woman, but especially for those near and dear to us by the ties of nature. Bless our family, and make it so happy and pure that the angels, our guardian spirits, may find within its walls an atmosphere akin to that of heaven. *Amen.*

Rev. M. M. Davis.
Dallas, Texas.

AUGUST EIGHTEENTH

How shall He not with Him * * * freely give us all things. — Rom. 8: 32.

O GOD, our Father, we thank Thee that we may come to Thee. Though Thou art holy, and we know how unfit we are to present ourselves before Thee, yet, our Saviour, Thy sufferings and death for us give us the precious knowledge that Thou dost love and will forgive us. We thank Thee that we may come so freely and tell Thee all that is in our hearts. We are deeply conscious of our weakness; we pray for strength and power. Many times we fail to do what we should; help us to make our lives useful and helpful to others.

Thou knowest, too, how many things fall to our hands to do; in the midst of it all, give us sweet hours of quiet and repose, keep us from becoming anxious or complaining. We ask for a trust in Thee that will still the soul and help us to see that Thou art in all our lives. Lord, Thou hast been so much to us, we want all the world to know Thee; help us ever to use Thy blessings that of those near and far away, some may be led to know and to love Thee. Help us to so live that our lives shall be a testimony of our love for Thee and thankfulness to Thee, for Jesus' sake. *Amen.*

Rev. Jacob W. Kapp,
Cincinnati. Ohio.

AUGUST NINETEENTH

Looking unto Jesus, the author and finisher of our faith. — Heb. 12:2.

FATHER, whenever we kneel in the quiet of the hour of prayer, the wonder of Thy love enthralls us. We are thrilled by the memory of Calvary; we marvel at the mercy which forgives sin; we are filled with awe at the thought of the goodness which has followed us all the days of our life.

But we find it hard to keep our hearts aglow when we arise from our knees and go forth to face the stress and the strife, the disappointments and the heartbreak of our common life. Then we are prone to forget Thy love. Oh,

131

help us each day, the bitterest as well as the brightest, to have so vibrant a sense of Thee that we shall act as those who are holden by the spell of an ineffable love. Give us each hour such an abiding memory of Thy mercy that we shall find it hard to be unmerciful to others. Keep us ever so alive to Thy goodness that evil shall be hateful to us. And may the vision of Calvary so impress itself upon us, that we may not hesitate to do the sacrificial deed that the need of some brother may demand. And do Thou walk with us in life; and in death take us, dear Lord, to dwell with Thee. *Amen.*

Rev. Albert E. Day, A.M.,
Cincinnati, Ohio.

AUGUST TWENTIETH

Pray unto Me, and I will hearken. — Jer. 29: 12.

OUR Father, we thank Thee for Thy presence, for home and health and strength, for the many friend3 we have. Help us to be friendly and worthy of friendship with all who are noble and pure.

Forgive us for the sins of the day. For the evil, known and unknown, for the thoughts and purposes of mind and heart which have not been right in Thy sight, we crave Thy pardon. It is written in Thy Word that if we confess our sin Thou wilt be faithful and just to forgive us our sin, and to cleanse us from all unrighteousness.

We ask a blessing upon all whom we love and upon those for whom we ought to pray. We think of our Church and Sunday School, and of all agencies everywhere which are seeking to establish Thy Kingdom. Give Thy favor to all.

Bless our family and make us a blessing to others. Help us to love and serve each other. Help us to be true in the home, in the school, in our work and play; and make us to be what, at our best, we appear.

We ask in the name of Jesus. *Amen.*

Guy Lamson, D.D.,
Philadelphia, Penna.

AUGUST TWENTY-FIRST

Thy word is a lamp unto my feet, and a light unto my path. I have sworn, and I will perform it, that I will keep thy righteous judgments. Accept, I beseech Thee, the freewill offerings of my mouth, O Lord, and teach me Thy judgments. Thy testimonies have I taken as an heritage for ever: for they are the rejoicing of my heart. — Ps. 119: 105, 106, 108, 111.

OUR dear Heavenly Father, we thank Thee that during the night we could rest and sleep under the shadow of Thy protecting wing. We are grateful for the opportunities for service which come with the new day. We pray for strength to overcome evil and perform our tasks. May we show the spirit of the Master in all we think, say and do.

Bless our absent friends and loved ones, and keep them in Thy holy will. Remember in mercy the tempted and tried and afflicted ones, and sustain them by Thy grace. Bless those in authority in our State and nation with wisdom to know and strength to do Thy will.

Sustain those who labor for the establishment of Thy Kingdom at home and abroad, and hasten the time when all men may know and obey Thee. For Jesus' sake. *Amen.*

Rev. Howard A. Kramer,
Cleveland, Ohio.

AUGUST TWENTY-SECOND

I called upon the Lord in distress: the Lord answered me. — Ps. 118: 5.

OUR Father, Who art in Heaven, we thank Thee that Thou art our Father, that we are not orphans, but sons and daughters of the Lord God Almighty! Hallowed be Thy Name. May it be the work of our lives to renden holiness to the Name of the Lord in all the earth. Thy Kingdom come in the plenitude of its power and the fullness of its blessing, and be spread abroad upon the face of the earth until the kingdoms of the world shall become the kingdoms of our Lord and His Christ.

Thy will be done on earth as it is in Heaven. We know that it is done gladly, joyfully and cheerfully by Thy creatures in Heaven, and may it be so done by Thy children on earth. Give us from day to day our daily bread, and teach us that, having food and raiment, therewith to be content, for godliness with contentment is great gain.

Lead us not into temptation, but deliver us from the Evil One with all his power and perils, and Thine shall be the Kingdom, and the power, and the glory forever, through Jesus Christ, our Saviour. *Amen.*

Rev. Z. T. Sweeney,
Columbus. Indiana.

AUGUST TWENTY-THIRD

Trust in the Lord with all thine heart; and lean not unto thine own understanding. In all thy ways acknowledge Him, and He shall direct thy paths. - Prov. 3: 3-4.

OUR Father, Thou hast given us the morning light so sweet to our eyes; give us also, we pray Thee, the morning blessing which shall fill the whole day with its sweetness and beauty.

May all the duties of the day, however distasteful in themselves, become a delight as we hear Thy voice calling us to go forward fearlessly into the heart of them, in the assurance that we shall find Thee waiting for us there, ready to give us the strength we need.

May all our relationships within and without this home be consecrated by the touch of Thy hand, by which all that is base, belittling and untrue shall be removed and destroyed.

When the night comes, may we be able to look back upon a day in which the burdens of others have been lightened, and in which hearts that have lost hope have been filled with new faith in God and His controlling love. In Christ's name we ask it. *Amen.*

Charles Wood, D.D.,
Washington, D. C.

AUGUST TWENTY-FOURTH

Let not sin therefore reign in your mortal body. — Rom. 6: 12.

OUR Heavenly Father, we thank Thee for Thy mercies to us in the past, and for Thy watch-care over us during the night. As we stand upon the threshold of a new day, we look to Thee for help and guidance. "We need Thy presence every passing hour."

Make us strong to resist temptation, and give us courage in all things to do Thy Holy Will. Open our eyes that we may see every opportunity for serving Thee and serving our fellow-men. Help us so to live as to commend the religion and service of Christ to all about us. Enable us to live "lives that are hid with Christ in God." May we daily grow in grace and in the knowledge of our Lord and Saviour, Jesus Christ.

Remember with us all for whom we should pray — the sick, the sorrowing, the distressed and the needy. Bless all efforts put forth for the extension of Thy Kingdom, and hasten the day when all men shall love and serve Thee.

Graciously forgive all that Thou hast seen amiss in our lives. Supply all our need according to Thy riches in glory.

Bless us and make us a blessing to others, we ask in Christ's name. Amen:

John William Lyell, D.D.,
Camden, N. J.

AUGUST TWENTY-FIFTH

God be merciful unto us, and bless us; and cause His face to shine upon us; That Thy way may be known upon earth, Thy saving health among all nations. Let the people praise Thee, O God; let all the people praise thee. O let the nations be glad and sing for joy: for Thou shalt judge the people righteously, and govern the nations upon earth. — Ps. 67: 1-4.

OUR God and Father, we render Thee our thanks and praise for all the good of this day. New were Thy mercies in the morning, and sweet is Thy love in the evening hour. We bless Thee that Thou hast given us this day our daily bread; that Thou hast not forgotten us even in those self-centered moments when we forgot Thee.

And now we pray Thee to watch over and preserve us, body and soul, during the hours of the day and night. May our rest and sleep be sweet to us. May we be brought to this new day refreshed and encouraged for all its duties and privileges, its sorrows and joys.

When we come at last to life's evening hour, and the night of death begins to fall about us, may we by faith look beyond its darkness to the breaking of the eternal day. We ask all in the name and through the merits of our Lord and Saviour, Jesus Christ. *Amen.*

Robert Hugh Morris, D.D.,
Philadelphia, Penna.

AUGUST TWENTY-SIXTH

Martha was cumbered about much serving, and came to Him, and said, Lord, dost Thou not care that my sister hath left me to serve alone? bid her therefore that she help me. And Jesus answered and said unto her, Martha, Martha, thou art careful and troubled about many things: But one thing is needful: and Mary hath chosen that good part, which shall not be taken away from her.
— Luke 10: 40-42.

O MERCIFUL Saviour, Who didst bless the little home at Nazareth with Thy meek and lowly life, inspire in us this day such a willing purpose to be about our Heavenly Father's business, that we may find no task too small for our patient regard, nor any burden too great for our earnest endeavor. Hear us and help us, we beseech Thee, that so each day, in home or temple, or in our daily work, our lives may be consecrated to the loving service of God and man, and that we, like Thee, may go about doing good, through Thy sufficient grace, Whose strength is made perfect in our weakness, and Who canst make us good and faithful servants, through Thine almighty power, to bless and to help, to seek and to save. We ask it in Thy name, Who art our Redeemer, our Example and our Friend. *Amen.*

Bishop James H. Van Buben, D.D.
Indianapolis, Indiana.

AUGUST TWENTY-SEVENTH

Blessed are the poor in spirit: for theirs is the kingdom of heaven. Blessed are they that mourn: for they shall be comforted. Blessed are the meek: for they shall inherit the earth. Blessed are they which do hunger and thirst after righteousness: for they shall be filled-. Blessed are the merciful: for they shall obtain mercy. Blessed are the pure in heart: for they shall see God. Blessed are the peacemakers: for they shall be called the children of God. Blessed are they which are persecuted for righteousness' sake: for theirs is the kingdom of heaven. Blessed

135

are ye, when men shall revile you, and persecute you, and shall say all manner of evil against you falsely, for my sake. — Matt. 6: 3-11.

OUR Father, we adore Thee as the center of all pure spirits, and we pray Thee to make us like unto Thyself. May our minds think pure thoughts. May our hearts love pure things. May our very lives be pure because Thou art pure.

Cleanse us and sanctify us, and constantly save us, our Father, lest we should break down under the wear and tear of the world and fall beneath temptations that without Thy purity and strength we could never resist. In Jesus' name. *Amen.*

E. E. Violett, D.D.,
Kansas City, Missouri.

AUGUST TWENTY-EIGHTH

The Lord is the strength of my life. — Ps. 27: 1.

OUR Heavenly Father, Thou hast promised us that as our day our strength shall be. We thank Thee for Thy sustaining grace through the day that has been, and Ave seek Thy favor and Thy help for the day that is to be. Help us to be kind to one another, and to all with whom we have to do. Suffer us not to be tempted above that we are able. May we be helpful to our fellow-travelers on life's way. May our lives be guided by the spirit of Him Who said, '"The Son of Man came not to be ministered unto but to minister, and to give His life a ransom for many." May we not be stumbling blocks to any, but may we walk worthy of the vocation wherewith we have been called. May we put conscience and heart into the performing of our several tasks. We claim the promise that Thou wilt give Thine angels charge over us to keep us in all our ways. If it be Thy will, keep us through the day and night from danger and death. May we be pure in heart that we may see God. May our speech be such as becometh those who have named the name of Christ. May we dwell in the secret place of the Most High, that we may abide under the shadow of the Almighty, and bring us all at last in peace to the Father's House in Heaven. *Amen.*

Frederick N. McMillin, D.D.
Cincinnati, Ohio.

AUGUST TWENTY-NINTH

Who shall separate us from the love of Christ. — Rom. 8: 35.

O GOD, kneeling at this family altar we hail Thee trustfully as our Father. As a family we worship Thee, and pray Thee to look upon us in love, and as we approach Thee for guidance and strength for the day with its unknown problems, grant that we may have no fear of Thee, or of the night, or of the morrow. Let perfect love cast out fear.

We acknowledge Thee to be our Lord. Help us to obey Thy law, and to do Thy will. Forbid that we should stumble through ignorance, or err through forgetfulness, or falter through fearfulness. Let us not lose our way, or our joy, or our souls.

We humbly confess our sins, and wait Thy word of forgiveness. Have mercy upon us, O God, have mercy! Make us pure, and kind, and unselfish. Grant us the blessedness promised to those who hunger and thirst after righteousness. From selfishness and indolence, from pride and hardness, from envy and vengefulness, do Thou in mercy deliver us, Lord!

Make Thou this day a good day for our family. Be Thou our shield, our refuge and our strong fortress. And help us to be eager to work — glad to be alive, glad to be the children of Thy care and love. For Jesus Christ's sake. *Amen.*

O. C. S. Wallace, D.D., LL.D.,
Montreal, Quebec, Canada.

AUGUST THIRTIETH

I love them that love me. — Prov. 8: 17.

'Father, we thank Thee for the night,
And for the pleasant morning light;
For rest and food and loving care,
And all that makes the day so fair."

W E are glad for the privilege of calling upon Thee. We love Thee because of what Thou art and because of what Thou hast done. Thou art the Creator and Preserver of our lives. In Thee we live, and move, and have our being. We thank Thee for Thy Son, in Whom we have redemption, the forgiveness of sins, and the hope of eternal life. We thank Thee for our country, and for our homes and schools and churches. Help us to love the right and despise the wrong. Prepare us for the duties of the day. We know not what is before us, but it is written, "Sufficient unto the day is the evil thereof." Give us grace whereby we may overcome evil with good.

Bless all our friends and neighbors. Bless Thy followers everywhere. Let Thy Kingdom come, and Thy will be done on earth as it is in Heaven. In Jesus' name. *Amen.*

Rev. J. W. Stiverson,
Cedar Rapids, Iowa.

AUGUST THIRTY-FIRST

Let us offer the sacrifice of praise to God. — Heb. 13: 15.

AS THE morning breaks gently upon us, O Lord, awaking us to consciousness and opening our eyes to the light and labor of each new day, before the blood-sprinkled mercy seat we bow. Here we would leave our sins, and loose and lose our weights, and find and cherish the full assurance of Thy favor. May Thy face be unobscured to us today. Give us grace to set our affections where Christ sitteth, that so we may be saved from all sordidness of thought, or word, or deed, and that our lives may draw their inspirations from high and holy springs. Help us to cherish a tender regard for all the children of God of every name.

Our eyes are unto Thee, God. Our hearts would find repose in the assurance of our acceptance in the Beloved. We would yield our members as instruments of righteousness unto Thee, that, by the gracious power of Thy Spirit, we may ourselves this day grow in grace and knowledge, and, by our ministry to others in Christ's name, bring some into an experience of His abounding grace.

Hear us, Lord, because we pray in that sweet Name in which all Thy exceeding great and precious promises are sure. *Amen.*

Rev. Thomas T. Shields,
Toronto, Ont., Canada.

September

SEPTEMBER FIRST

O Thou, my God, save Thy servant that trusteth in Thee. — Ps. 86: 2.

IN THY mercy and love, God, we are permitted to greet another day. Thy guardian angels have watched over us when we have not been able to care for ourselves. Sweet sleep has refreshed us, and now we look into another day confident that Thou wilt guide and strengthen.

Help us this day to walk uprightly, that no good thing may be withheld. Forbid that any of us should be careless or indifferent to the opportunities of service that may be ours. May Thy Word which we have just read be a source of strength and uplift, and may we treasure it more as the days and the years slip by.

God bless the sick and the tempted. Strengthen the weak ones and comfort all who sorrow. Bless our ministers and missionaries and deaconesses, and all who devote their lives specially to the work of Thy Kingdom.

And now, our Father, as we separate for the day's duties, may Thy loving presence be with us, in our home, and at school, and at business. And at the close of the day may we realize that "the trivial round and the common task" have indeed brought us nearer Thee.

We ask all through Jesus Christ our Lord. *Amen.*

Rev. S. E. Marshall, B.A., B.D.,
St. Catharines, Ont., Canada.

SEPTEMBER SECOND

Behold what manner of love the Father hath bestowed upon us, that we should be called the sons of God: therefore the world knoweth us not, because it knew Him not. Beloved, now are we the sons of God, and it doth not yet appear what we shall be: but we know that, when He shall appear, we shall be like Him; for we shall see Him as He is. And every man that hath this hope in him purifieth himself, even as He is pure. — I John 3: 1-3.

OUR Father, in thankfulness we come to Thee, remembering the night of rest, and the new light of another day. Every day is the record of Thy tenuer mercy, Thy providing care, Thy patient love. No need have we to put Thy love to the test, for Thou hast overwhelmed us with blessings beyond our most eager asking. Thou art in Thyself promise and fulfillment, and we have found the yoke easy and the burden light in our co-work with Thy Son, Jesus, the Christ.

Once more we renew our purpose to serve Thee; once more we lift our praises to Thee, for to us has come down through the years the story of Thy patient love to mankind everywhere, and the experience of it in our daily toil. Father, be with us in all that we do in the fulfilling of Thy will, and save us for service in Jesus' name. *Amen.*

Philip Eugene Howard, B.A.,
Philadelphia, Penna.

SEPTEMBER THIRD

Your heart shall live that seek God. — Ps. 69: 32.

O LORD, our gracious Father, we would bring to Thee our thanksgiving for all Thy great kindness and love to us. We bless Thee for all remembered or forgotten of Thy providences. We bless Thee for all the way by which the Lord our God hath led us, and whilst Thou hast been so gracious in the past, we thank Thee that we can hope in Thee perfectly for all the future.

Strengthen us, we pray Thee, that we may draw near to Thee with lowly and obedient spirits. Do Thou quicken us, that we may call upon Thy Name with more earnestness of desire, and more true submission, and more true faith than we sometimes have. We acknowledge that, as we go about our daily work, we too often forget Thee, for Whose sake and by Whose strength it should all be done. We confess that we yield far too much to the temptations that are around us, drawing us away from Thee. We live as if the present world were all we had to do with or depend upon. Do Thou deliver us, we pray Thee, from all foolish over-estimate of the worth of transitory things here, and enable us to rise above the temptations of the fleeting present, and to find in Thyself the treasure that the world cannot give, and no change can take away. *Amen.*

Rev. W. A. Cameron, B.A.,
Toronto, Ont., Canada.

SEPTEMBER FOURTH

He is a buckler to all them that trust in Him. — II Sam. 22: 31.

ALMIGHTY GOD, pour out Thy Spirit upon us in this morning hour, and give us the blessed consciousness of Thy presence as we stand upon the threshold of this new day. Guide us unerringly through each hour by Thy Spirit that we may enter wider fields of usefulness. Strew our common pathway with beautiful and fragrant flowers, and set upon our daily board the plate of plenty and the cup of good cheer. Multiply the qualities of our hearts and the excellencies of our lives, and thrust us out into new regions of experience and service. Help us, loving Father, to interpret life at its highest levels, and with a deep sense of the world's awful need. Enable us, by Thy abounding grace and infinite love, to reflect the Spirit, life and purpose of Jesus Christ to the men whom we meet this day. May we be, in the truest sense, reflectors of God, so that men shall say as did one in the long ago: "I have seen Thy face as though I had seen the face of God." Give us an increasing appreciation of the glorious Gospel of Jesus Christ, a Gospel that uplifts, redeems and beautifies the lives of men. Speak to us, gracious Father, that we may go forth to the tasks of this day in faith, hope and love, through Jesus Christ our Lord. *Amen.*

Rev. Edwin L. Davis,
Cincinnati, Ohio.

SEPTEMBER FIFTH

Pray, lest ye enter into temptation. — Mark 14: 38.

O GOD, our Father and our Mother! We thank Thee that like as a father pitieth his children, so dost Thou pity us, and like as a mother comforteth her children, so Thou wilt comfort us.

We thank Thee for our home, and for the home that it suggests to us, where we hope to be forever with Thee, and with each other. For all the good things that come to us, we praise Thee, and we beseech Thee that we may never forget to be grateful to Thee.

Our eyes are closed, for we would shut everything out; we bow before Thee, for we are dependent upon Thee; we have nothing in our clasped hands, nothing with which to buy blessings, and no weapon. God, wilt Thou keep us from doing anything to grieve Thee, and make us all the day eager to serve Thee in serving others. Help us, that we shall bring gladness into human lives, and never sorrow or pain. We pray for the whole world in its great need of Thee. God keep us, and all whom we love.

Hear us, in Jesus' name. *Amen.*

Frank S. Dobbins, D.D.,
Philadelphia, Penna.

SEPTEMBER SIXTH

Whoso putteth his trust in the Lord shall he safe. — Prov. 29: 25.

OUR Heavenly Father, we thank Thee for this day with its opportunities for service. We thank Thee for food and raiment. We thank Thee for friends, companions and loved ones. We bless Thy Holy Name for letting us have a part in the great work of telling a lost world of Jesus.

We pray Thee to make us channels of blessing this day. May the radiance of our Redeemer be reflected in our lives. May all who come in contact with us take knowledge that we have been with Thee.

Bless us as we go about our daily tasks. In the home; in business; in the classroom; yea, everywhere, may we be true to Thee and to Thy teaching. Whether we eat or whether we drink, or whatsoever we do, may we do all to the glory of God.

Be with our absent loved ones. Bless our city, and those who are in authority. Bless our Church and our pastor. Bless all who are engaged in Thy service.

Lead us not into temptation, but deliver us from the evil one. We ask it all in Jesus' name. *Amen.*

Allen Fort, D.D.,
Nashville, Tennessee.

SEPTEMBER SEVENTH

Bow down Thine ear, Lord, hear me: for I am poor and needy. Preserve my soul; for I am holy: O Thou my God, save Thy servant that trusteth in Thee. Be merciful unto me, O Lord: for I cry unto Thee daily. Rejoice the soul of Thy servant: for unto Thee, O Lord, do I lift; up my soul. For Thou, Lord, art good, and ready to forgive; and plenteous in mercy unto all them that call upon Thee.

— Ps. 86: 1-5.

O GOD, our Heavenly Father, we worship Thee. We thank Thee for rest through the night, and for the light of the morning. Thou art the light of our spirits! As in all nature the plants turn toward the sun, and the flowers even in dark and shady places reach out toward the light, so we look up to Thee, Thou Sun of Righteousness! May the influence of Thy Spirit be felt in our hearts all the day long, cleansing our thoughts, purifying our motives, strengthening us in every good purpose.

Be with us, whether in work or in study, in recreation or repose. If trials fall to our lot, may we be patient; if crosses come to us, may we bear them with courage; if sorrows, may we find consolation in communion with Thee. We pray for our friends and our neighbors. We think of those who are in spiritual darkness, in want and loneliness. Manifest Thy mercy to all mankind, through Jesus Christ our Lord. *Amen.*

James Buckley Faulks, D.D.
Chatham, N. J.

SEPTEMBER EIGHTH

Hast thou not known? hast thou not heard, that the everlasting God, the Lord, the Creator of the ends of the earth, fainteth not, neither is weary? — Isa. 40: 28.

OUR Heavenly Father, with reverence and humility we would bow at the Throne of Grace to obtain mercy and find grace for our daily needs. Conscious in some measure of our weakness and sinfulness, we earnestly seek Thy forgiving mercy, rejoicing to know that "Like as a father pitieth his children, so the Lord pitieth them that fear Him." We thank Thee for our home, and for the love that sweetens and beautifies home life. To each member of our family circle grant such blessings as are specially needed. Enlarge and deepen our sympathies. Preserve us from selfishness. Help us to learn patience and self-control. Keep us from hasty, thoughtless and unkind words, and from misunderstanding and misjudging others, and deliver us from anxiety and complaining. Fill Thy Church with missionary zeal and with the presence and power of the Holy Spirit. Strengthen the weak, comfort the sorrowing, restore the wandering. Remember with special mercy the homeless, the widow and the fatherless and all who are lonely and friendless. Help men everywhere to have the spirit of true brotherhood, and grant the speedy triumph throughout the whole world of the principles of the Gospel of Peace. All of which we ask in the name of Jesus Christ cur Lord and Saviour. *Amen.*

J. W. Conley, D.D.,
Fresno, California.

SEPTEMBER NINTH

Seeing then that we have a great high priest, that is passed into the heavens, Jesus the Son of God, let us hold fast our profession. For we have not a high priest which cannot be touched with the feeling of our infirmities; but was in all points tempted like as we are, yet without sin. Let us therefore come boldly unto the throne of grace, that we may obtain mercy, and find grace to help in time of need.
— Heb. 4: 14-16.

O GOD, our loving Father in Heaven! We look up to Thee now with reverence and trust and love. We thank Thee for teaching us to "come boldly unto the Throne of Grace."

With penitence we confess our sinfulness, and ask for forgiveness. With trust we bring our weakness to Thee, and ask for strength. With love we bring our hearts to Thee, and ask Thee to enter and possess. Lead us onward step by step. Order the pathway of life for us as Thine own wisdom and love shall see to be best. Help us to be found faithful throughout.

Bless with us our dear ones, and all for whom we should pray. Let Thy peace possess the world. May Thy Kingdom come, O Christ, come quickly! All this we ask in the name of Jesus our Saviour. *Amen.*

Anson P. Atterbury, D.D.,
New York City, N. Y.

SEPTEMBER TENTH

Whatsoever ye shall ask the Father in My name, He will give it you. - John 16: 23.

O GOD, Who art the Father of all the families of the earth, and Who makest men to be of one mind in a house: Bless this household, we beseech Thee, and grant that its members may be so united to one another in Thy faith and fear, that Thou mayest have Thy dwelling in them, and through them draw others to know Thee, to love Thee, and to serve Thee.

Set us free, we beseech Thee, from all the sins which we have committed in the years that are past, showing us how we have displeased Thee, making us sorry for all our selfishness, our pride, our anger and every other wrongdoing.

Grant us courage this day to be true to Thee, in thought and word and deed. Make us patient and humble, pure in heart and speech, cheerful and self-forgetful, temperate and just. Strengthen us to stand for the rights of the poor, the oppressed, the forsaken, against the insolence of the rich and the tyranny of the powerful. And bring us at last to Thy Heavenly Kingdom. All this we ask for the sake of Thy dear Son, Jesus Christ, to Whom, with Thee and the Holy Ghost, be glory now and forever. *Amen.*

Rev. James O. S. Huntington,
West Park, N. Y.

SEPTEMBER ELEVENTH

I will praise Thy name for Thy loving kindness. — Ps. 138: 2.

O GOD, our Heavenly Father, we thank Thee this day for our health and strength, for our homes, for our loved ones, for all the blessings and privileges Thou art giving us every day, but more than all these we thank Thee for the gift of Thy dear Son Jesus Christ We thank Thee that Thou didst give Him up for thirty-three years, and that He shed His precious blood, and gave His life, a ransom for our sins.

And so, O God, help us to die to self and sin this day. Forgive us for the mistakes of yesterday, and may they be stepping stones to higher and better things today. Breathe into our lives Thy Christlikeness, shine through our eyes, speak with our lips, grip with our hands, throb with our hearts, and may we help bring the world back to Thee.

We would pray Thee for those who are m trouble, for those who are sick, for those who know Thee not. Grant us in our weakness, strength; in our ignorance, knowledge; and in our sickness, Thy healing touch. Bless all the families we represent, and bless our loved ones wherever they are.

We ask these things, with pardon for all our sins, in Christ's name. *Amen.*

Rev. Gypsy Smith, Jr.,
Haddon Heights, N. J.

SEPTEMBER TWELFTH

Hear, O Lord, when I cry with my voice: have mercy also upon me, and answer me. When Thou saidst Seek ye my face; my heart said unto Thee, Thy face, Lord, will I seek. Hide not Thy face far from me; put not Thy servant away in anger: Thou hast been my help; leave me not, neither forsake me, O God of my salvation. When my father and m3 r mother forsake me, then the Lord will take me up. Teach me Thy way, O Lord, and lead me in a plain path, because of mine enemies.
— Ps. 27: 7-11.

WE BOW humbly before Thee, O Lord, our Father, and render to Thee our praises for all Thy loving-kindness and tender mercy toward us. All that we have and are and hope, we owe to Thy goodness. We humbly beseech Thee to forgive our sins, and cleanse us from every stain of iniquity. Help us to walk before Thee blameless, resisting every temptation, and faithfully performing every duty which devolves upon us. Bless our absent loved ones as Thou seest they have need. Grant unto them and us abundant grace, and the guidance of Thy Spirit, that we may all be strengthened to be and to do as Thou wouldst have us.

Finally bring us all into Thy everlasting Kingdom, we ask, through riches of grace in Christ Jesus, our Lord. *Amen.*

Rev. Andrew J. Lamar,
Nashville, Tennessee.

SEPTEMBER THIRTEENTH

Love suffereth long, and is kind; love envieth not, love vaunteth not itself, is not puffed up; Doth not behave itself unseemly, seeketh not her own, is not easily provoked, thinketh no evil; Rejoiceth not in iniquity, but rejoiceth in the truth; Beareth all things, believeth all things, hopeth all things, endureth all things. Love never faileth. — I Cor. 13: 4-7.

MOST merciful God, Whose we are and from Whom we receive our daily supplies, accept the adoration and gratitude of our hearts for Thy fatherly care and bounty. We have sinned and come short of Thy glory. Be merciful unto us in the forgiveness of all our sins, for the sake of Him Who loved us and gave Himself for us. May the love of Christ abound in our hearts, and manifest itself in our daily lives. May the Holy Spirit enlighten our minds, and enable us to understand and appropriate the Word of God, in order that it may be food for our souls and light unto our pathway. May He comfort our hearts and help us to lay down every burden that hinders our Christian progress. Deliver us from the power and temptations of Satan and wicked people. Employ our lives every day in Thy service, and make them a blessing to others. In mercy deal with the afflicted and save the lost, for Jesus' sake. *Amen.*

J. J. Hill, D.D.,
Red Springs, N. C.

SEPTEMBER FOURTEENTH

Now our Lord Jesus Christ Himself, and God, even our Father, which hath loved us, and hath given us everlasting consolation and good hope through grace. Comfort your hearts, and stablish you in every good word and work.
— II Thess. 2: 16-17.

O MERCIFUL GOD and Heavenly Father, we give Thee hearty thanks for all Thy benefits and blessings of the past. Continue to us this day, we beseech Thee, Thy watchful care and protection, as Thou hast through all our days. Keep all the members of this household from all accidents which may happen to the body, and from all evil thoughts that may assault and hurt the soul. Teach us what things are right to do, and make us wise and strong to do Thy will.

Comfort all the sick and sorrowful, the poor and distressed, and put it into our hearts to help them, and show us how to do it.

Bless and direct Thy Church. Give its ministers wisdom, zeal and faithfulness, and make each member of it faithful to Thee, and ready to do Thy will. Call sinners to repentance, and inspire all Thy people to obedience to Thy law and to service of their fellowmen. All this we ask through our Lord and

Saviour Jesus Christ. *Amen.*

Bishop Francis Key Brooks,
Oklahoma City, Oklahoma.

SEPTEMBER FIFTEENTH

Thanksgiving ... be unto our God for ever and ever. — Rev. 7: 12.

O THOU God of Heaven and earth, Thou Who hast established the home and sanctified it, bless, we pray Thee, this our home. May it be a place where Thou canst dwell, a place in which Thy Spirit shall reign supreme, a place which is a real home in every sense of the word.

Mav the home-maker be conscious this day of Thy presence, and may she lean upon Thee f or strength and for help, and may the home-provider be led by Thee as he goes out to his work, and be sustained by Thee as he meets the trials and temptations that shall beset him, and be returned in health when the work of the day is all over, to this our home and resting place.

May nothing be allowed to mar our home relations and may each member of this home be faithful and true May the parents be all they ought to be to the children, teaching them by example as well as by precept and may the children hold dear the lessons they learn from the parents, and may both parents and children be what they ought to be in the sight of the Lord.

This we ask in the name of Jesus our Redeemer. *Amen.*

Llewellyn L. Henson, D.D.,
Pueblo, Colorado.

SEPTEMBER SIXTEENTH

Let us come before His presence with thanksgiving. — Ps. 95: 2.

O LORD GOD, our Father, Saviour and Guide, by Whose gracious and bountiful providence we have been nourished and sustained until this hour, and in Whose redemptive, all-embracing love we greatly rejoice, accept, we beseech Thee, the sincere and profound gratitude of our hearts for Thine un-failing mercy and goodness. Pardon, we implore Thee, all our failings, faults and follies. By the Spirit dwelling within us, sweeten our dispositions and chasten all our appetites and desires. Sanctify our home, light it with the lamp of Thy presence continually, and warm it with the fire of Thy love.

Make Thy way plain before our eyes, and lead us onward and upward. Sanctify unto us all our trials and difficulties. Help us over the hard places, and in the smooth places suffer us not to forget our constant need of Thee. Quicken and intensify our love to Thee, and help us to be compassionate and generous in all our dealings with our fellow-men. Enable us to do justly and to love kindness, and to walk humbly with Thee. May we not be overcome of evil, but may we overcome evil with good.

let the wickedness of the wicked come to an end, but establish Thou the righteous. And may the whole earth be filled with Thy glory! *Amen.*

W. H. Cline, D.D.,
Georgetown, Ont., Canada.

SEPTEMBER SEVENTEENTH

Bless the Lord, O my soul: and all that is within me, bless His holy name. Bless the Lord, O my soul, and forget not all His benefits: Who forgiveth all thine iniquities; Who healeth all thy diseases; Who redeemeth thy life from destruction; Who crowneth thee with loving kindness and tender mercies; Who satisfieth thy mouth with good things; so that thy youth is renewed like the eagle's.

— Ps. 103: 1-5.

ALMIGHTY GOD, Father of all grace, we adore Thee as the Author of our being, our Preserver, and our Redeemer. Cleanse us from all inherent iniquity, and from all the defilements of sin contracted as we have lived and moved in a sinful world. Command a double portion of Thy Spirit's power upon Thy ministers, upon all Christian workers, and upon all Thy people who constitute Thy Kingdom upon earth. Grant that Thy children may show that spirit of kindness and helpfulness which was manifested by our Lord Jesus Christ when upon earth. Work in us the spirit of forgiveness towards all who may have in any way offended against us. Give us that which is necessary for the health of our bodies and endue us with the spirit of contentment. Give us a just conception of the things with which we are surrounded, and make us faithful in the discharge of all our duties.

We ask in the name of Jesus Christ our Lord. *Amen.*

Rev. William Megginson,
Richmond, Virginia.

SEPTEMBER EIGHTEENTH

Let no corrupt communication proceed out of your mouth, but that which is good to the use of edifying, that it may minister grace unto the hearers. And grieve not the holy Spirit of God, whereby ye are sealed unto the day of redemption. Let all bitterness, and wrath, and anger, and clamour, and evil speaking, be put away from you, with all malice. — Ephes. 4: 29-31.

ALMIGHTY GOD, our Father and Preserver, Who, having refreshed us with night's slumber, hast awakened us to the duties of a new day, grant us, we humbly beseech Thee, Thy heavenly presence, that we may be able to do our work as in the great Taskmaster's eye.

Thou Who hast redeemed us through Thy mercy, be pleased to defend us by Thy grace from the evil without us, and within. Save us from the power of our own lusts; the subtle suggestions of our own thoughts; the treachery of our own hearts; and cause Thy face to shine upon us, Thou in Whose presence there is no night, that this day and all our days may be pure and holy, and that we may walk in the light as children of the light. We beseech Thee to hear us, through Jesus Christ our Lord. *Amen.*

Rev. T. B. McCorkindale, M.A.
Chesterville, Canada.

SEPTEMBER NINETEENTH

And whatsoever ye shall ask in my name, that will I do, that the Father may be glorified in the Son. If ye shall ask any thing in my name, I will do it. If ye love Me, keep my commandments. And I will pray the Father, and He shall give you another Comforter, that He may abide with you for ever. — John 14: 13-16.

O ALMIGHTY GOD and Heavenly Father, Who hast safely preserved us through sleep and darkness, and hast brought us again to light and the joy of living, we adore Thy name and bless Thee for Thy mercies daily renewed.

Let Thy truth guide our footsteps, and Thy Spirit rule in our hearts through all the changes of this fleeting life, that we never be surprised into sin or error but preserved with calmness and courage in the way 'set before us, having always a conscience without offense and without recrimination. Accept the dedication of our full and hearty service of body, soul and spirit, not regarding our thoughtlessness and distractions, but sustain us in our purpose of righteousness and true holiness, that we may live to the glory and praise of Thy Holy Name, through Jesus Christ, our only Saviour and Redeemer. *Amen.*

Bishop Cleland K. Nelson,
Atlanta, Ga.

SEPTEMBER TWENTIETH

Blessed is that man that maketh the Lord his trust. — Ps. 40: 4.

OUR gracious Lord, we beseech Thee to so guide and bless us this day, that we may become more like Thy Blessed Son, in all the gracious and wonderful perfections of His being. We earnestly pray that we may possess the mind of Christ — the mind of perfect humility; that His cross of self-denial and sacrifice may be willingly assumed and carried as one of the coveted privileges of the Christian life; that we may enjoy the Spirit of Christ, for we have learned that human wisdom is not sufficient to equip us to meet the demands of life and service; that we may possess the purity of Christ, in

Whom there was found no fault; that the confidence of Christ may be ours, the confidence which perfect faith ensures; that the joy of Christ may fill our souls, the joy of perfect peace — peace enjoyed because there exists between Thy heart and ours nothing to create division or friction.

Grant, we beseech Thee, Lord, that we may so live as to be fit to represent Thy dear Son as ambassadors; that we may be epistles known and read of all men, as telling the story of a wonderful redemption; that the influence of our lives may be such that men may constantly take knowledge of us that we have been with Christ Jesus and have learned of Him. *Amen.*

Rev. George R. Stair,
Portland, Maine.

SEPTEMBER TWENTY-FIRST

I command thee this day to love the Lord thy God. — Deut. 30: 16.

OUR Heavenly Father, we come to Thee this morning with praise and thanksgiving for Thy care and love. We are grateful for the temporal blessings Thou hast given us, and for the loved ones we have to enjoy. We thank Thee for the gift of Thy Son, and for the* Holy Spirit.

We ask Thee to forgive our sins, and to cleanse us from all unrighteousness. Be with us this day, and help us to be kind and courteous. Help us to be more like Thee. May our eyes be opened to the opportunities for serving Thee and helping others to know Thee, Whom to know aright is life eternal.

May Thy Spirit be with those, at home or abroad, who preach or teach salvation, and grant that the word preached may not return unto Thee void. Be with those in authority, and may they rule with justice and equity. Comfort "as one whom his mother comforteth" those in trouble and sorrow, and strengthen those in sickness.

Our Father, hear our petition, and keep us this day without sin, for the sake and in the name of Jesus, our Saviour. *Amen.*

Claeence B. Mitchell,
Haverhill, Mass.

SEPTEMBER TWENTY-SECOND

All the ways of a man are clean in his own eyes; but the Lord weigheth the spirits. Commit thy works unto the Lord, and thy thoughts shall be established.
— Prov. 16: 2-3.

OUR Father, Who art in Heaven, Thou art our Father, though we are of the earth, and impure in Thy sight. Thou dost love us, and we are Thy children. Thy goodness is shown in that Thou hearest our prayers.

We thank Thee for so many tokens of Thy favor and abiding love. Help us to live as Thy children should live every day that we tarry here. May we learn more of Thee as the days rush on into eternity. May all our powers and service be devoted to Thee. May it be our constant joy to serve Thee and follow where Thou dost lead. Thou dost always design the best possible course for us — therefore we are safe in doing Thy will.

Teach us Thy way, and help us to keep our feet therein. In the hard places of life's pathway, help us, Lord, for we are weak, and sometimes we fall. "We need Thee every hour." Keep us from falling into sin. Save us now and evermore, for the sake of Jesus, our Master. *Amen.*

Rev. W. W. Van Dusen,
Boise, Idaho.

SEPTEMBER TWENTY-THIRD

Let Thy mercies come also unto me, O Lord, even Thy salvation, according to Thy word. S» shall I have wherewith to answer him that reproacheth me: for I trust in Thy word. And take not the word of truth utterly out of my mouth; for I have hoped in Thy judgments. So shall I keep Thy law continually for ever and ever. — Ps. 119: 41-44.

OUR Father, Who art in Heaven; Thou art also upon the earth. Thou didst stretch forth Thy hand and darkness came over the earth, Thou hast stretched it forth again and light has flooded the world. We give Thee thanks for the morning light and for the sleep and rest of the night. Grant to us this day wisdom for our problems, courage for our tasks, patience for our toil, strength for our burdens, and faith for our enterprises. Enable us to so spend this day that our work shall be our worship. May we be "the glory of Christ" among men, commending Him and His salvation. Enable us to so spend the day that our spiritual life shall be enriched by its experiences, and our fellowmen helped by our influence. Help us to maintain a conscience void of offense toward God and man. We ask it all in Christ's name. *Amen.*

William Robert King, D.D.
St. Louis, Missouri.

SEPTEMBER TWENTY-FOURTH

For there is not a word in my tongue, but, lo, O Lord, Thou knowest it altogether. Search me, O God, and know my heart: try me and know my thoughts: And see if there be any wicked way in me, and lead me in the way everlasting.
— Ps. 139: 4-23-24.

O GOD, we give Thee thanks for Thy great goodness, and Thy unfailing kindness. Day after day Thou hast bestowed upon us gifts according to our need. Teach us so to use them that in all our doings we may glorify Thy name, and further Thy righteous cause.

Above all, Most Merciful Father, we bless Thee for Jesus Christ, Thy Son, our Saviour. For His sake, do Thou receive us, and grant us Thy Spirit, that we may be enabled to follow in His footsteps, and to grow in His likeness. Prepare us, Heavenly Father, for all the appointments of Thy wise and loving Providence. May we be found, in them all, diligent, brave and faithful!

We commend to Thy love and care all that are dear to us, and all men everywhere in their need of Thee. May Thy gracious hand. lead and keep them till the discipline of life is over! Then may we and they be brought into Thy glorious presence, and find a place in Thine everlasting kingdom, through Jesus Christ our Lord. *Amen.*

T. B. Kilpatrick, D.D.,
Toronto, Canada.

SEPTEMBER TWENTY-FIFTH

Thy Word have I hid in mine heart, that I might not sin against Thee. Blessed art Thou, O lord: teach me Thy statutes. — Ps. 119: 11-12.

DEAR Father in Heaven, we come to Thee in love and praise for all the blessings we enjoy; for the food we have to eat, for the water we drink, the raiment we wear and the fresh air we breathe. We thank Thee for our home, our loved ones, and that we live in a land and an age when we can worship Thee openly. We thank Thee for the open Bible, but above all else we thank Thee that Thou didst lead us out of darkness into light through the gift of Thy dear Son.

O Father help us to become more worthy of Thy watchful care and love. Keep us in the straight and narrow path. Bless us in our plans and purposes, but defeat us in them if they lead us from Thee. Help us to let our light shine, and give us souls for our hire, in the name of Jesus we ask it. *Amen.*

Rev. John L. Brandt,
St. Louis, Missouri.

SEPTEMBER TWENTY-SIXTH

And in every work that he began in the service of the house of God, and in the law, and in the commandments, to seek his God, he did it with all his heart, and prospered. —II Chr. 31: 21.

OUR kind Heavenly Father, we come to give Thee worship this morning. We have rested safely beneath the cover of Thy care through the night, and can say as Thy servant of old, "When I awake, I am still with Thee." Blessed be Thy name. "Thy mercies are new every morning, and Thy thoughtfulness renewed in the night." We thank Thee for morning light and morning gifts, and for the opportunities to serve Thee through this new day. Help us, our

Father, to enter into all the work of the day with cheerful minds. Give us strength for our toil, clearness of mind for all decisions we must make, and grace to overcome every temptation to do wrong. Help us to walk before our fellow-men in such manlier that others can see that we "have been with Jesus." Remember graciously all our loved ones; parents, brothers and sisters, and all dear to us.

> "Though sundered far, may we often meet
> Around one common Mercy seat."

and realize that Ave have a common Father over us all. Bless this day all efforts put forth to win men from sin. Give success to all teaching and preaching and living Thy word at home and abroad. Give us, dear Lord, the joy of winning a soul for Thee today, and to Thy name be glory forever. *Amen.*

H. L. Yarger, D.D.,
Chicago, Illinois.

SEPTEMBER TWENTY-SEVENTH

Happy is he that hath the God of Jacob for his help. — Ps. 146: 5.

WE REJOICE, O God, that we are not lonely orphans in the world. We gladly realize that we can look unto Thee and call Thee "our Father." Lead us to note Thy nearness. In the midst of the hurry and flurry of the day, quiet our lives and prompt us to listen to Thy voice, and to interpret aright Thy message. We thank Thee for the bright sunshine and the blue heavens, for fresh air and wholesome food. We praise Thee for the privilege of study and meditation; for uplifting books and ennobling thoughts. We are grateful for good friends and loving companions. May our lives, as well as our lips, tell Thee of our gratitude. Speak with our tongues; work with our hands; send our feet on Thy errands; possess our whole being; "Let that mind be in us which was in Christ Jesus."

Save us from listlessness and laziness; keep us from flimsiness and frivolity; deliver us from selfishness; fill us with cheer, and lead us to brighten the lives of all we meet. Remove from us all malice and meanness. Help us to flee from evil, follow after righteousness, and fight the good fight of faith. Broaden our vision, deepen our earnestness, lengthen our love, intensify our reverence and increase our usefulness, we ask in our Master's name.

Francis Harvey Green, A.M., Litt.D.,
West Chester, Penna.

He is faithful and just to forgive us our sins. — I John 1: 9.

ALMIGHTY GOD of the Heaven, the earth and the sea! God of our fathers and God of the nations! Hear us, we pray Thee. Forgive our sins, remove our transgressions far from us. Help us, that we may behold Thy glory.

Help us to see the beauties of Thy law, and to feel the quickening power of Thy wonderful love. Give us, we pray Thee, broad faith, bright hopes, strong love and a firm step to meet the duties of life.

Let our hearts sing for joy in the remembrance of Thy goodness. Keep us in strength, that we may serve Thee. We praise Thee for Thy many and signal blessings vouchsafed to us, not only as individuals, but also as a people and a nation. We thank Thee for our forefathers, for Thy manifold blessings bestowed upon them, and through them upon us, their children. We pray Thee, O God, for grace to enable us to live useful lives, helpful to our fellow-men.

May wars and strife cease, and the kingdoms of this world become the kingdoms of our Lord and His Christ. Hear our prayer for our Redeemer's sake. *Amen.*

Lucian J. Fosdick,
Dorchester, Mass.

SEPTEMBER TWENTY-NINTH

Peace be to the brethren, and love with faith from God the Father and the Lord Jesus Christ. Grace be with all them that love our Lord Jesus Christ in sincerity. Amen. — Ephes. 6: 23-24.

DEAR Father, at the beginning of another day we come before Thee, after the quiet rest of the night, to thank Thee that Thou hast spared our lives to see this day, for all the days are Thine; the cattle on a thousand hills are Thine; the water in the brook is Thine and the fish in the sea are Thine; so why should we concern ourselves about the temporal things of this life, knowing and believing that Thou art able and willing to take care of us, and provide for our every need. So we come to Thee with great boldness, trusting in Thee for all that is necessary to sustain us. We most humbly beseech Thee to pour out Thy Holy Spirit upon us, and to guide us in all that we may do or think or say, that we may be kept from harm and sin, and be made pure and good within. Help us to praise and adore and magnify Thy Holy Name, for all Thy goodness and love for us this day of our lives on earth, for Jesus' sake. *Amen.*

J. Frank Fox,
Philadelphia, Penna.

SEPTEMBER THIRTIETH

Unto Thee lift I up mine eyes, Thou that dwellest in the heavens. Behold, as the eyes of servants look unto the hand of their masters, and as the eyes of a maiden unto the hand of her mistress; so our eyes wait upon the Lord our God, until that He have mercy upon us. — Ps. 123: 1-2.

OUR Heavenly Father, in the light of another day we rise to do Thy will. We bless Thee for the comfort and rest of the night, and for the promise of strength for the new day.

May we find joy in our toil, and much quiet in the clamor and strife of the street. May the still, small voice guide us in the way of all good, and may Thine own spirit throughout this day keep our eyes from tears, our feet from falling, and our souls from death.

Bless all our kind, and those everywhere that we hold dear, and do for them, we beseech Thee, beyond what we know how to ask. Forgive every wrong thing in our lives for which we repent. Keep us this day near to Thee in all our thoughts and words and deeds. Let Thy joy live in our hearts, and Thy peace abide in our homes, and all these things we ask in Jesus' name. *Amen.*

William Chalmers Covert, D.D.,
Chicago, Illinois.

October

OCTOBER FIRST

The Lord is my light and my salvation. — Ps. 27: 1.

OUR Heavenly Father, we of this household, with varied needs, unite to revere Thy name. We would glorify Thee in our ordinary life. We thank Thee for the quiet shining of the light upon the world, and for the quiet shining of Thy light in the souls of men. Light us on our path, lest we lose the way. We would make league with Thee for the Master's presence. May Jesus be guest and chiefest friend at our fireside, the listener to every conversation, counsellor in every day of doubt, light in every hour of darkness, refuge in any time of storm, solace in the night of grief. Bless us in basket and in store. Make us rich in all the things of the Kingdom of God.

Give us all the gladness Thy love and wisdom can trust us with, and only enough of trial and of storm to make us pure. When our feet shall have grown tired upon the road of the years, and death shall scatter the mist upon our faces, and we grope with blind fingers for the latch of the gate of Thy house, may He guide us with the unfailing cunning of His love, and give abundant entrance into the graveless, deathless, nightless city which is Thy home and ours.

Forgive us our trespasses. And this we pray for all who name Thy name. For Christ's sake. *Amen.*

Rev. Lincoln A. Ferris,
Baltimore, Maryland.

OCTOBER SECOND

Thou art my God; early will I seek Thee. — Ps. 63: 1.

OUR Heavenly Father, Who hath kept us through the night and given us a new day, we thank Thee for all Thy gifts. We thank Thee for renewed strength of body, and for refreshment of mind. We thank Thee for the new opportunities that come with the new day — the opportunity to learn, the opportunity to be kind, the chance to work, and the chance to pray. We failed yesterday in leaving undone things that we should have, done, and in doing things that we ought not to have done; but Thou hast given us today in which to begin anew. We look to Thee, the Giver of all good, for help to spend the day in ways Thou dost approve.

May Thy peace possess our hearts. Grant us that perfect love that casteth out fear. In all our ways we would acknowledge Thee, that Thou mayest direct our paths. We beseech Thee to give unto us that measure of Thy sustaining grace that will make us victorious over temptation, patient when tried, kind and helpful and loving in all our relations with others. Help us to be faithful in the little things of daily life, and in everything to seek first the Kingdom of God, that our lives may conform to Thy perfect plan, and that we may glorify 'Thee in accomplishing the work Thou dost give us to do. We ask it for Christ's sake. *Amen.*

Rev. M. F. McCutcheon, B.A.,
Montreal, Canada.

OCTOBER THIRD

Her sins, which are many, are forgiven. — Luke 7: 47.

HEAVENLY FATHER, through the darkness Thou hast blessed us with Thy gift of sleep and rest. We thank Thee for it. The new day, too, is Thy gift, and for it we give Thee thanks. Help us to begin the day with a glad sense of Thy reality, Thy nearness, Thy love, Thy gracious Fatherhood.

Grant us, We beseech Thee, a fresh sense of Thy forgiving grace, that the sins of the past may not haunt and accuse us. Grant us Thy helping grace, that we may be steadfast in the presence of temptation; that we may be cheerful and faithful in the performance of our "tasks; that we may carry our cross of trial, if such shall be laid upon us, bravely and unflinchingly; that we may put away our selfishness and unkindness, and live today a loving life with our dear ones and all others with whom we shall have to do. Our help is in Thee.

Bring to our remembrance Thy great promises. Make the Saviourhood of Christ real in our hearts today. Shed forth Thy Holy Spirit anew within us. And what we ask for ourselves, grant, we beseech Thee, in Thy great goodness, to others. Through Jesus Christ our Lord. *Amen.*

Prof. Thomas Trotter. D.D.
Toronto, Ont., Canada.

OCTOBER FOURTH

He that loveth father or mother more than me is not worthy of me: and he that loveth son or daughter more than me is not worthy of me. And he that taketh not his cross, and followeth after me, is not worthy of me. He that findeth his life shall lose it: and he that loseth his life for my sake shall find it. — Matt. 10: 37-39.

O LORD, our Heavenly Father, we adore Thee for Thy loving kindness and tender mercies. Thou hast surrounded us with evidences of Thy care and protection. We thank Thee for every blessing Thou hast bestowed upon us — our life, sustenance and hope. May we be conscious this day of Thy presence to guide, protect and help us. In our trials, give us patience to endure; in temptation, make a way for our escape. May we all be under the influence of Thy Holy Spirit; may He make effectual our holy purpose to be knit together as one family in Jesus Christ our Lord, that in our individual and social life we may reflect the character of our Saviour in the love we bear to God and to our fellow-men. Help us to walk in His footsteps, in holy obedience to Thy will. Increase our faith to claim the promises Thou hast so richly given for spiritual sustenance, and the inspiration of hope, that our life on earth may lead to everlasting life in Heaven. Through Jesus Christ our Lord. *Amen.*

Henry Wheeler, D.D.,
Ocean Grove, N. J.

OCTOBER FIFTH

Therefore being justified by faith, we have peace with God through our Lord, Jesus Christ. — Rom. 5: 1.

WE BOW before Thee in united worship, our Father and our God, praising Thee for Thy faithful shepherd care. We thank Thee for every support of life, but especially for Thy Son, our Saviour, through Whom we have been made children of God. Take from us the guilt and power of sin. Teach us today our dependence upon Thee. Impart to us faith, patience, love and hope.

Lift us above living for this world alone. May we as members of the family be helpful one to another in days dark and bright. Deliver us from dangers seen and unseen. And may we so love and serve our fellowmen that others may see Thee in us. Hear us on behalf of all who are dear to us by ties of nature or of grace. Heal the sick, comfort the sorrowing, lift the fallen and destroy the works of the devil.

Speed the day when earth's utmost bounds shall hear and turn unto Thee. May Thy people everywhere today live valiantly for God. And so guide us each one, all through life, that we may at last be one unbroken family circle around Thy throne in Glory. For Jesus' sake. *Amen.*

John Alvin Ore, D.D.,
Pittsburgh, Pa.

OCTOBER SIXTH

Happy is he that hath the God of Jacob for his help, whose hope is in the Lord his God: Which made heaven, and earth, the sea, and all that therein is: Which keepeth truth for ever: Which executeth judgment for the oppressed: Which giveth food to the hungry. — Ps. 146: 5-7.

WE SALUTE Thee, God of the Sunrise! "My voice shalt Thou hear in the morning, O Lord; in the morning will I direct my prayer unto Thee, and will look up."

Give us to go through this day with head erect, heart full-beating, eyes open to see, mind responsive to know. Let us be thankful for what we have, without covetousness, and grant us to share gladly with others what Thou dost drop in our laps. We do not pray for a bank full of gold, but for a mind full of noble thoughts. We do not pray for a house full of treasure, but for a home full of Thy love.

Help us to walk to the end of this day with Thee. Then, when the lamps are lighted, may this home, yes, and the great world, find Thy promise fulfilled to the soul, that at evening time it shall be light. In His name Who is the Light of the world. *Amen.*

Rev. Fred Winslow Adams,
New York City, N. Y.

OCTOBER SEVENTH

Now God Himself and our Father, and our Lord Jesus Christ, direct our way unto you. And the Lord make you to increase and abound in love one toward another, and toward all men, even as we do toward you: To the end He may stablish your hearts unblamable in holiness before God, even our Father, at the coming of our Lord Jesus Christ with all His saints. — I Thess. 3: 11-13.

ALMIGHTY GOD, our Father, help us to receive this day as a fresh gift from Thy loving hand, and to use it earnestly and joyously. Give us for its tasks, we pray Thee, vigor of body, clearness of mind and definiteness of purpose, but above all, the right spirit and the pure heart.

Look graciously upon our loved ones; place upon them Thy guiding and restraining hand. Comfort all who are sick and in sorrow; heal the wounded in spirit; recall the wandering. Strengthen all who are working earnestly for the Kingdom of our Lord, and grant that throughout the world this may be a day of great progress toward righteousness and peace.

Thy Kingdom come. Thy will in us and in all men be done, through Jesus Christ our Lord. *Amen.*

Alexander MacColl, D.D.,
Philadelphia, Penna.

OCTOBER EIGHTH

Blessed are the undefiled in the way, who walk in the law of the Lord. Blessed are they that keep His testimonies, and that seek Him with the whole heart. They also do no iniquity: they walk in His ways. Thou hast commanded us to keep Thy precepts diligently. O that my ways were directed to keep Thy statutes!
— Ps. 119: 1-5.

OUR Father, Who dost love us with everlasting love, may we rejoice in that love, and endeavor day by day to show our love for Thee by glad obedience to Thy will. Keep us pure, strong, and full of trust in Thee, that we may be victorious over temptations to wrong-doing, and may ever know the joy and help of Thy presence in our lives.

Banish all selfishness, and inspire us with desire for justice to all men, and stir up our wills to establish the rule of Christian brotherhood on earth. May we look upon Thy whole family and respond to every call for sympathy and compassion, and to every challenge to heroic and self-sacrificing service for our fellow-men.

In all things give us the guidance and direction of Thy Holy Spirit, that we may serve and please Thee. In the name of our Lord and Master, Who loved us and gave Himself for us. *Amen.*

Rev. Romilly F. Humphries,
Baltimore, Maryland.

OCTOBER NINTH

My praise shall be continually of Thee. — Ps. 71: 6.

ALMIGHTY GOD, our Heavenly Father, from Whom all good thoughts proceed, grant us the presence of the Holy Spirit, that we may walk humbly before Thee this day. Thou art the fountain of our light and the source of all our strength. We render thanks to Thee for this home with all its

comforts and blessings. We thank Thee for all the tokens of Thy loving kindness and Thy mercies which we have experienced. Be with us this day, God!
May each member of our household be conscious of Thy presence. May
Christ Jesus be exalted in all that we shall say and do. We thank Thee for salvation; we ask Thee to make us ready for service. May each one of us surrender absolutely to Jesus, Thy Son. May we give ourselves, our time, our money
and our influence unreservedly to Him. May we care for the lowly and neglected; may we visit the sick and those in distress; may we encourage the
tempted and the discouraged, and not forget to be fishers of men.

Make us wise, Blessed Master, with Thy wisdom and strong in Thy
strength. May we be loyal to Jesus Christ, our Saviour and Lord. Give us vitali-
ty of body and make us able to endure. Grant us the spirit of prevailing prayer, for Jesus' sake. *Amen.*

W. D. Powell, D.D.,
Louisville, Kentucky.

OCTOBER TENTH

My mouth shall show forth Thy praise. — Ps. 51: 15.

ALMIGHTY and most merciful God, we gratefully acknowledge Thee
as the ruler of our lives. Thou art Infinite God; we are creatures of the earth.
Yet Thou hast exalted us to be Thy children. Thou hast endowed us with reason and will, and hast given us a nature that seeks after Thee. Thou hast
placed us in this beautiful world and lavished its bounties upon us, and Thou
hast made provision for the pure enjoyment of every sense. Thou hast set us
in families amidst neighbors, and hast endowed us with love.

Above all, because we have fallen into sin, Thou hast manifested redeeming love by the sacrifice of our Saviour upon the cross. We humbly confess
our personal sinfulness and failure to render a full measure of service to
Thee and to our fellow-men. In mercy grant Thy forgiveness, and enable us
to live more nobly.

Look with compassion upon all men. Awaken true repentance and desire
for salvation in every breast, both in heathen lands and at home.

Widen Thy Kingdom, and manifest Thy power in the earth. Bring all rulers
and peoples under Thy sway, and soon, Lord, soon manifest Thyself in Thine
eternal glory. Through Jesus Christ our Lord. *Amen.*

L. Stanley Hughson, B.A., D.D.,
Stratford, Ont., Canada.

OCTOBER ELEVENTH

God is our refuge and strength, a very present help in trouble. — Ps. 46: 1.

MOST gracious Father, from Whom all good gifts come, grant us, we entreat Thee, the gift we need above all others, Thy Holy Spirit to help our infirmities, that our worship may be purged from all unreality. Free us from selfishness in our prayers; deliver us from asking for those things that will minister chiefly to our pleasure. Help us to covet the best gifts, the gifts which we do not always ask for by reason of our ignorance, or do not dare to implore Thee to grant us because of our sin. We are conscious of our sinfulness, but cannot be truly sorry for our misdoings until Thou dost move us to honest contrition. We would be grateful to Thee for the multitude of Thy mercies, but it is not until Thou dost grant us a due sense of Thy goodness, and awaken within us gratitude, that, our hearts are ready to praise Thee. Our love languishes and dies except Thy Spirit shall quicken it into a living flame. We would live the prayer life; we would learn what it is to pray without ceasing. To this end do Thou come and dwell within us, Thou Spirit of Christ! Grant us Thy grace, that our lives may show forth Thy praise, until at length we behold Thee in the face of Jesus Christ, Whom, now unseen, we love. *Amen.*

Samuel P. Rose, D.D.,
Montreal, Que., Canada.

OCTOBER TWELFTH

Fight the good fight of faith. — Tim. 6: 12.

WE THANK Thee, our Heavenly Father, for the care, the rest and refreshment vouchsafed unto us during another night. We thank Thee for the privilege of being able to present ourselves again before Thee, we trust, in the spirit of worship and of consecration, for the life and work of this new day. We recognize that the highest, as well as the holiest, possible ideal of life is the doing of Thy will and the accomplishment of Thy purposes concerning us. We recognize also, that even as Thou hast said, the way of man is not in himself, that it is not in man that walketh, to be able always and everywhere to direct his steps aright, and so we look to Thee for the strength and wisdom and grace necessary to discharge faithfully and earnestly the responsibilities and duties of the day. Make us deeply sensitive to Thy presence, and to the other privileges and blessings of the day, so that they shall not pass from us unappreciated and unused.

Grant unto us the spirit of patience, of sympathy and of willingness to help any who may not be as highly favored as we are. Remember those in weakness, in suffering or in sorrow, and should we ourselves be called upon to pass through any of these experiences, may there also come with them the grace of resignation and of trust. *Amen.*

Rev. Robert Milliken, B.D.,
Regina, Sask., Canada.

160

OCTOBER THIRTEENTH

If we ask anything according to His will, He heareth us. —I John 5: 14.

WITH gratitude for Thy protection, during the night watches, we begin, O Lord, the new life of a new day. Our paths will be the busy thoroughfares — walk Thou with us unseen. Our thoughts will be of our business — let not our hearts cleave to these things, but through the sweet influence of Thy Spirit, incline us to seek things that endure. We shall be tempted today, we may be drawn to the verge of some awful mistake — in the swift moment of danger, when we cannot withdraw to our closet of prayer, give us to know the right, and the power to do it.

Let not trifles ruffle our temper, nor disappointments unman us; let not exacting duties make us selfish and churlish; give us rather a sunshiny face, a forthright hand, and the joy of a word fitly spoken to some timid, discouraged soul.

Strength for the day's service give us in such measure as Thou wiliest; pass by our sins of omission; and when the shadows fall, bring us again, unsullied by thought, or word, or deed, to sweet refreshing sleep. For Christ's sake. *Amen.*

(Not original; heard by him several years ago.)

Hon. John Stites,
Louisville, Kentucky.

OCTOBER FOURTEENTH

Pray without ceasing. — I Thess. 5: 17.

OUR blessed Saviour, Who dost dwell in our hearts by faith, grant us such a clear consciousness of Thine indwelling that each may be able to say, "I live, and yet no longer I, but Christ liveth in "me." Show us that our interests and Thine are one. Enable us so to surrender ourselves to Thee that Thou mayest work in us both to will and to work for Thy good pleasure. Establish Thy rule over every part of our nature. Subdue our passions and energies to Thy will. In Thy light may we see our faults and failures, and, as they are revealed, do Thou remove them, and finish in us the work Thou hast begun. Grant us grace today to let Christ live out His life in us. May He so possess our spirits and so govern our lives, that men, beholding us, may think of Him; listening to us, may hear His message; and in fellowship with us, may feel the influence of His Spirit. Keep us from stifling the voice within. Keep us from becoming so engrossed with our worldly pursuits that we lose sight of the Christ Who reigns in our souls, and Who is our very life. Lord Jesus, make us Thine instruments, prepare us for Thy service, and use us as Thou wilt for the fulfilment of Thy purposes. Then grant us the joy of Thine approval. For Thine own name's sake. *Amen.*

George C. Pidgeon, D.D.,
Toronto, Canada.

OCTOBER FIFTEENTH

Follow righteousness, faith, charity, peace. — II Tim. 2: 22.

ALMIGHTY GOD, our gracious Heavenly Father, we, Thy needy children, would draw near to Thee. We come with confidence, for Thou hast already manifested Thy interest in us this day. Thou hast called the light out of darkness, and so ushered in for us a new day. Thou hast raised us from rest in slumber, and so given us a new opportunity to do Thy will.

Add, we beseech Thee, to these evidences of Thy favor, all needed goodness and mercy; goodness to provide for our ever-returning wants of body and soul; mercy to pardon our past transgressions, and to protect us against future temptations. Grant us also grace this day to manifest the Spirit of Jesus Christ in all we shall think, and say, and do.

Show Thy loving favor to all who are near and dear to us. Guide, we pray Thee, all who occupy positions of authority and trust in Church, in State, in industry, in education, in society, and in the home. Hasten, God, the time when every knee shall bow in the name of Jesus, and every tongue shall confess Him as Lord. These blessings, and whatever else Thou seest we shall need this day, we ask through the merits and mediation of Jesus Christ, Thy Son and our Saviour. *Amen.*

Lewis Seymour Mudge, D.D.
Harrisburg, Penna.

OCTOBER SIXTEENTH

Believe that ye shall receive, and ye shall have. — Mark 11: 24.

OUR Father in Heaven, in the name of Jesus Christ, Whom having not seen we love, we draw near to Thee in prayer.

We are unworthy of Thy many mercies, for we have sinned against Thee, but we know Thou wilt not despise the humble and contrite heart.

We thank Thee for life and its sustenance; for home, with all its comforts; for our loved ones and friends; and above all, for Jesus, Who loved us and gave Himself for us. May we be enabled to follow in His footsteps, doing as He would have done, speaking as He would have spoken, and denying ourselves that others may be blessed.

Bless to us Thy holy Word. Enable us to live according to its divine teaching. In all our intercourse with our fellow-men, give us grace to be patient, forgiving, loving and kind, and to influence others for good. Forgive us our many sins, and keep us by Thy almighty power through faith unto salvation.

We ask everything in the name and for the sake of Jesus Christ, our adorable Redeemer. *Amen.*

William H. Scott,
Philadelphia, Penna.

OCTOBER SEVENTEENTH

Follow after righteousness, godliness, faith. — I Tim. 6: 11.

OUR Father, teach us how to speak to Thee. May Thy Spirit lead us into the light, for we know so little about Thee and are so dull and slow to learn. Wilt Thou forgive us when we do wrong, and keep us from going away from Thee. Good Shepherd, the wilderness is so large, and we are weak and so easily lose our way. Keep us from the wild beasts of sin, and may we never miss the path that leads to Thy fold.

Bless our home today, and all who are in it. May we always be gentle and loving, and seek to make all about us happy. Help us to have a shining face, and especially when we meet Thy other children who are sad and in trouble. Teach us to do as Jesus did when He forgot all about Himself in trying to help others.

We thank Thee for all the good and beautiful things Thou art giving us every day. We pray Thee to help us to help Thee to make Thy world good and happy.

And this we ask in the name of our Elder Brother, Christ, Who loved us and gave Himself for us. *Amen.*

Charles R. Flanders, D.D.
London, Ont., Canada.

OCTOBER EIGHTEENTH

The prayer of the upright is His delight. — Prov. 15: 8.

LORD, teach us how to pray; for we know not how to pray as we ought. Thou hast bidden us in everything, by prayer and supplication with thanksgiving, to make our requests known unto Thee. Thou hast given us so many wonderful promises in respect of prayer that we cannot but believe that prayer is the open way between us and Thee.

Thou art our Father, and we trust Thee and know that Thou canst never contradict Thy love for us as manifested in the coming and living and dying of our Lord Jesus Christ. How shalt Thou not with Him freely give us all things? No withholding or even denial of our requests can make us doubt Thee. And then we remember that Thy "No" is just as real an answer to prayer as Thy "Yes," as when Thou didst say to Moses and Paul "No"; and yet, later, how wonderfully Thou didst answer those seemingly unanswered prayers.

Be Thou our light in darkness; our comfort in sorrow; our wisdom when we are perplexed; our strength when we are in weakness. Our desire is to be used of Thee. We do not want to be idle or unfruitful in Thy service, even when limited in our opportunities. Grant this our prayer, Father, for Jesus' sake. *Amen.*

George F. Pentecost, D.D., LL.D.
Philadelphia, Penna.

OCTOBER NINETEENTH

The God of love and peace shall be with you. — II Cor. 13: 11.

OUR Father in Heaven, Thou Who carest for all the families of the earth, grant to this family a consciousness of Thy presence and love. May we be ever careful lest by word or deed we bring dishonor to Thy matchless name. Follow us as we go to the tasks of today. May we be strong in Thy strength; courageous because of Thy promises; and humble, in view of our constant dependence upon Thee.;

May the Angel of the Lord encamp round about the absent ones; guard them from evil, and inspire them for service. Give us all hearts of pity for those who are in need, sympathy for the weak, and willingness to lift up the fallen. Forbid that we should be content with our own plenty, or proud in our own accomplishments, but as children may we ever be anxious for the glory of our Father's name, and thankful for His care. Forgive us for that wherein we have failed; forgive us for willfulness and downright sin.

When the great homecoming takes place, and we are in the Father's house, may every member of this family be among the "multitude that no man can number," serving Thee as we cannot here. This we ask for the sake of Jesus Christ, Thy Son and our Saviour. *Amen.*

Rev. J. R. Webb,
Peterborough, Ont., Canada.

OCTOBER TWENTIETH

Believe ye that I am able to do this? — Matt. 9: 28.

O GOD, our Heavenly Father, we give Thee thanks for all that makes Thee known to us, and for all the good things that Thou hast given us. We praise Thee that our household has once more been preserved to meet in health and to join in common thanksgiving unto Thee, the Most Holy God, the Eternal Providence.

We pray Thee to forgive all our sins, and to cleanse our hearts by the inspiration of Thy Holy Spirit. Accompany us into the duties of each day, and give us strength for every need.

Preserve us from all danger, defend us from all error of heart, deliver us out of every temptation, save us from murmuring against our lot or grieving over our losses, save us from envy and pride, from hate and untruth, from waste of time and excessive pleasure, and from all worldliness. May we be diligent in business, fervent in spirit, serving Thee, our Lord. We pray Thee in behalf of our neighbors and friends. May both we and they be blest in our mutual intercourse. Bless the poor and needy, the sick and desolate and defenseless, and bring back the lost ones to Thy home and heart.

We ask it all in the name of Thy dear Son, our Saviour and Lord. *Amen.*

W. T. G. Brown, B.A., B.D.,
Toronto, Canada.

OCTOBER TWENTY-FIRST

The fruit of the Spirit is love, joy, faith. — Gal. 5: 22.

OUR Heavenly Father, we turn to Thee in gratitude for Thy goodness, and in loving dependence upon Thy grace. Thou art our shield, our strength, our guide. Through Jesus Christ, our Lord, Thou dost forgive our sins. We trust in Thee alone. Our feeble strength can give no security in temptation, nor firmness in trial. We humbly pray for Thy sustaining grace today. May Thy companionship transform our daily tasks and make our weakness strong.

Grant to us hearts of compassion for the sorrowing, tempted, hopeless ones whose lives shall touch ours today. May we follow our Saviour in helpful ministry, and may His Spirit go out from us to lead men unto Him Who alone can bless.

May Thy Holy Spirit enable us to set ourselves firmly against the evils which destroy the souls of men, and do our part of the work that is needed for the coming of Thy Kingdom. Help us to be faithful and true in thought, word and deed, that we may not add to the sum of the world's evil, but may purify and enlighten all the life about us.

These things we ask in the name of our Lord and Saviour, Jesus Christ. *Amen.*

Robert E. Vinson, D.D.,
Austin, Texas.

My tongue shall speak of Thy righteousness and praise. — Ps. 35: 28.

OUR Heavenly Father, we rejoice in Thy love. The knowledge of Thy love for us casts out all our fear as we approach Thee in prayer. Thy love has redeemed us, and moment by moment we are kept by the power of Thy love. That we may glorify Thee, that the world may know that we love Thee, help us to be kind and courteous and honest in all the relations of life. Give us the mind that was in Christ Jesus. Show us our duty and privileges as His followers. Help us with open eye to see the truth, and with open heart to receive it, and grant us grace in all things to do Thy holy will. We thank Thee, Heavenly Father, that Thou hast supplied all our needs. We have wanted for no good thing. We confidently trust Thee for the future. We put our all in Thy hands, knowing Thou wilt never fail us. Be about our homes and loved ones today. Beat back all that disturbs human peace and mars human happiness. Deliver us from all evil.

Bless and prosper the cause of Christ our Saviour in the Church and throughout the world. Bring many today, by the way of the cross, into Thy Kingdom. Save the lost. We ask all this, with the forgiveness of our sins, through Jesus Christ our Lord. *Amen.*

Rev. Charles Henry Pinchbeck,
Baltimore, Maryland.

Save Thy people, and bless Thine inheritance. — Ps. 28: 9.

OUR Gracious and kind Heavenly Father! We lift our hearts to Thee at dawn, though we painfully recognize and feel our unworthiness of Thy uncounted mercies which are new every morning and fresh every evening. We throw ourselves upon Thy clemency. Put Thy protecting hand, with its tender touch, upon our drooping heads, and though we venture not to look up, may we hear Thy reassuring and forgiving voice. Here we are grouped together at the foot of Thy cross, because we know Thou hast room for us all in Thy great yearning heart. We long for Thy tender caress and Thy smile of forgiveness. Put about us Thy everlasting mighty arms, and carry us safely through this day. As we take up life's business afresh and hasten out into the wild hurry of the world, be Thou ever near us. Be Thou our traveling companion. We need Thy presence every passing moment. For the gift of Thy Son, our adorable Christ, we thank Thee, O God. He brought eternal calm to our surging hearts, and made our sin-tattered lives to rejoice. Give us a new vision of Him as we toil this day. May we see the rift in the clouds as we look up to behold Him. Soften our hearts, direct our thoughts, steady our step, and shelter us by Thy care until our traveling days are done, we humbly ask in Jesus' name. *Amen.*

Rev. F. W. Mueller,
Cleveland. Ohio.

OCTOBER TWENTY-FOURTH

And make confession unto Him. — Josh. 7: 19.

OUR Heavenly Father, we thank Thee for keeping guard over us during the night. We laid us down and slept; we awakened because Thou didst sustain us. Thou hast opened to us the gateway of this new day and set before us open doors of fresh opportunity and privilege. As we go forth to new duties and responsibilities, we pray for Thy presence to go with us. Strengthen us in our weakness, guide us in our ignorance, and inspire us both to will and to do according to Thy good pleasure. Enable us to present our bodies a living sacrifice, wholly acceptable unto Thee, which is our reasonable service. We commit to Thee all our loved ones, and beseech Thee that Thy Spirit may so control their hearts and guide their lives as to save them from forgetfulness of Thee, and from neglect of Thy claims. Remember those in authority over us. Put Thy fear in their hearts, that they may faithfully discharge their responsible duties. May Thy Spirit rest on all our people, causing us to lead peaceable, quiet and orderly lives. Hasten the triumphs of Thy Kingdom, until all hearts shall be brought under the rule of Christ, and the whole family of man shall constitute a brotherhood bound together by the bond of Christian love. These blessings we ask, with the forgiveness of our sins, in the name of Jesus Christ. *Amen.*

R. C. Reed, D.D.,
Columbia, S. C.

OCTOBER TWENTY-FIFTH

He hath showed thee, O man, what is good; and what doth the Lord require of thee, but to do justly, and to love mercy, and to walk humbly with thy God.
— Micah 6: 8.

ALMIGHTY GOD, Whom truly to know is everlasting life, we draw near to Thee at the beginning of this day, desiring to know Thee as the Father of our spirits, and to refresh our spirits in Thy eternal goodness. As we draw near to Thee in worship, we pray that Thou wilt draw near to us in blessing and in inspiration. Grant us, we beseech Thee, the things of which Thou seest our need. We ask for health, for opportunity, and for a willing mind that finds delight in fruitful labor. Grant us the consciousness of sin forgiven, that in our labors and undertakings there may be no sad friction of remorse and shame.

Grant us the blessing of friendship greatly widened. We would not think of ourselves as too good to mingle with the humblest. We would not live apart from others in hope and sympathy. Rather do we seek from Thee the gladness of the common life of all Thy children, and the sweetness of its universal hope. Thou Who hast made us of one blood, help us to toil and hope and suffer and rejoice as brethren, that in our common life Thy purpose may be glorified, through Jesus Christ our Lord. *Amen.*

Rev. Howard Chandler Robbins,
New York City, N. Y.

OCTOBER TWENTY-SIXTH

They believed the Scripture. — John 2: 22.

OUR Father Who art in Heaven, we praise Thee for the grace which permits us to look upon another day. Wondrous is Thy love. We frail children of earth bow for a moment to receive the benediction of Thy infinite Motherhood and omnipotent Fatherhood. Forth we go to battle and to toil. We dare not go alone. Temptation will crouch beside our pathway. Some of us may come upon dangers suddenly. Do Thou befriend us. When the duties of the day are done, may it please Thee to gather us at eventide an unbroken, happy family, with no stain of sin upon our garments. The Church we love, do Thou bless it. May the Holy Spirit abide with the pastor and all the people. We love our native land. Do Thou save it. For the whole world we offer our humble prayer. Thy Kingdom come. Great Son of God, dear Prince of Peace, why dost Thou tarry? Humanity dies. Give us hearts to bleed and hands to bless. Pity the men who have no home, and protect the women who toil and are weak. Send us from this trysting place to laugh and love and labor in the strength of Him Who said, "Inasmuch as ye did it unto one of the least of these, ye did it unto me." Lord, we thank Thee for Thy promised strength. *Amen.*

Rev. David Otis Cowles,
Jersey City, N. J.

OCTOBER TWENTY-SEVENTH

Ye are My friends if ye do whatsoever I command you. — John 15: 14.

OUR Heavenly Father, we bless Thee for Thy great gifts to us, Thy children— that there is provision for all our needs. We thank Thee for the power given to men to bless and gladden one another by the warmth of love, the truth and tenderness of friendship, and to support each other in all good. Mav we accept this great gift with a sense of responsibility. Let not the wealth of human love bestowed upon us be wasted or despised— the tender care lavished on us in our early days, the love of parents, the patience of

168

teachers, the wisdom of counsellors, all the sweet charities of home, the joy and strength of true human intercourse.

As we have received of love, so may we give. May we learn the deep lessons of love— self-denial, patience, helpfulness, sympathy, and growth in gracious living. May the discipline of love train us in constancy and true virtues. May we use the love with which we have been dowered to panoply us against evil, to preserve us under the manifold dangers and temptations of the world.

Bless our friends— may they and we be friends of God. Above all, may our experience of earthly love bring us nearer to Thy love, Thou Lover of our souls! *Amen.*

Hugh Black, D.D.,
New York City.

OCTOBER TWENTY-EIGHTH

The Lord is good, a strong hold in the day of trouble; and He knoweth them that trust in Him. — Nah. 1: 7.

OUR Father, we thank Thee for Thy revelation of love through Jesus Christ, and for all that He has brought to our lives of inspiration and guidance and hope. We thank Thee for the tasks Thou hast given us, and for Thy presence and help as we undertake them. Help us, we pray, to live in unbroken companionship with Thee; to draw life from Thy life; to show Thee forth as we have to do with our fellowmen in the ways of common life. Be quick to strengthen us when the lure of the world is strong upon us, and when we are tempted to put the things that perish above the things that are eternal. Give us a great hunger after righteousness, and help us to be genuine in all that we do and say and think.

As Thy disciples, Christ, may we come to be more like Thee each day, as in ever-increasing measure the spirit which was in Thee comes to dwell in us. Help us to love God and our neighbors with all our hearts. Keep us from selfishness. Forgive our sins, for Thy name's sake. *Amen.*

Lathan A. Crandall, D.D.,
Minneapolis, Minn.

OCTOBER TWENTY-NINTH

While ye have Light, believe in the Light. — John 12: 36.

ALMIGHTY GOD, our Heavenly Father, we come with reverence to Thy mercy seat, honoring and praising Thy Holy Name.

We thank Thee for the revelation Thou hast made of Thyself in Thy Holy Word; in the beautiful works of nature; and by Thy Spirit in our hearts.

We confess our unworthiness of Thy blessings, for we have sinned, forgetful of Thy commands and of Thine infinite, eternal, unchangeable love. Father, forgive us for Christ's sake.

We thank Thee for our home and loved ones, and for all of life's comforts and joys. Bless every member of our family. Abide with us in our home; and when our days on earth are numbered, may our hearts rejoice in the assurance that our Saviour has prepared a place for us in His house of many mansions — the house not made with hands, eternal in the heavens — and there may we meet again our dear ones who have gone before us, and all who may come after us; and the glory of our salvation shall be. not unto us, but unto Thee, Father, Son, and Holy Spirit, the only living and true God, as it was in the beginning, is now, and ever shall be, world without end. *Amen.*

Francis B. Reeves,
Philadelphia, Penna.

OCTOBER THIRTIETH

If ye shall ask anything in My name, I will do it. —John 14: 14.

OUR Father, Who through another night hast kept us with the loving care a mother might show to her infant child, while in the land of sleep and all unmindful of the world about us, we have been with Thee; though to the darkness of the night has been added the closing of our eyes, Thou hast seen us. Unconscious we have been, as though we dwelt in the land of death, but Thou hast been mindful of us.

From dangers all unseen Thou hast protected us; from the land of mystic shadows to the light of a new day Thou hast brought us. We give Thee thanks. And now, O Father, the day is ours — Thy priceless gift. Help us this day to love Thee. Help us this day to do Thy will. Help us to be patient, kind and true.

Through all this day may we remember that all men are Thy children. Help us to show our love to Thee by being helpful to our fellows. Help us to be clean in thought and word and deed. And when again we return to the land of refreshing sleep, if we no more should awake on earth, may we awake with Thee. *Amen.*

Rev. F. B. Stockdale,
Brooklyn, N. Y.

OCTOBER THIRTY-FIRST

Forgiving one another, as God for Christ's sake hath forgiven you.

— Eph. 4: 32.

OUR Heavenly Father, we thank Thee for protection and sleep through the night, and for the blessing of a new day. We beseech Thee to guide us through all its hours, giving us wisdom to understand and grace to do Thy will. Among ourselves, and among all with whom we have to do, enable us to keep and show the Spirit of Christ.

We pray Thee to bless the children, with their companions and teachers, and do Thou teach them always to be fair, to love truth and hate a lie. Guard our absent dear ones, keeping their hearts pure and their hands clean, and grant them health and prosperity, according to Thy will.

We ask Thy blessing upon our neighbors, and especially upon any in sorrow or sickness or business trials, or any trouble, that their faith and courage fail not, and that under Thy blessing they may come to a better day. We pray for all who have yielded to temptation, and all who refuse Jesus Christ, that through repentance and faith Thou mayest bring them to an assured salvation. Keep us humble and watchful and prayerful through all the day, and help us to consider others rather than to please ourselves. Forgive our sins; fit us for our tasks, in Jesus' name. *Amen.*

George N. Luccock, D.D.
Oak Park, Illinois.

November

NOVEMBER FIRST

Now abideth faith., hope, love. — 2 Cor. 13: 13.

OUR Father, Who art in Heaven, we thank Thee for Thy wonderful love to us — a love that is infinite and eternal, a love that will not let us go. We love Thee, we adore Thee, we praise Thee, yet we humbly confess that we have not always loved Thee with our whole hearts, and that we have not always loved our neighbor as ourselves. In many ways we have sinned and come short of Thy glory. Have mercy upon us, God, according to Thy loving kindness and according to the multitude of Thy tender mercies blot out our transgressions. Abide in our home today. May it be none other than the house of God, and the very gate of Heaven. Send us to our daily duties with the conviction that we are about our Father's business. May we live and labor and love as seeing Him Who is invisible. Grant that we may be Christlike in all of our dealings with others, whether it be in the home, or in the social circle, or out in the business world. Unify and purify Thy Church, Christ. Make it a great soul-winning Church. Thy Kingdom come! Thy will be done on earth as it is in Heaven. Our prayer we humbly make in the name of the Lord Jesus, Who loved us and gave Himself for us. *Amen.*

Walter L. Lingle, D.D.,
Richmond, Virginia.

NOVEMBER SECOND

Commit thy way unto the Lord. — Ps. 37: 5.

O GOD we come to Thee as children come to their father to ask for Thy loving care and protection We know not what awaits us of joy or sorrow, of life or death, and before we enter this untried, unknown future we would commit our way to Thee, remembering Thy promise that Thou wilt direct our paths. We thank Thee for the common blessings of life which have come to us so noiselessly as to be almost unnoticed and forgotten. We thank Thee for the special blessings which are the evidences of Thy personal care over us. Because of Thy promise of forgiveness, we come and ask Thy mercy for our sins, through Jesus Christ, our Lord. We pray that Thou wilt give us moment by moment both spiritual and material blessings. Help us to trust Thee when we cannot understand, knowing Thy word is true that all things work together for good to them that love God. We pray that all those who belong to us may belong to Thee, and that Thy benefits and blessings may extend to all mankind everywhere. Hasten the day when Christ shall reign in every home and heart throughout the entire world. May not one of our dear ones and friends be missing in that land of glad and blessed reunion beyond the valley of the shadow. We give Thee praise for the privilege of prayer and for the gifts which have been and will be ours because of Thy loving kindness and tender mercy. *Amen.*

Johnston Myers, D.D.,
Chicago, Illinois.

NOVEMBER THIRD

Jesus departed into a solitary place and there prayed. — Mark 1: 35.

O GOD, our Father, in the opening of the new day we look up into Thy face to thank Thee for the care of the night and for the joy of another morning.

The new day will bring its blessings; may we be able to see and seize them. In the new day we shall have opportunity — opportunity to be kind — may we remember that kind words can never die.

We shall have opportunity to bear or share another's burden; may we, like the Great Burden Bearer, tenderly, tactfully enter into and share the needs of others.

Joys may come, sorrows may fall upon our hearts, surprises may wait us at some turn in the way, but do Thou, ever-present, loving Father, show us that no joy or sorrow or surprise can come to us, Thy children, without Thy knowledge.

Teach us to thank Thee for the joys; to remember, when we must weep, that "Jesus wept"; and to trust all the unexpected — the surprises — to Him Who doeth all things well, and to radiantly hope for the day when "we shall know, even as we are known." *Amen.*

A. E. Piper, D.D.,
Wilkes-Barre, Penna.

NOVEMBER FOURTH

Believe that ye shall receive them, and ye shall have them. — Mark 11: 24.

ALMIGHTY GOD, our Father in Heaven, God and Father of our Lord and Saviour Jesus Christ, we would wait on Thee that Thy Holy Spirit may enable us to worship Thee. We are not worthy of the least of Thy mercies, yet hast Thou enriched us in all needed good things. We pray Thee to search us and show us our sins; and, as we confess, we would trust Thee to forgive, and to cleanse us from all unrighteousness. We would thank Thee for the blessings Thou hast bestowed upon us, and trust Thee to give us what is best for us. We pray Thee to bless all who are dear to us, and if we have any enemies, bless them and give us right spirits toward them. If any dear to us are unsaved, bring them to repentance and faith in our Saviour, to serve Him as Lord. Jesus is the true vine. We who are His disciples are the branches. Enable us to abide in Him, and may the Holy Spirit bring forth from His life the fruit of the Spirit in our lives. Bring Thy people up to the help of the Lord against the mighty. Send forth Thy light and truth. Send forth laborers into Thy harvest, and bless the labors of those whom Thou hast already sent forth. Give us some place and part this day in Thy service. We ask all for Jesus' sake. *Amen.*

A. D. McClure, D.D.,
Wilmington, N.C.

NOVEMBER FIFTH

We trust in the living God, who is the Saviour of all men, specially of those that believe. — I Tim. 4: 10.

OUR God and Father, for the protecting care of the night we give Thee thanks. For the new day, a free gift of Thine, with its message of renewal and tireless interest on the part of our Father, we give Thee thanks. Teach us anew with this new day the meaning of home, friendships, and opportunity to do our work for God and our fellow-men.

Set our faces in the right direction as we go out to live another day. Fortify us that we may not be overcome by any evil. Restrain us from any untoward tendencies. If the way grow dark, cause us to see Thy light. If loneliness should be our lot, let us be mindful of Thy companionship.

By Thy help may we add some joy to other lives, and live out this day with the blessed thought of having done something worth while.

And as the shadows of the evening creep over us we would again give thanks and commit ourselves anew to Him Who careth for all. We make our requests in the name of Christ Jesus our Lord. *Amen.*

Rev. Clarence W. Kemper,
Minneapolis, Minn.

NOVEMBER SIXTH

As thou hast believed, so be it done unto thee. — Matt. 8: 13.

OUR Father in Heaven, as children come to an earthly parent, so we, Thy children, come to Thee. We acknowledge Thy goodness in keeping us in safety during the night, and in the mercies renewed to us with the return of the day. While we have been locked in slumber, Thou hast not suffered any harm to befall us. We have lain us down in peace and slept because Thou hast sustained us, and the morning of a new day finds us with renewed vigor for its labor and toil.

As the day brings to us fresh obligations, fit us for their discharge. As new temptations make their appeal to us, strengthen us for their resistance. In new battles we may have to fight, lead us to victory. Fortify us against the evil we may have to meet, and make us responsive to every uplifting and helpful influence. May the evil tendencies in our nature constantly grow less insistent. May the spirit of love to Thee and to all become the fixed characteristic of our lives.

Accept our gratitude for daily renewed mercies. Give us pardon for all our sins. Keep us as a family from harm and evil today, and when our days on earth are past, bring us to the Heavenly home. We ask it in Christ's name. *Amen.*

Rev. J. W. Stewart,
Owen Sound, Ont., Canada.

NOVEMBER SEVENTH

This is His commandment, that we believe. — I John 3: 23.

OUR Father, Who art in Heaven, hallowed be Thy name. We thank Thee for the day that is before us, with its opportunities, its privileges, its unexpected pleasures, and its disappointments as well. We rejoice in the opportunity to serve Thee, to witness for Thee in our intercourse with men. May we be ever ready to display a sympathetic interest in the welfare of those with whom we mingle in the home, the train, the busy street, the office and the shop. A3 we look back over the life of our Lord, we find that wherever He moved among men they were conscious of a rising hope within them, their spirits were quickened, and they faced life's tasks with new courage and hopefulness. Grant, our Father, that we, too, may be used this day, through the Holy Spirit, in making Christ very real to someone. May we find keen enjoyment in the work which we have been called upon to do, and may we seek to know Thy will in the commonplace duties which in Thy providence have been assigned to us. When discouragement confronts us and when obstacles are placed in our paths — yes, even when perhaps we may not have any tangible evidence on which to base our hope — may we then trust Thee fully and completely, for Thou art our Father and our God. *Amen.*

S. Earle Hoover,
Philadelphia, Penna.

NOVEMBER EIGHTH

Wherefore laying aside all malice, and all guile, and hypocrisies and y envies, and all evil speakings. As newborn babes, desire the sincere milk of the word, that ye may grow thereby. — I Peter 2: 1-2.

O LORD our God, we desire to thank Thee sincerely for Thy never-failing love and mercy unto us. For all the great temporal blessings, and especially for the gift of Jesus Christ our Saviour, we bless and praise Thy Holy Name.

Cleanse our hearts, we beseech Thee from all unrighteousness, and forgive wherein we have failed to do Thy will. Grant unto us the strength we need to overcome temptation, and to be brave and cheerful amid the trials and sorrows of life. May the light of Thy truth shine into our hearts, dispelling the darkness of fear and unbelief.

Help us, O Lord, to be more generous in our judgment of others. May Thy wondrous love fill and flood our hearts, making us to be kind and sympathetic in our treatment of those whose lives we touch day by

da We pray that Thy blessing may descend upon the people of all lands. May the day soon come when the good news of salvation shall have been made known to all mankind. Through Jesus Christ our Lord. *Amen.*

Rev. Joseph Janes, M.A.,
Ingersoll, Ont., Canada.

NOVEMBER NINTH

Be not afraid, only believe. — Mark 5: 36.

OUR Heavenly Father, we thank Thee for the child's right of approach and of expectancy. Humbly pleading Thy promises, relying alone upon the merits of Thy Son, we pray; in our sorrow, send the Comforter.

In our helplessness, supply efficiency for service. In our ignorance and loneliness, show us the way wherein Thou wilt walk with us.

Dwell Thou within us, that we sin no more against Thee, that Thy will be our pleasure, Thy cause our masked passion. Give us the courage of faith, the consolation of conscious forgiveness, and the blessed assurance that underneath are the everlasting arms. Make us to cleave to that which is good, and abhor that which is evil.

Above all, Thou Giver and supreme Lover of life, we pray for ourselves not only, but for all men and women, and particularly for all children, that Thou wilt give everlasting life — saving spiritual life, vigorous physical life, pure social life, beneficent mental life — all the life there is that is worth having, for we ask it in His name Who lovingly confided to us, "I am come that ye might have life, and that ye might have it abundantly." *Amen.*

Ira Landrith, D.D., LL.D.,
Boston, Massachusetts.

NOVEMBER TENTH

It is a good thing to give thanks unto the Lord, and to sing praises unto Thy name, O Most High; to show forth Thy loving kindness in the morning and Thy faithfulness every night. For Thou, Lord, hast made me glad through Thy work: I will triumph in the work of Thy hands. — Ps. 92: 1-2, 4.

OUR loving Father in Heaven, we come to Thee as the good All-Father that cares for us here below, realizing our many wants, but "our God can supply all our needs according to His riches in glory by Jesus Christ." Teach us also, dear Lord, to realize fully our many infirmities. "Teach me to know how frail I am," and notwithstanding all, may we go to Thee as children to an earthly parent — *trustfully, believingly,* and in full confidence that Thou wilt lead our steps aright. Bless our children, loving Saviour, and as they grow up to manhood's and womanhood's stature, may they grow into the measure of the stature of the fullness of Jesus Christ. Prepare us today for all that Thou art preparing for us. Make us patient, loving, thoughtful and helpful. Bless each one of us, and, what is far better, make us a blessing. For Jesus' sake we ask it. *Amen.*

Rev. P. C. Cameron, B.A.,
Berlin, Ont., Canada.

NOVEMBER ELEVENTH

Ye shall see Me, and find Me, when ye shall search for Me with all your heart.
— Jer. 29: 13.

O THOU, with Whom to dwell is the light of life and from Whom to depart is the shadow of death, grant us the joy of Thine abiding presence this day, that in us there may be no darkness at all. We are not children of the darkness, Father, but our paths this day may lead us into the midst of human sorrow and strife and sin. May we walk as befits the children of the Light!

Give us, we pray Thee, open and alert minds to discover Thy will, and a holy purpose both to love and to do it. Help us to be true in the midst of all that is false, pure where evil most abounds, friendly to the friendless, and bearers of our brothers' burdens for our Saviour's sake. Take away, we pray Thee, all the guilt of our sin, and give us the joy of the victorious life through our divine Redeemer.

At the close of this day bring us, with spirits untroubled and unashamed, to our own firesides, where, by Thy grace, we may find rest, and the peace that passeth understanding.

All of this we ask for the sake of Jesus Christ, Thy Son, our Saviour. *Amen.*

William Hiram Foulkes, D.D., LL.D.
Philadelphia, Penna.

NOVEMBER TWELFTH

We will show forth Thy praise. — Ps. 79: 13.

AS WE present ourselves before the throne of Thy power, Lord, we come to praise Thy name and to bring with us a large petition. We ask, nay, even with boldness we claim the inheritance left us by our Elder Brother, His peace — the peace which the world cannot give, and which the world cannot take away.

We dare not ask for wealth, with all its allurement to worldliness; we dare not ask for length of days, with prospect of aged weakness and dependence; we dare not ask for preferment among our brethren, realizing that if we honor ourselves, our honor is nothing; we dare not ask for freedom from sorrow, remembering that they who are not of this world shall in the world have tribulation; but we do ask, our Father, that in perfect peace we may rest in Thee, knowing that He that spared not His own Son, but delivered Him up for us all, shall with Him also freely give us all things. Grant, Lord, that the peace of God which passeth all understanding, may keep our hearts and minds through abundance of grace in Christ our Redeemer.

This our prayer we make in the name of Him Who loveth us and gave Himself for us, even Jesus Christ our Righteousness. *Amen.*

John W. Friend,
Petersburg, Virginia.

NOVEMBER THIRTEENTH

Let my mouth be filled with Thy praise. — Ps. 71: 8.

WE THANK Thee, Lord, that Thou hast been our dwelling place in all generations. Before the mountains were brought forth, or ever Thou hadst formed the earth and the world, even from everlasting to everlasting Thou art God.

We thank Thee that the Word became flesh and dwelt among us, full of grace and truth. We are grateful to Thee that He took upon Himself the form of a man like other men, and that He became obedient unto death - even death upon the cross - that we might have life, and have it more abundantly.

Grant, Lord, that we, the children of men, through the power of Thy Holy Spirit, may become like the Son of Man in mind and heart and will. May we be brothers to the race. Enable us to toil patiently up the slopes of service. Teach us to be willing to forgive as He forgave. We pray for all the nations of the earth whom Thou hast made of one blood. Speed the coming of Thy Kingdom upon the earth, that nation may no longer make war against nation. Hasten the coming of the day when the knowledge of God shall cover the earth as the waters now cover the sea, and bring us all at last up to that city whose Maker and Builder is God. *Amen.*

Hoyt M. Dobbs, D.D.
Fort Worth, Texas.

NOVEMBER FOURTEENTH

It Is good to sing praises unto our God. — Ps. 147: 1.

OUR Father, for such Thou hast taught us to call Thee, we thank Thee that we may be brought into Thy family through living, loving faith in Jesus Christ, Thy Son and our Elder Brother. And we thank Thee for all that may mean to us. We thank Thee for a Father's love. Keep us ever, we pray Thee, within the circle of that love. We thank Thee for the oversight and protection that Thou dost give us day by day. As we go out from the home, go Thou with us, and when we return at eventide may we bring Thee with us, to be with us in the breaking of bread and through all the hours of darkness, until morning break and the shadows flee away. Draw all members of the family circle into real fellowship with Thy Son, that we may be cleansed from all sin, and may be kept by His power from falling, and may be presented at last faultless before Thy presence with exceeding great joy. Make us to be more tender and thoughtful one of another, and of all our companions. Forgive all display of temper and hasty speech, give us the love that suffereth long and is kind. Bless with us all the needy and distressed. Bless all mankind. Redeem the world lying in sin, and hasten the coming of Thy Kingdom, through Jesus Christ our Lord. *Amen.*

Ernest Thompson, D.D.,
Charleston, West Virginia.

NOVEMBER FIFTEENTH

I love the Lord, because He hath heard my voice and my supplications. Because He hath inclined His ear unto me, therefore will I call upon Him as long as I live. The sorrows of death compassed me, and the pains of hell gat hold upon me: I found trouble and sorrow. Then called I upon the name of the Lord; O Lord, I beseech Thee, deliver my soul. Gracious is the Lord, and righteous; yea, our God is merciful. — Ps. 116: 1-5.

OUR Heavenly Father, we thank Thee for this new day, with its privileges and opportunities. May we in gratitude for Thy love and mercy, serve Thee today with sincere hearts. Give us grace to do Thy will, and to accept Thy purposes for us in the spirit of joyful obedience, believing that Thy will is always best.

Keep our hearts from sin, our minds pure, and our motives true. Forgive us when we fail. Grant that we may consecrate the commonplace duties of the day with the consciousness of Thy presence. Whether the day brings prosperity or loss, sunshine or shadow, blessings or bereavement, may our faith remain firm, our love unfailing, our hope undaunted. Through us today may mankind be blessed, and the coming of Thy Kingdom hastened, for His name's sake, *Amen.*

Rev. H. H. Bingham, B.A.,
London, Ont., Canada.

NOVEMBER SIXTEENTH

Ask what ye will, and it shall be done unto thee. — John 15: 7.

O GOD our Father, Thou hast watched us during the hours of sleep, and under the shadow of Thy wings we have rested in safety. Grant that now, when we awake, we may be still with Thee. May we walk with Thee and work with Thee through all the hours of the day, seeing Thee in all the life about us, and finding it our meat to do the will of Him Who sent us, and to finish His work.

In the busiest moments, may we never quite lose sight of Thee, or slacken the hold of our souls upon the things that are eternal.

Defend us from all dangers, but above all from our own faults and weaknesses. Help us so to pass through this day that we shall cast no shade on other lives, but shall bring brightness into the world about us.

And when the day draws to an end, may we have the quiet joy of knowing that, by Thy grace, we have been able to win and to manifest something of that eternal life which is found in doing justly, with loving kindness, and walking humbly with God. In the name of Jesus Christ. *Amen.*

William Pierson Merrill, D.D.
New York City, N. Y.

NOVEMBER SEVENTEENTH

Praise the Lord, call upon His name. — Isa. 12: 4.

ALMIGHTY GOD, our Heavenly Father, in Whom we live and move and have our being, from Thy kind hand comes down every good and perfect gift; and we humbly thank Thee for all Thy loving kindness to us.

We come before Thee confessing our sins, for which we ask Thy forgiveness. Bless us in our bodies and our spirits, which are Thine. Grant us food and strength and clothing and shelter as we need. And give us grace to know and do Thy holy will. Make the path of duty plain before us; keep us from temptation and from sin, enabling us to glorify Thee upon the earth.

Bless, too, all our loved ones whom, in the arms of our prayer, we would bring before Thee. Heal any who are sick, comfort the sorrowful, and strengthen any who are faltering; grant them each one Thy favor, in which is life; Thy loving kindness, which is better than life.

Remember graciously the community in which we dwell, in all its interests temporal and spiritual. Prosper Thy Church among us, and give success to its work. Bless our country, and make us that happy people whose God is the Lord. Send out Thy light and Thy truth, and hasten the coming of Thy Kingdom.

In Jesus' name. *Amen.*

Thomas H. Law, D.D.,
Spartanburg, S. C.

NOVEMBER EIGHTEENTH

Praying always with all prayer and supplication in the Spirit. — Eph. 6: 18.

WE COME before Thee, our Father and our God to worship, to praise Thy name, and to thank Thee for Thy great mercy and Thy many blessings. We confess our sins, but we come with boldness to Thy throne of grace, for our trust is in Him Who is our Advocate and our Mediator. We pray that Thou wilt show to each one of us Thy will for this day and help us to do it, not going in our own selfish and sinful ways. O Lord, grant that Thy will may be done more and more by all men, and that Jesus may not only be given a place in the throne room of our hearts but may we let Him be seated on the throne and crown Him Lord of all. Our Father, we ask that Thy Holy Spirit may be our comforter, our guide and our helper this day. May we let our light so shine today-in the home, on the street, at work or at play —that others may be drawn to Him Who is the Light of the World. We pray that it may be our earnest desire to know Christ better, and to make Him known. Help us to watch and be faithful, so when He comes He may find us with lamps trimmed and burning. And all we ask is in His own blessed name. *Amen.*

Rev. J. L. Read,
Little Rock, Arkansas.

NOVEMBER NINETEENTH

Being then made free from sin, ye became the servants of righteousness.
— Rom. 6: 18.

HEAVENLY FATHER, we thank Thee for the rest which has come to our bodies in sleep. During the long hours of the night Thou hast been watching over us. Thou art always mindful of us, not only in the night, but also in the workaday. Help us, dear Father, to be as mindful of Thee as Thou art thoughtful 1 of us. Forbid that we forget our God. May we not become so occupied with worldly affairs that we have no time or place for Thee.

As we talk to Thee, our sins rise like mountains from the deep. We are ashamed of our weaknesses. We confess everything, and plead for Thy forgiveness. Leave us not in our humiliation, but take us by the hand and lift us up. Give us the assurance that our sins are pardoned, and help us to live this day as the blessed Jesus lived every day.

We pray for the discouraged and distressed; Lord, give them cheer. We pray for all the people who are living in darkness; Lord, give them light. Wet pray for those who fight against themselves, against each other and against God; Lord, give them peace. We ask it all in the name of Jesus, for Thy glory and for our good. *Amen.*

Luther E. Todd, D.D.,
St. Louis, Mo.

NOVEMBER TWENTIETH

He that dwelleth in the secret place of the Most High shall abide under the shadow of the Almighty. I will say of the Lord, He is my refuge and my fortress: my God; in Him will I trust. He shall cover thee with His feathers, and under His wings shalt thou trust: His truth shall be thy shield and buckler. — Ps. 91: 1-2, 4.

IN THY wisdom, Whose ways are past finding out, Thou hast appointed our dear ones unto tears. Thou hast called them into sorrow's Gethsemane, where great loneliness and anguish wring their hearts. Grant, Father, that they may meet Jesus there. This is all that we can pray. Our blundering lips cannot comfort them and our blind eyes cannot discern the purpose of Thy providence. But, O Father of love, draw these sorrowing ones close to Thyself in the person of the sympathetic Saviour. Through their tears may they see

Jesus. There is no comfort but in Thee, O God Triune; may all who weep find Thee. Be Thou companionship for their perplexity, strength for their weakness and courage for their new life of bereavement. Show them that all Thy plans for Thy children include two worlds. Reveal unto them the tenderness and humaneness of Thy sympathy; comfort them as those whom a mother comforts. This we ask in the name of the Saviour Who sorrowed and wept. Amen,

Rev. William T. Ellis, LL.D.,
Swarthmore, Penna.

NOVEMBER TWENTY-FIRST

Ye are the salt of the earth: but if the salt have lost his savour, wherewith shall it be salted? it is thenceforth good for nothing, but to be cast out, and to be trodden under foot of men. Ye are the light of the world. A city that is set on an hill cannot be hid. Neither do men light a candle, and put it under a bushel, but on a candlestick; and it giveth light unto all that are in the house. Let your light so shine before men, that they may see your good works, and glorify your Father which is in heaven. — Matt. 5: 13-16.

OUR Saviour and our Intercessor, Thou earnest into the world not to be ministered unto, but to minister, and to give Thy life a ransom for many. Thou didst go about doing good. Looking upon the young man, Thou didst love him.

Thou didst weep over Jerusalem. In the spirit of Thy love and sacrifice for lost souls, inflame our hearts with a sacred passion for the redemption of men. Thou, the sinners' Christ, pour upon us a tender and undying yearning to save precious souls! Give us a greater zeal than our fathers had. May we take no neighboring saint for our standard, but dwell with our God for power. *Amen.*

Arthur S. Phelps, D.D.,
Waterville, Maine.

NOVEMBER TWENTY-SECOND

Ye that fear the Lord, praise Him.— Ps. 22: 23.

HELP us, God, this day to recognize ourselves as Thy children. May we call to mind and refresh ourselves with the teachings of Thy servant, who declared that our birth is a forgetting; that the soul that rises with us, our life's star, hath had elsewhere its setting, and cometh from afar. May we remember that we come from God, who is our home, and may we mourn the fact that we have forgotten the Imperial Palace whence we come and the glories we have known. May it be in our hearts to thank Thee, O Lord, that there is something in each of us which the weights and frosts of earth cannot suppress, which lives as the embers of primeval fires; those high instincts, those first affections— shadowy recollections which are the master light of all our seeing; a primal sympathy, a faith that looks through death.

We thank Thee, Lord, for the seasons of calm weather, when we have sight of that immortal sea over which we voyaged to this y world, and back over which again, when the work of life is done we shall travel to our eternal home. In full knowledge of Thy way, Thy truth, Thy life, as declared through Thy Son, our Lord Jesus Christ, may we live to serve Thee every day of our lives. *Amen.*

James W. Lee, D.D.,
St. Louis, Mo.

NOVEMBER TWENTY-THIRD

Ask, and ye shall receive, that your joy may be full. — John 16: 24.

O GOD, our Father! We worship Thy name, and bless Thee for Thyself. We acknowledge Thee to be the source and stay of our lives. We are Thy creatures. Thou wilt not leave us to suffer eternal want; Thou wilt not leave us to lack for daily bread. We are Thy children; we believe ourselves descended from Thee. grant that we may not plead Thy Fatherhood in vain! Let us not stand either as aliens or orphans, but as the heirs of God through promise. Give us, we beseech Thee, Thy Holy Spirit, that He may perfectly reveal to us Jesus Christ the Son. Give us to know Him, that we may abide in Him, and that His Word may abide in us. May neither prosperity nor the enticements of the world wean our thoughts and faith from Him. Pardon our sins and cleanse our hearts, that we may become a habitation of God through the Spirit; that Christ may dwell in us and we in Him. Guide and direct us in our intercourse with men. May our words and influence become a savor of life unto life. Show us how we may help to bring Thy Kingdom upon the earth. Admonish us in the days of health, nor forsake us in sickness and the hour of death. When our change shall come, give us to dwell forever in the house of Thy Fatherhood in Heaven, through the merit and grace of Jesus Christ Thy Son. *Amen.*

Horace M. DuBose, D.D.,
Nashville, Tennessee.

NOVEMBER TWENTY-FOURTH

Evening, and morning, and at noon, will I pray, and cry aloud: and He shall hear my voice. Cast thy burden upon the Lord, and He shall sustain thee: He shall never suffer the righteous to be moved. — Ps. 55: 17, 22.

OUR Father in Heaven, look upon us, we beseech Thee in Thine infinite love and compassion. Dwell Thou in us, that, being molded by Thy good Spirit, we may have fellowship with Thee as my children. Help us at all times to trust Thee. Appoint for us what Thou wiliest, and make us ready to receive with thankfulness whatsoever seemeth good to Thee concerning us. Go with us in every mission on which Thou art pleased to send us, and in my service may we find rest.

Lighten our darkness, we entreat Thee, that we may behold Thy face, and, in Thy tender mercy, do Thou temper the storm lest our weak faith fail, forgive our sins, and day by day deliver us from their power. We commit all our loved ones to Thy keeping. Do Thou watch over them and bless them. And as Thou givest us a taste of Thy joy in loving our friends lead us into the fullness of the joy of loving all whom Thou lovest, through Jesus Christ our Lord. *Amen.*

William Farquharson, D.D.,
Agincourt, Ont., Canada.

NOVEMBER TWENTY-FIFTH

Walk in love, as Christ also hath loved us. — Eph. 5: 2.

OUR Heavenly Father, we thank Thee for having mercifully kept us in health and strength, and for filling our lives with so much of comfort and happiness.

We pray for each one of those near and dear to us, and we beseech that Thou wilt keep them, and defend them from all evil. Enrich them with the blessing of Thy Holy Spirit.

Likewise we pray for all Thy disciples of every creed, wherever they may be, and that Thou wilt bring all those now separated from Thee to a vital knowledge of Thy goodness to them, and to a desire to become Thy humble followers.

As we pray "Thy kingdom come, Thy will be done on earth as it is in heaven," so, Lord, may we daily strive by all our acts to do all that we can for the upbuilding and extension of Thy kingdom on earth, and may our lives show to all men that we are Thine.

May we honor Thee by striving to obey Thy command to do unto others as we would that they should do unto us, and so bring men to acknowledge Thee as their Lord and Saviour. *Amen.*

Alba B. Johnson,
Philadelphia, Penna.

NOVEMBER TWENTY-SIXTH

I will, therefore, that men pray everywhere. — I Tim. 2: 8.

OUR Father, we art Thy children by faith in the Redeemer. We are Thy children when we are obedient and Thou art pleased; we are Thy children when we are wayward and in grief Thou dost chasten us We know that our sins are wholly displeasing to Thee, and they are painful to us. For Jesus sake,

Accept our deepest gratitude for Thy tender mercies in all our past, for the promise of Thy grace in all our needs, for the assurance of Thy presence always.

Bless us in the duties to which we have been called. Deliver us from the fear of man. Keep us from measuring our duties by the conduct of others, and help us to be great in Thy sight. Let us remember that there are but twelve hours in the day, and the night cometh. Help us to see that the great questions are issues of eternity, and may we be kept in the love of God.

Guide, O Great Jehovah, in the affairs of state; bless all movements and men that promote our Redeemer's Kingdom; and give Thy holy benediction upon the homes wherein our loved ones dwell. In Jesus' name. *Amen.*

Rev. J. M. Dawson,
Waco, Texas.

NOVEMBER TWENTY-SEVENTH

Gad! said, Ask what I shall give thee.— 1 Kings 3: 5.

O LORD, our Father, we lift our hearts in love and gratitude to Thee. Thy constant mercies come with the morning light, and fall upon us with the evening shadows; without them we could not live. The only return we can make to Thee, for Thine own sake, is to love Thee and to praise Thee. All else we must give to others, whose needs are like our own. Help us to know, also, that when we worship Thee, we ourselves are most benefited, by minds exalted and hearts purified in coming into Thy holy presence. May every day make Thee more real to us, until at last no other friend shall be so near. Give us to know Thy will concerning us, so that we shall not grope our way through life, but follow Thy plan. While we would thankfully enjoy every creature comfort bestowed upon us, keep us from setting our hearts too much on things that perish in the using. Help us to know our weaknesses, that we may have sympathy for all who fail and sin because they do not lean on Thee. Enable us so to live as not to spoil a single day or grieve a single heart by deeds that might never be undone, or words that might never be recalled. And this we can do only by His help Who is our Saviour, and through Whom we ask it. *Amen.*

George W. White, D.D.,
Oakland, California.

NOVEMBER TWENTY-EIGHTH

By faith Abraham, when he was called to go out into a place which he should after receive for an inheritance, obeyed; and he went out, not knowing whither he went. * * * For he looked for a city which hath foundations, whose builder and maker is God. — Heb. 11: 8, 10.

OUR Father, Who art in Heaven, we thank Thee for Thy presence in our hearts and in our home, for Thy loving kindness and Thy tender mercies. We desire to give Thee the largest possible place in our life, that Thine ideals for us may be realized and that we may fulfill our little part in Thy great plan. So humbly pray Thee to pardon anything in our lives that hinders our fellowship with Thee or our usefulness to our fellow-men, and correct in our characters whatever is not Christlike. Teach us to trust Thee for all our needs, both of soul and body.

Defend us in the time of temptation and help us to realize that we are citizens of the spiritual kingdom. Bless all our fellow-disciples the world around. Empower Thy Church that she may win great victories over evil, and at last receive us to be with Thee, through Jesus Christ our Lord. *Amen.*

Rev. W. O. Rodgers,
Terre Haute, Indiana.

NOVEMBER TWENTY-NINTH

He ever liveth to make intercession for them. — Heb. 7: 25.

ALMIGHTY and everlasting God, because of Thy good hand upon us in mercy, we have been spared during another night. Help us to trust in Thee, to have no will but Thy will, and to desire to be only what Thou wouldst have us be. We pray that Thou wilt show us how large is Thy pity, how great is Thy love, and how infinite is Thy goodness; give us to feel that Thou hast called us with a holy calling; that Thou hast put us here to do Thy pleasure, and hereafter to enjoy Thee forever. Breathe into us the spirit of prayer and teachableness, and enable us to give earnest heed to the truths taught in Thy Word. We thank Thee for Thy holy Word, for Thy Church, and for all the ordinances of Thy house, and for the way of salvation through Christ. We bless Thee, our Heavenly Father, for all Thy gifts, but above all for Thine unspeakable gift, our Saviour, Jesus Christ. We rejoice in the assurance that He is now interceding for us. May the weary and heavy-laden come unto Thee and find rest unto their souls. We pray that Thou wilt send forth laborers into Thy harvest. Be Thou to all Thine own as the shadow of a great rock in a weary land. Speedily fill the whole earth with Thy glory. Make us all, Christ, joyful in hope, patient in suffering, active in service and abounding in love. We ask all these blessings in the name of Jesus Christ, Thy Son, our Saviour. *Amen.*

Robert Stuart MacArthur, D.D.,
Boston, Mass.

Before they call, I will answer. — Isa. 65: 24.

JEHOVAH, our God, "How excellent is Thy name in all the earth." We come to Thee, acknowledging Thy goodness and greatness, reverently bowing in the name of Jesus Christ, to give Thee praise and seek at Thy hands the strength needed for the duties of today. Most humbly do we confess our sins. In thought, word and deed we have transgressed Thy holy laws and "done despite unto the Spirit of grace." We recognize, God, our weakness and failures in life; when we would do good, evil is ever present. We have brought shame upon Thy sacred name and dishonor to Thy cause. Led from the path of righteousness by the alluring influences of sin around us. But in Thy infinite love Thou wilt not refuse to hear or grant our petition. Forgive us of our many sins, and make possible, O God, a greater work of grace in our lives. Help us to be true to Thee each day. Help us to remember Thy mercies and to acknowledge Thee at all times. Strengthen us, dear Father, that in the hour of trial we may stand true as Thy children. Grant Thy blessing to all who seek Thee in truth. Bring back those who have wandered from Thee, that all may be saved. Accept this petition in the name of Jesus Christ, our Saviour and Redeemer. *Amen.*

Rev. Joseph Keevil,
Cincinnati, Ohio.

December

DECEMBER FIRST

I am the Lord thy God which teacheth thee to profit, which leadeth thee.
— Isa. 48: 17.

O GOD and Father of all the families of the earth, Thou art worthy of our daily love and constant gratitude. Thou knowest we can never be other than children crying to Thee for food, raiment and shelter for our sustenance and protection. We stretch our hands toward Thee to be led through paths we cannot know, beside which temptations lurk and snares are set. Deliver us, we beseech Thee, from the evil one.

Help us to appreciate our earthly family relations, established and wondrously blessed by Thee. Grant that our home may be kept in peace and good-will among all of its members by that love for one another which casts out suspicion and fear. We consecrate it with all its interests to Thy care and service, that the yearning of our hearts for Thy approval and indwelling may bring to us godliness with contentment.

Today, in our family worship, we confess our sins that He Who is faithful may forgive and cleanse us from all unrighteousness. As we go forth to our individual tasks, give us courage, strength, patience and that wisdom which cometh down from above, which is first gentle, peaceable, easily to be entreated, full of good works. All of these blessings we ask in the name of Christ Jesus our Lord. *Amen.*

President I. N. McCash, LL.D.
Spokane, Washington.

DECEMBER SECOND

But they that wait upon the Lord shall renew their strength; they shall mount up with wings as eagles; they shall run, and not be weary; and they shall walk, and not faint — Isa. 40: 31.

OUR dear Heavenly Father, we thank Thee for the rest, refreshment and safety of another night and for the light of another day. Thou art the giver of every good and perfect gift, and we give Thee our thanks for health preserved and life continued, and for another day with its opportunity of service. Give us stronger faith and confidence that we may go day by day, relying only on Thy sustaining strength and guidance.

Preserve us from temptation and sin, and grant that something of good may be accomplished by us during the hours of light, and that we may then find, as the day closes, that there have been some victories won and some development in our spiritual experience; and we do most humbly pray Thee that we may so spend all the days and nights of our earthly lives that when Thou dost call us hence, we may go into Thy presence shining and without shame, trusting only in the merit of Thy dear Son, our Lord, and this we pray for Jesus' sake. *Amen.*

Walter Duncan Buchanan, D.D.,
New York City.

DECEMBER THIRD

But' we all, with open face beholding as in a glass the glory of the Lord, are changed into the same image from glory to glory, even as by the Spirit of the Lord. — II Cor. 3: 18.

LOVING LORD, renew in us the image of our Creator.

We have marred, we have lost, through sin, the holiness which makes men like to Thee. Transform us, conform us to the image of Thy dear Son — Himself the express image of the Father's Person — Who came and died and rose again that we might be fashioned anew in the likeness of God. Give us the vision of Thee in Thy blessed Word, so that reflecting as in a mirror the glory of the Lord, we may be changed into the same image from glory to glory.

Let the light of Christ's love shine in our faces as we go among our brothers day by day. Make us so like Him in all our ways that in us they shall see Him and be drawn to Him. Enable us to say in truth, "To me to live is Christ."

Deepen within us the yearning to see His unveiled face in the day when we shall be satisfied when we awake in His likeness, Who liveth and reigneth with the Father and the Holy Ghost, one God, world without end. *Amen.*

Rev. C. Armand Miller,
Philadelphia, Penna.

DECEMBER FOURTH

My grace is sufficient for thee. — II Cor. 12: 9.

OUR Heavenly Father, we Thy children would bless Thee for the dawn of this new day, for we regard it as Thy gift to us. Help us, we humbly pray Thee, to use it wisely and well; conduct ourselves through all its hours that to some extent we may prove ourselves worthy of such a gift, and in it do something worth while, so that at its close we may feel we have not lived it in vain. For all the difficulties that may confront us, give us grace sufficient; for all the questions we may have to decide, give wisdom; and for all the temptations we may have to meet, give us overcoming power. Keep us all the day conscious of Thy companionship, and of the realities of the things unseen; may we increase in knowledge of things that matter most, and understand better the things we now only know in part. Reveal Thy will more clearly to us, and may this day see that will better fulfilled in us. For 'all bound to us by the ties of nature, faith and love we r>ray; enrich their lives with every good, and use them in the furtherance of Thy most gracious will on earth. And very earnestly do we pray for the hastening of the day when among all peoples on earth Thy kingdom will come, Thy will be done perfectly. Hear us, we pray Thee, gracious God, for we pray in the name of Thy blessed Son, our Saviour and Lord, Jesus Christ. *Amen.*

Rev. Lewis C. Hammond,
Cincinnati, Ohio.

DECEMBER FIFTH

For I am now ready to be offered, and the time of my departure is at hand. I have fought a good fight, I have finished my course, I have kept the faith: Henceforth there is laid up for me a crown of righteousness, which the Lord, the righteous judge, shall give me at that day: and not to me only, but unto all them also that love His appealing. — II Tim. 4: 6-8.

OUR Father, we thank Thee for the revelation of Thyself in Jesus Christ our Lord. We thank Thee for Thy kindly care over us. We pray that the Holy

Spirit may lead us into the light of truth. Give to us a larger vision of Thy glory and make us more faithful to Thee and to the needs of our fellow-men. Teach us how to pray.

Give us more faith and love. Give us clearer vision to see the deeper meaning of Thy truth. Bless our land, and Thy Church in all lands. Bless the young, the aged, the sick and the troubled. Fill our hearts with sympathy and hope. Let us live to be of service to Thee, and to our fellow-men. Thine shall be the kingdom, the power and the glory, for we ask in the name of Jesus Christ our Lord. *Amen.*

William M. Anderson, D.D.,
Dallas. Texas.

DECEMBER SIXTH

Be careful for nothing; but in every thing by prayer and supplication with thanksgiving let your requests be made known unto God. And the peace of God, which passeth all understanding, shall keep your hearts and minds through Christ Jesus. — Phil. 4: 6-7.

OUR Father, we bring home and hearts to Thee this day for the blessing which Thou hast planned for them. May there be in us nothing to hinder Thy coming, nothing to cloud the vision of Thyself, nothing to deaden the sound of Thy voice. We would open the ears and eyes within us to hear and see Thee; we would open the whole soul that Thou mayst come in. Come in, Father of us all, into our home, into our hearts.

Many things we need this day. One thing, best of all, is all that we ask; we ask for Thyself, and having Thee, we have all. Bless the home with Thy presence, and the sun shall shine through the darkest clouds of the sky; bless our hearts with Thy love, and no burden shall be too heavy for us to bear for Thee.

And then, out of a home where Thou dost dwell, may we take Thee in our hearts, in our lives, to bless our brethren wherever we go. In Thy name. *Amen.*

Bishop Theodore S. Henderson,
Chattanooga, Tenn.

DECEMBER SEVENTH

Finally, brethren, whatsoever things are true, whatsoever things are honest, whatsoever things are just, whatsoever things are pure, whatsoever things are lovely, whatsoever things are of good report; if there be any virtue, and if there be any praise, think on these things. — Phil. 4:8.

OUR Father, we thank Thee for Thy goodness to us during the night. Thou hast watched over us whilst we slept. Now we pray Thee to guard and guide us through this day. May Thy presence be with us. As our day, so may our strength be.

May Thy love be in our hearts and manifest in our conduct. Enable us to resist evil, to endure trial, to overcome difficulties, and in all things to do Thy will. Whatsoever our hands find to do, may we do it with our might.

Keep us from becoming discouraged. May Thy joy be our strength. May we not grow weary in welldoing. May Thy word be a lamp to our feet and a light to our path. Keep our hearts and minds. May we think of the things which are pure and lovely and of a good report. Supply all our needs this day. Make all things work together for our good. We ask in Jesus' name. *Amen.*

David McKinney, D.D.,
Cincinnati, Ohio.

DECEMBER EIGHTH

Forgive, and ye shall be forgiven. — Luke 6: 37.

OUR Heavenly Father, we turn for a little while at the threshold of this new day to be with Thee. Refresh us with a new vision of Thy face. Speak to us Thy will that we may do it. Make all the day cheerful by Thy presence and fellowship.

We thank Thee for life and work in such a beautiful world. Give us, we beseech Thee, that due sense of all Thy mercies that our hearts may be thankful, and that we show forth Thy praise not only with our lips but in our lives. Perfect us in love, that we may conquer all selfishness and learn how to pardon as we pray for forgiveness.

May our home life be sanctified today, and all the days, by the presence of the divine Guest. As we go out among men to do our work, touching the hands and lives of our fellows, make us friends of all — true representatives of Thine. Ballast our activities for the day with high purposes. Show us how to fill it with enriching service, that night may bring a peaceful pillow. Bless the home life of our nation, and all the nations. Let every palace, mansion and cottage in the whole earth become the house of God and the gate of heaven. *Amen.*

Bishop H. H. Fout, D.D.,
Indianapolis, Indiana.

DECEMBER NINTH

Hitherto hath the Lord helped us. — I Sam. 7: 12.

O LORD, our Lord, Creator, preserver and bountiful benefactor of men, in Whom we live and move and have our being, we adore Thee for Thy loving kindness and tender mercies. With shame in our hearts we confess before

Thee our many sins. Our lives do not meet Thy requirements. Our footsteps have wandered from the pathway of rectitude. Our Father, look upon us in mercy, and do Thou be pleased to have pity upon us in our sins. Look upon Thy Son, Who died for us, and do Thou for His sake accept us as righteous before Thee. Grant that our sins may not only be blotted out of the book of Thy remembrance, but that by the power of the Holy Ghost we may be enabled to die unto sin, and to live unto righteousness. Comfort the disconsolate, cheer the saddened, bring friends to the friendless, teach the ignorant, give visions to trembling faith, set the star of hope in the overhanging clouds, and hurry the forces of truth towards the consummation of Thy Kingdom. We can trust all to Thee. As our Shepherd, lead us today. As our King, defend us from the enemies that watch for our souls. As our priest, teach us the will of God for our salvation. God, our Father, overshadow our pathway with Thy merciful providence, and let each one of us bear some part in the advancement of the Redeemer's glorious Kingdom. Through Jesus Christ our Lord. *Amen.*

W. J. McMillan, D.D.,
Baltimore, Md.

DECEMBER TENTH

Remember the sabbath day, to keep it holy. Six days shalt thou labor, and do all thy work: But the seventh day Is the sabbath of the Lord thy God. - Ex. 20: 8-9.

(For Sunday Morning.)

WE THANK Thee, Lord, for the holy Sabbath, so full of blessings for Thy children. We adore Thee for this memorial of the precious work of our redemption, and type of the rest that remains for the people of God. Help us to keep the day holy. May we be richly blessed in reading Thy Word, in listening to Thy Gospel, and in all the services of the holy day. Be with all ministers of the Gospel, and especially with those who preach Thy Word today. Bless our children, at home and in the Sabbath school. Give to the teachers the power to mold character and to guide the children along the path of the just. Comfort all that mourn, especially such as have not been allowed to attend Thy house today. Give us grace not merely to hear the Word, but to help in the spread of light and life over the world. Enable us to live nearer to Thee. May each Sabbath be a spiritual benediction to all Thy people. Look upon those who are yet sitting in darkness and in the shadow of death. Send abroad Thy light and Thy truth into the benighted portions of our globe. Turn the nations from idols to serve the living God. Let the people praise Thee, let all the people praise Thee; and blessed be Thy glorious name forever and ever. *Amen.*

A. M. Mayo,
Lake Charles, Louisiana.

DECEMBER ELEVENTH

Then shalt thou call, and the Lord shall answer. — Isa. 58: 9.

O THOU Who art so distant that no reach of our thought can compass Thee, and so near that we are apt to overlook Thee, hear our prayer. Our Saviour taught us to address Thee in the endearing names of our homes. We can call ourselves Thy sons, and we can call Thee our Father and our Friend. And we are not as unimportant as sometimes we seem, for if we are less than the child, to care for us Thou art more than the mother. As in spring days men walk in their gardens to see how their flowers and fruits are growing, so may we go through our souls to observe what the divine nature is bringing forth there. May we see much love, aspiration, hope, courage and other riches of Thy grace. Here we promise more faithfully to cultivate the good seeds and eradicate the weeds. And our promise is not a passing wish, but we pray that it may be a consecrated purpose. Bless our country with strength for righteousness. Bless our homes with children that shall develop in integrity and usefulness. Forgive us for misemphasizing the things of time more than those of eternity. In all trouble, help us to say, "If God be for us, who can be against us?" Aid us to hold within our thought and love and hope dear ones who have gone to their heavenly home. May we prepare for reunited fellowship with them, and unveiled communion with God, by nobler living. In our Master's name. *Amen.*

Rev. John W. Langdale,
Cincinnati, Ohio.

DECEMBER TWELFTH

Pray now unto the Lord our God. — Jer. 37: 3.

WE THANK Thee, our Heavenly Father, for Thy care over us through the past night. We thank Thee for the Bible. Help us to understand it, to believe it, to obey it and to love it. We thank Thee, Blessed Saviour, that Thou didst come from heaven to earth that we might go from earth to heaven; that Thou didst die that we might live. We thank Thee that Thou didst rise from the dead, ascend up on high, and dost ever live to intercede for us. We thank Thee that Thou didst say, "Come unto me all ye that labor and are heavy laden, and I will give you rest." We come to Thee. Have mercy on us. We have done wrong. Forgive us. We want to do right; help us. We are sinners; be Thou our Saviour. Fill us with Thy Spirit; consecrate us to Thy service. Comfort the troubled; guide the perplexed; strengthen the weak; succor the tempted. Bless our country. Bless Thy Church everywhere, and bless all Christian workers. Fill the whole earth with Thy glory. We ask all in the name of our Lord Jesus Christ, and for His sake we pray,

"God bless our going out,
Nor less our coming in,
And make them sure.
God bless our daily bread,
And bless whate'er we do, whate'er endure.
May death unto His peace awake us,
And heirs unto His salvation make us."

Amen.

Richard Boyd Webster, D.D.,
Wilkes-Barre, Penna.

DECEMBER THIRTEENTH

Watch and pray. — Mark 13: 33.

O GOD, Lord of Heaven and earth, the builder up of the universe, Thou art the rock of our salvation, unchanging in holiness and loving kindness. We lift up our hearts unto Thee; we know that Thou carest for us and hearest us. Lord Jesus, Thou art the Son of God, the Son of Man, the Son of David. Thou didst come and share our life, teaching, healing, tasting death on the cross as a sin-bearer, triumphing over evil, and pledging Thyself to come again in glory. Bless all dear to us; lead them in the way everlasting; be with them and us in all times of suffering, sorrow and anxiety (especially * * *). We thank Thee for the Gospel message, and for the Bible, which is the record of what Thou hast said and done in the past, and of what Thou hast promised for the future. May it be to us increasingly the guide to life, the key to history, and the revelation of hope. Help us to do our share in spreading the knowledge of it throughout the world. Look with pity on Thy scattered people Israel. Open their eyes to see the truths contained in their own Scriptures, and to recognize the Lord Jesus as their Prince and their Saviour. We offer these our prayers and praises in the name of our King, Jesus Christ. *Amen.*

Rev. Canon R. B. Girdlestone, M.A.,
Wimbledon, England.

DECEMBER FOURTEENTH

He shall * * * save them because they trust in Him. — Ps. 37: 40.

OUR Father, as Thy children we, in this new day, hope for Thy presence and listen for Thy voice. That we may be sensitive to Thy touch and alert to Thy word, make us eager to know Thy will and resolute to do it. To know Thee in close intimacy is our need and our prayer.

In Thee is food for all our hungers; light for all our gloom; tasks for all our energies; love — warm, throbbing, sacrificing, to purge away our selfishness.

This is our faith — make it our living experience.

Look in pity upon all the sons of men. Bring strife to an end. Establish righteousness in the affairs of nations. Help all rulers to decree justice. Let reason prevail, and love bind together the hearts of men.

Be our sufficiency all day. Be our defense if we are threatened by evil forces; keep us rigid when we are tempted; give us fresh inspiration when our purposes flag; keep us unselfishly, deliberately, eagerly kind all day, and when night falls may we have the consciousness of Thy favor, and the peace which passeth understanding, through Jesus Christ our Lord. *Amen.*

Wallace MacMullen, D.D.,
Madison, New Jersey.

DECEMBER FIFTEENTH

Let this mind be in you, which was also in Christ Jesus: Who, being in the form of God, thought it not robbery to be equal with Gad: But made Himself of no reputation, and took upon Him the form of a servant, and was made in the likeness of men: And being found in fashion as a man, He humbled Himself, and became obedient unto death, even the death of the cross. Wherefore God also hath highly exalted Him, and given Him a name which is above every name. — Phil. 2: 5-9.

OUR prayer to Thee, Father, is in the name of Thy Son, Who forgave our sins on the cross. Help us by Thy Holy Spirit to separate ourselves from sin and enter into the inheritance of Thy redeemed children. May we this day give the world in spiritual blessing far more than we receive in material gain. May we realize that our safety of soul and body is in Thee, and upon Thee we can depend for all our need. May we have a genuine love for all humanity, and seek the salvation of all people. May we be of real help to someone, and may *all* see in us more of Christ than they can see of self.

Unto God our Father, Christ our Saviour, and the Holy Ghost our Comforter, be all glory. *Amen.*

Rev. James B. Ely,
Philadelphia, Penn.

DECEMBER SIXTEENTH

If a man love Me, he will keep My words.— John 14: 23.

ALMIGHTY GOD, our Heavenly Father, we thank Thee for Thy goodness, Thy loving kindness to us and to all men; for the health that gives strength, and for the sickness that brings patience; and most of all for the forgiveness of sins for Christ's sake, for the means of grace, and for the hope of glory.

We beseech Thee, give Thy guidance in what we ought to do and in the ways wherein we ought to go, and vouchsafe Thy grace to enable us to walk in them aright. Save us from being so busy as to forget Thee, or so contented as to feel no need of Thee.

Fill our hearts with grateful love of Thy dear Son, our Saviour and our King; and open our eyes to the light, and our souls to the grace of Thy Holy Spirit, that He may come in and take possession and work in us the holiness without which no man shall see the Lord.

God, be merciful to us sinners as we tread the dusty way of active life, and when the evening comes bide with us near, and give light for the way home, through Jesus Christ our Lord. *Amen.*

Bishop Daniel S. Tuttle, D.D.,
St. Louis, Missouri.

DECEMBER SEVENTEENTH

Thou that hearest prayer, unto Thee shall all flesh come. Ps. 65: 2.

MOST Gracious Father, from Whom all good gifts come, grant us, we entreat Thee, the gift we need above all others, Thy Holy Spirit to help our infirmities, that our worship may be purged from all unreality. We long to pray to Thee sincerely, but we cannot unless Thou dost cleanse our hearts from the dross of vain desire. Free us from selfishness in our prayers; deliver us from asking for those things that will minister chiefly to our earthly pleasure. Thou must inspire the petitions which Thou alone canst answer. We are conscious of our sinfulness, but cannot be truly sorry for our misdoings until Thou dost move us to honest contrition and unfeigned repentance. We would be grateful to Thee for the multitude of Thy tender mercies, but it is not until Thou dost grant us a due sense of Thy goodness, and awaken within us sincere gratitude, that our cold hearts are ready to praise Thee.

Our love languishes and dies except Thy Spirit shall quicken it into a living flame. Our good deeds cry aloud to Thee for pardon, if Thou dost not inspire them and purify them by Thine own indwelling.

We would live the prayer life; we would learn what it is to pray without ceasing. To this end do Thou come and dwell within us, O Thou Spirit of Christ! We want day by day to glorify Thee, our Father, and to serve our fellows, even as did Jesus, Thy well-beloved Son. In His name. *Amen.*

S. P. Rose, D.D.,
Montreal, Canada.

DECEMBER EIGHTEENTH

With my spirit within me will I seek Thee early. — Isa. 26: 9.

OUR Father in Heaven, we call unto Thee because we have called before and Thou didst hear us. Come unto us, Lord, when all is dark, and when trouble weighs us down. Lift us up again, that we may praise Thee and smile in our heart. For the labors of this day, give us free grace; for the hard road, the iron shoes of good resolution; for the hour that casts us down, calm us and lift us up again. Make us gentle, Lord, with our loved ones. May we never give way to harsh words or unjust thoughts. Lord Jesus, listen to our prayer as we confess our sins before Thy Holy Cross. May we meet the Man of Sorrows now while we bend before Thee, so shall our sins fade away, and our hearts rejoice with a new joy. May we be resigned to Thy will, no matter what we must yield. Gather this little family about Thyself as doth the bird when the storm falls. Cover us with Thy love, and protect us in the hollow of Thy hand. Lord, give us the power to pray aright, for we pray in Thy might. At last, Gentle Shepherd of our home folks, gather us all to Thyself in the dear Homeland, when the morning breaks and the shadows flee away. And this we ask in Jesus' name. *Amen.*

C. H. Woolston, D.D.,
Philadelphia, Penna.

DECEMBER NINETEENTH

Let us hold fast the profession of our faith. — Heb. 10: 23.

ALMIGHTY GOD, our Heavenly Father, the Giver of all good things unto Thy children, in Whom we live and move and have our being, Who hast brought us in safety to see the light of another day, we, Thy humble servants, offer Thee our heartfelt praises for Thy preservation of us throughout all our lives, and especially through the hours of darkness, for the rest and peace which we have enjoyed, and for the opportunities of another day. We thank Thee for all Thy mercies to us, for home and friends, for health and strength, and for all the blessings with which Thou hast crowned our lives.

Grant especially that this day we may have grace in all our thoughts and words and deeds to glorify Thy Holy Name, and to brighten the lives of those about us, and to help them to better things. Help us to do with our might whatsoever our hands may find to do for Thee and for our fellow-men. Keep far from us all sin and evil, and, if it please Thee, deliver us from all sickness, sorrow and anxiety. Whatsoever Thou mayest have in store for us, grant at least that in all things we may be drawn nearer to Thee.

We ask it all through Jesus Christ, Thy Son, our Lord. *Amen.*

James Goodwin, D.D.,
Hartford, Connecticut.

DECEMBER TWENTIETH

He shall save the children of the needy. — Ps. 72: 4.

O LORD, our Heavenly Father, we praise and magnify Thy Holy Name
for all Thy loving kindness and Thy tender mercy which Thou hast bestowed
upon us. Thou hast opened Thy hand and supplied all our wants. We thank
Thee, O Lord, that when we were without strength, in due time Christ died
for the ungodly, that He might ransom our souls from sin and death, and give
unto us eternal life. Grant, Lord, that each one of us, now in Thy presence,
may receive Christ Jesus as our eternal Saviour. We praise Thee, God, for the
gift of Thy Holy Spirit, Who tabernacles in our hearts, and Who takes of the
things of Jesus and reveals them unto us day by day, moment by moment.

Grant Thy blessing, we beseech Thee, upon every member of this household, and upon all our loved ones, wherever they may be at this hour. We
thank Thee that "in Jesus' keeping we are safe, and they." Remember in mercy, O Lord, any who are in distress at this time, in mind, body or estate. Comfort all who mourn. Let all the earth remember and return to Thee, O God; let
all the kindreds of the nations worship Thee, in spirit and in truth. Grant unto
us the forgiveness of all our sins, in the name of our Lord and Saviour Jesus
Christ. Amen,

Rev. Charles George Smith, B.D.,
Belleville, Ont., Canada.

DECEMBER TWENTY-FIRST

I will magnify Him with thanksgiving. — Ps. 69: 30.

GOD of all mercies, Saviour and Sanctifier of men, we worship Thee, the
Triune God, and call upon our souls and all that is within us, to praise and
magnify Thy Holy Name.

We confess our sins, but rejoice that they are constantly being blotted out
by the blood of our blessed Lord, and because He is righteous, we who have
our lives hid in Him are also righteous.

We come to Thy mercy seat with joy and thanksgiving, as we count our
innumerable blessings, knowing that no good thing shall be withheld from
those who love Thee and put their trust in Thee. As Thou hast delivered us
from all perils, sorrows and trials in the past, so we are assured that Thou
wilt keep that which we commit to Thee for the future. Enrich our hearts

with Thy Word, that we may lead clean, holy lives, and have power to be winners of souls for our Master.

We pray for Thy rich grace to be upon our beloved in our home and elsewhere, and for the world which lies in sin, that Thy Kingdom may come, and Thy will be done, through our Lord Jesus Christ. *Amen.*

J. H. Jefferis,
Philadelphia, Penna.

DECEMBER TWENTY-SECOND

I have loved thee with an everlasting love. — Jer. 31: 3.

OUR Father in Heaven, we would praise and magnify Thy Holy Name. Thy love watches over us, protecting us from every kind of danger, and provides for our every need. Thou dost never fail us. We trust in Thee.

We have sinned against Thee in thought and word and deed, but we come with contrite hearts, confessing our unworthiness, and pleading for Thy forgiveness, through the merits of the shed blood of our Saviour Jesus Christ.

We thank Thee for all Thy good gifts unto us, and we pray Thee to accept us and to use us as Thou canst. Bless each of us as we need Thy blessing. And, with us, bless all the ill, the sorrowing, the discouraged, the sinning, and all Thy needy ones. We would pray also for all those engaged in lowly or great tasks for the extension of Thy Kingdom in the hearts of men everywhere.

And now do Thou be with us in our daily task of hand or mind. May we be workmen in things material and spiritual of whom Thou needest not to be ashamed. Gather us home after while, without one. missing. We ask it in Jesus' name. *Amen.*

Rev. Stewart Winfield Herman,
Harrisburg, Penna.

DECEMBER TWENTY-THIRD

They that trust in the Lord shall be as Mount Zion, which cannot be removed, but abideth for ever. As the mountains are round about Jerusalem, so the Lord is round about His people from henceforth even for ever. For the rod of the wicked shall not rest upon the lot of the righteous; lest the righteous put forth their hands unto iniquity. Do good, O Lord, unto those that be good, and to them that are upright in their hearts. — Ps. 125: 1-4.

OUR gracious Heavenly Father, we thank Thee for the light this morning. Endue our hearts with gratitude and love for the blessings of the past week, and direct our conversation and daily walk through the coming week. May all we do be acceptable in Thy sight. Grant that we may render Thee service that will not only give us joy and comfort, but that our example and influence will lead others to love and serve Thee. God grant that we may realize and appreciate every day of our lives that we owe all to Thee and that all the good things of life come from Thy mercy and gracious kindness. All this we ask for Christ's sake. *Amen.*

George T. Jester,
Corsicana, Texas.

DECEMBER TWENTY-FOURTH

His ears are open unto their prayers. — I Peter 3: 12.

AROUND this, our family altar, we come, O God, to seek Thy face. Keep us today, sheltered in the light of Thy countenance. Help us to do only the things that please Thee. At every step may we be conscious that Thou art at our side.

We seek Thy very best, both for ourselves and for those, our loved ones, absent from our altar of prayer. As parents, may we guide our household aright; as children, may we walk worthy of the Lord unto all pleasing.

Mid the darkening shadows, keep us walking in the light; may our hearts be garrisoned with peace. Fill us, O God, with the knowledge of Thy will in all wisdom and spiritual understanding; make us fruitful in every good word and work. As we bow around, this family altar, Lord, help us to comprehend the atoning efficacy of Thy death, the keeping power of Thy life, and the blessed hope of Thy coming.

We ask Thy presence with us during the day; we dare not walk alone. The tempter is too subtle, the pleasures of the world too luring, and the lust of riches too strong. Lead us, O Lord, in the train of Thy triumph; make us more than conquerors in Thee. *Amen.*

Rev. R. E. Neighbour,
Athens, Georgia.

DECEMBER TWENTY-FIFTH

And the angel said unto them, Fear not: for, behold, I bring you good tidings of great joy, which shall be to all people. For unto you is born this day in the city of David a Saviour, which is Christ the Lord. — Luke 2: 10-11.

WE ARE filled with joy and gratitude this morning for the gift of the Saviour, Jesus. We are especially thankful that He is not a Saviour afar off, but linked to our nature in the manner of His birth, in childhood, in humility, in love and sympathy. He who saw the light of day in the midst of the beasts of burden when first He threw the mantle of humanity over Himself, has lifted from us the burdens of sin and anxiety. In Him we are glad.

With all the angels who celebrated His nativity we add our voice of joy. With the humble who inquired what these things meant, we still search for the truth of the incarnation. Give joy this day to all people, we earnestly pray. Bless all children, the babes of the land. Be with the poor, and give to us all, and to all others, the spirit of good-will and of charity. Bring peace to earth, a reception of the good tidings also. May the gifts of love manifest the spirit of Jesus, we ask in His name. *Amen.*

Rev. Robert W. Thompson,
Pittsburg, Kansas.

DECEMBER TWENTY-SIXTH

We have peace with God through our Lord Jesus Christ. — Rom. 5: 1.

OUR Father, Thou Who sittest upon a throne high and lifted up, Whose glory fills the Heavens, make us conscious this morning that Thou art not far from any one of us, Thy children. Thou hast revealed Thy nearness to us in Jesus Christ our Lord. Help us to see that our selfishness is the only thing that can separate us from Thee. Take out of our hearts every selfish impulse, and fill them with a holy love for Thee. Then we know that there shall be fulfilled for us the promise of Jesus, that Thou, our Father, and He, our Brother, shall come in and dwell with us this day. Speak to us by Thy still, small voice.

Christmas Day has come and gone. We have given and we have received the tokens of friendship and love. We cannot repeat these gifts every day, but we earnestly beseech Thee that the Christmas spirit may abide in our hearts and in the hearts of mankind everywhere. Take out of our hearts every trace of jealousy and hatred toward any of Thy children, and give us the attitude toward all mankind which was in Jesus Christ our Lord. Hasten the day when our ears shall hear the morning stars singing together and all the sons of men joining with the angelic choir in the anthem of the first Christmas morning, "Peace on earth among men of good will." Through Jesus Christ our Lord. *Amen.*

Rev. Frank W. Padelford,
Boston, Massachusetts.

DECEMBER TWENTY-SEVENTH

And He said to them all, If any man will come after Me, let him deny himself, and take up his cross daily, and follow Me.

For whosoever will save his life shall lose it: but whosoever will lose his life for My sake, the same shall save it.

For what is a man advantaged, if he gain the whole world, and lose himself, or be cast away? — Luke, 9: 23-25.

O LORD, Thou Whose eye seest everything, even into the secrets of our hearts, and with Whom is all wisdom and power, be not silent to our petition. In our suffering let us observe Thy presence, and, out of pain, teach us submission.

We cannot always understand what Thou art doing with us, but O Thou Watcher of men, make our souls to know that Thou arc always just and good, ever long-suffering in Thy mercy. Give us Thy strength to bear the burden.

Teach us that if we would be most serviceable to Thee, we must be marred and hurt and made to bleed. Then we shall come forth as gold tried in the furnace, and Thy righteousness shall be our robe, and Thy glory our diadem. *Amen.*

Peter Ainslie, D.D.,
Baltimore, Maryland.

DECEMBER TWENTY-EIGHTH

Giving thanks always for all things unto God and the Father, in the name of our Lord. Jesus Christ. — Eph. 5:20.

But thanks he to God, which giveth us the victory through our Lord, Jesus Christ. — I Cor. 15: 57.

OUR Heavenly Father, for all Thou hast given and all Thou hast forgiven, we thank Thee. For every gift of nature, and Thy favoring providences, and Thy great salvation through Christ, we thank Thee.

For blessings within us and around us; for everything by which Thou hast brought good and drawn us to Thyself through all our lives and the lives of our kin; for our power of understanding, of loving, of homemaking, of sharing friendships; for the good hope concerning loved ones who have gone from the ways of earth, and for our own expectation of sharing heaven's joy with them through Christ's saving merit — we thank Thee.

Help us, O Father, to live and work with the cheer of a grateful spirit, overcoming all trouble by the patience of hope and the wisdom of love. So may we share the fellowship of all who follow Christ, both near about us and in all the world. *Amen.*

Rev. William Allen Knight, LL.D.,
Boston, Massachusetts.

DECEMBER TWENTY-NINTH

For the love of Christ constraineth us. — II Cor. 5: 14.

OUR Father in Heaven, we are Thy children, redeemed by Christ our Saviour and Elder Brother, and we come to Thee in His name. Forgive our sins. Deliver us from all the guilt and power of sin, and from its consequences. Take the love of it out of our hearts. Make our love of Thee to glow. Let it burn out all the dross of evil, and impel us constantly to gracious acts of kindly ministry done to others in the Master's name and for His sake. Give us a clear vision of our ever-present Saviour as an abiding Friend. Grant that we may be transformed by thus beholding Him, growing daily more and more like Him in the desires of our hearts, the words of our lips, and the things we do and refrain from doing.

Bless with us all others, supplying their every need, and giving them grace and guidance. Make the Gospel light shine out brightly in all lands, bringing peace and spiritual prosperity, and drawing all men to Christ, and together in the bonds of Christian unity and brotherliness. We ask all this, as we pray for grateful hearts, in the name of Him Who died on Calvary. *Amen.*

J. H. Bomberger, D.D.,
Cleveland, Ohio.

DECEMBER THIRTIETH

The Lord is good to all: and His tender mercies are over all His works.

— Ps. 145: 9.

O GOD, our Father, we are about to enter upon a new day. To meet well all duties and responsibilities that come to us; to resist firmly every distraction and temptation that seeks to draw us from our path; to be utterly prepared for any danger or any crisis that may this day befall us; to be found, when the evening is come, pure and holy — this is our desire.

And we would be friendly with all men; strength to the weak, hope to the despondent, joy to the sorrowing, power to the tempted.

We wait, therefore, our Father, for the coming of Thy Spirit upon us ere we venture into all that this day holds for us. In the quiet of this early morning hour, bowed before Thee, our souls wait. Touch us with that hand which has been laid in blessing upon others before us; speak to us with that still, small voice of power; fill us with Thine own righteousness.

Give us of Thyself, that we may this day so live for ourselves and before men that through us Thy Kingdom may in part come, and Thy will more fully be done among men. For Jesus' sake. *Amen.*

Rev. Seeley K. Tompkins,
Cincinnati, Ohio.

DECEMBER THIRTY-FIRST

We love Him, because He first loved us. — I John 4: 19.

O GOD of Light, Who, in Thy omnipotent power drove away the darkness of primeval chaos, be pleased to let the Sun of Righteousness so illumine our dark hearts that we shall go forth to the duties of this day in the joy of faith, the gladness of obedience, and with a clear vision of truth and duty.

O God of Liberty, Who hast bestowed upon us, the children of bondage, that sublime yet awful heritage, the freedom of the will, help us to realize the responsibility which it involves. Perfect us in the practice of that self-denial, that choosing of the better portion, until we learn to know from experience as well as revelation that to be Thy bond servant is to enjoy the only perfect freedom which the soul of man can ever know.

God of Love, Who hast loved us, wretched sinners, with an everlasting love, help us, Thy unprofitable servants, to reflect Thy love more and more, and show our constantly increasing affection by more loyal devotion, more faithful service and more complete obedience.

O God of Life, Who hast promised here and hereafter life yet more abundantly to all who truly seek it, help us on this last assured day of all time to strive for that deeper, fuller experience which comes only through Thee. Help us to live this day a nobler, purer, more devoted, more obedient life than ever before, to the glory of Thy name, Thou God of Light, Liberty, Love and Life. *Amen.*

John E. Mulholland,
Philadelphia, Penna.

Prayers for Occasions

A Sentence Prayer.

LORD, speak to me, and then speak through me.
Pres. Henry Churchill King, D.D., LL.D.,
Oberlin, Ohio.

A Prayer for Easter Morning.

WE THANK Thee, God, for the day in which life and immortality were brought to light through the resurrection of our blessed Lord from the dead. We remember that crimson footprints marked His way into the dark tomb, and that with wounded hand the door of death was unlocked. We thank Thee, God the Father, and Jesus the Saviour, for the love of the Cross and the power of the divine Spirit, whereby the grave was robbed of its victim and a living Saviour appears to cheer and bless. May we live our lives upon the earth as those who are united to Him, raised up with Him, seated with Him in the heavens, and as those who look for the blessed hope and appearing of the glory of the great God and Saviour Jesus Christ. May the light of His glory shine far this day, revealing and healing the sins of many hearts. We ask in His name. *Amen.*

Rev. Robert W. Thompson,
Pittsburg, Kansas.

A Prayer for Mother's Day.

LORD, I thank Thee for the tender care and constant prayer of a godly mother. May the "unfeigned faith" that dwelt in her dwell in her son also. Help me to keep ever before me the high ideal of service and character which she impressed upon the mind of my youth. Help me to make bright the sunset of her days and by my life and faith to be a living answer to her prayers; and when I mourn "as one that mourneth for his mother," may her memory still be with me, a star to guide me on my journey through the broken and uneven ways of life till traveling days are o'er. In the name of Him whose last earthly thought was for His mother, when He said to that disciple whom He loved, "Son, behold thy mother." *Amen.*

Clarence Edward McCartney, D.D.,
Philadelphia, Penna.

An Evening Prayer.

WE THANK Thee, Lord, for the work of the day, and for the rest of the night. We will lay us down both in peace and sleep, for Thou, Lord, only, makest us to dwell in safety. Keep watch around us throughout this night, to protect us against the assaults of the evil one, to suggest to us holy thoughts, to defend us from all dangers, to lead us in the perfect way of peace, and to prepare us for the happy service of a new day. For Jesus' sake. *Amen.*

Rev. John Edgar Park,
West Newton, Massachusetts.

A New Year's Prayer.

STRONG Son of God, on the threshold of the New Year we pray:
May nothing false pass our lips. May our lives be real, our hearts pure, our spirit right. May all that is unseemly be eliminated. May our hearthstones be centers of wholesome influence. May God be a partner in our business. May our social life be elevating; our Church life as becometh saints. Grant this our prayer, O God the Sanctifier, in Jesus' name. *Amen.*

G. Bickley Burns, D.D.,
Philadelphia, Penna.

A Prayer for Trust.

The joy of the Lord is your strength. — Neh. 8: 10.

THOU, God, Who hast created us for Thy joy, teach us to know ourselves held in the hollow of Thy hand; help us to know that as Thou hast breathed into us the breath of life, so Thou wilt sustain us according to Thy pleasure. Help us to accept what comes to us as that which Thou hast chosen for our development, and the expression of an eternal will and wisdom. So with courage and with trust, help us to grow, to love and to accept Thy creation and all our fellow-creatures until we too become loving co-workers in the great field of preparation. Cleanse us, God, of fear, of self-will, of childish desires. Open our minds and hearts, so that in such measure as we are able, we may comprehend and trust the working of Thy goodness in us. *Amen.*

Louise Collier Willcox,
Norfolk, Virginia.

(For Thanksgiving Day.)

HEAVENLY FATHER, we bring Thee a psalm of thanksgiving. Thou hast put a new song in our hearts, and there is a new hymn of praise upon our lips. Thou hast done wonderful things for us and in us, for which we are glad. Old things have passed away and behold all things have become new. We call upon our souls and all that is within us to praise Thy Holy Name. Thou hast set us in a high place. Our hearts are enlarged. Christ has come to be the chiefest among ten thousand and the One altogether lovely. His will is our delight, His church is like the gate of Heaven to our souls; His words are sweeter than honey to our lips, and His service is joy beyond compare. Forgive us for the sins of omission, for slowness of belief, for poverty of prayer, for ignorance of Thy Word, for besetting sins, for neglect of duty.

Help us to redeem the time, to be instant in season and out of season, if only we may hasten the harvest of souls and more speedily usher in the Kingdom of our Lord. Help us to dare great things for Thee and to expect great things from Thee, as Thou hast promised. Make us worthy of Thy confidence, that we may be worthy of Thy commendation when the day is done. *Amen.*

Frederick T. Keeney, D.D.,
Syracuse, N. Y.

www.ingramcontent.com/pod-product-compliance
Lightning Source LLC
Chambersburg PA
CBHW030529100426
42813CB00001B/189